2003 11 27

DATE DUE
DATE DE RETOUR

CARR McLEAN   38-296

Web Radio

Web Radio
Radio Production for Internet Streaming

Chris Priestman

Focal Press

OXFORD AUCKLAND BOSTON JOHANNESBURG MELBOURNE NEW DELHI

Focal Press
An imprint of Butterworth-Heinemann
Linacre House, Jordan Hill, Oxford OX2 8DP
225 Wildwood Avenue, Woburn, MA 01801–2041
A division of Reed Educational and Professional Publishing Ltd

⊖ A member of the Reed Elsevier plc group

First published 2002

British Library Cataloguing in Publication Data
Priestman, Chris
  Web radio: radio production for Internet streaming
  1. Internet radio broadcasting
  I. Title
  384.5'4'0285'4678

Library of Congress Cataloguing in Publication Data
A catalogue record for this book is available from the Library of Congress

ISBN 0 240 51635 4

For information on all Focal Press publications visit our website at:
www.focalpress.com

Composition by Genesis Typesetting, Rochester, Kent
Printed and bound in Great Britain

FOR EVERY TITLE THAT WE PUBLISH, BUTTERWORTH-HEINEMANN
WILL PAY FOR BTCV TO PLANT AND CARE FOR A TREE.

Contents

Preface   xi

Acknowledgements   xix

1 What is radio on the Web?   1

What's new about the New Medium?   3
The Internet on the phone system   4
The Web floats on the Internet   6
Bringing radio to the Web   6
Radio *was* an interactive medium   8
Vertical versus horizontal radio communication   12
Radio listening was shaped in the Broadcast Century   13
A note on DAB   25
Summary   26
Further reading   27

2 . . .And what web radio isn't   28

Convergence of digitalized media technologies   29
Divergence of media uses   30
Radio's relationship with the music industry   31
The many forms of audio on the Internet   34
Streaming   34
Downloading and shopping for music online   35
Downloading radio programmes at high sound quality   38
Web radio's relationship to other radio transmission routes   39
Radio in the visual world of multimedia   43
The website is the web radio station's 'front door'   45
Websites with additional audio   45

Interactivity and the visual   46
Web TV   48
A summary of intersections for web radio   49
Further reading   50

3 Stream receivers and how the listener listens   **51**

How streaming works – an overview   52
'Packet switching' technology   54
A note on 'embedded' audio files   56
Starting the stream   56
ISP connections, bandwidth and connection speeds   57
The common tools of compression – streaming software products   59
Desktops and laptops as radios   65
Off the shelf dedicated web radio devices   67
Portable radio around the house   71
Web radio back in the ether?   72
Summary   74
Further reading   76

4 Streaming radio output   **77**

Scalability   78
Who runs the server?   78
Host streaming services   78
Running your own server   81
Selecting your audience   82
Measuring your audience   88
Encoding and streaming server software products   88
Managing the server   93
The streaming studio   94
Summary   97
Further reading   98

5 Established radio broadcasters on the Web   **99**

Interactivity on the station website   100
Virginradio.co.uk case study   101
The simulcast stream of the terrestrial output   105

Radio Netherlands case study   106
Archive streams of parts of the terrestrial output   109
CFUV FM case study – a small Canadian university and
    community station   109
The addition of 'side channels'   113
Summary   114

6 Internet-only stations and other adventures in web radio   116

Interactivity and the website   117
RadioValve case study   118
Using a host to handle radio streaming   122
Pulse Radio case study – Global Dance Radio   122
Exploring speech radio alternatives   125
Radio Voix Sans Frontières (Voices Without Frontiers) case study   126
Web radio across the digital divide   130
Kothmale Community Radio Internet Project (KCRIP) case study   131
Summary – web radio is an experiment   134

7 One voice in a very large crowd: getting heard   135

Some audience principles – push and pull   136
The hyperlink is the key   138
Web radio portals or aggregating sites   140
Other online radio tuners   141
Web radio directories, large and small   142
Outsourcing promotion   145
Registering your own domain name   146
The front end – web page design   147
Reputation   150
Offline promotion   151
Building a brand   152
Summary   153
Further reading   154

8 Copyright on web radio   155

Established music copyright arrangements for terrestrial broadcasts   157
Music copyright in the digital environment   161

National versus international agreements   166
The precautionary approach   167
A copyright checklist   169
Ownership versus consumption models   172
Non-musical copyright   173
Protecting your own copyright   175
Summary   176
Further reading   177

9 Free speech on web radio   **178**

Reasons for regulating radio   180
Problem areas   188
Zoning and filtering   193
Horizontal media and centralized control   194
Case study: Radio B92, Belgrade   194
Summary – is freedom of speech safe on web radio?   195
Further reading   196

10   Redefining radio content   **197**

Music presentation on web radio   198
Factual speech on web radio   203
Non-factual speech on web radio: drama, comedy, entertainment   208
Audience participation and talk on web radio   210
Experiments in horizontal radio on the Web   213
Summary   214
Further reading   215

11   Scheduling for redefined audiences   **217**

Programmes versus programming   218
Patterns of listening   220
Time shifting   222
The locality of the listener   224
Global communities   225

Addressing a community of interest 227
Individual programmes for specific communities 228
Feedback and the effects of accurate audience measurement 228
Summary 229
Further reading 230

12 So how is web radio different? A checklist 231

Review of the characteristics the Web adds to radio 233
Web radio as part of the mosaic of radio platforms 235
Ways of being a web station 237
Regulation and control 239
Content 241

Appendix 1 Glossary 244

Appendix 2 Useful websites 252

Appendix 3 Bibliography 259

Index 265

Preface

Radio has reached a crossroads. After a century of broadcasting on AM and FM, we are told that – starting in the technology-rich countries perhaps as soon as 2010 – those more or less dependable analogue electromagnetic transmissions will be turned off. Some fundamental decisions about what radio is and how we want to continue to use it cannot be avoided. Neither by practitioners, nor listeners, nor indeed by students of this venerable, once magical, now taken for granted medium.

Radio has reached a crossroads in two senses – both of which are the consequence of our tentatively embracing digital transmission technology. The first sense is technical: by which routes shall we decide to send and receive radio programmes? DAB? DRM? Digital DSB? The Internet? Cable? The second sense is social (and cultural and political and economic and so forth): as the availability of individual listening choice increases exponentially, is there a single road ahead we can still call radio 'broadcasting', in the familiar, unifying, collective meaning of the word? If everyone in a street of a hundred houses is tuned to a different radio station, if each of those stations targets their audiences in the low thousands or less, can we still call that public broadcasting? Is there a minimum number of regular listeners below which the 'broad' becomes redefined as the 'narrow'?

I don't have an answer to any of these questions, but as a teacher and a sometime practitioner of radio I know they must be answered – and soon. A great deal of research urgently needs to be done at the user end of the chain – in some kind of proportion to the huge investments that are going into rolling out the various technologies. In contemplating these crossroads we cannot discount the listener and, for instance, the possibility they may remain unmoved by any of these digital options. For most people who've grown up with it, analogue radio broadcasting is a fully realized medium, one that's stood the tests of time and television, and does more or less exactly what listeners want it to: it works extremely efficiently, receivers are cheap and good value, tuning in is free and its programmes can accompany us almost anywhere.

Though I am no seer into the future of radio what I hear today – exactly 100 years after Guglielmo Marconi first demonstrated that he could transmit Morse signals on radio waves across the Atlantic from Cornwall to Newfoundland – is a mature analogue radio industry, surrounded by a mosaic of much smaller, infant, digital versions of itself. Most of these offspring have distribution systems that are broadcast in character, more or less in the sense we understand the term today; one does not.

DAB is being groomed in Europe and elsewhere as the natural successor to analogue. But progress on bringing portable, affordable receivers to tempt more than a handful of enthusiasts into buying has been painfully slow since DAB transmissions began in 1995. Meanwhile, the outside contender DRM, with potentially lower cost transmission infrastructure, has been able to stake a claim as a serious alternative – and gained substantially more interest in the US than its European rival. In terms of audience coverage, transmission areas would be very much like those we're used to today, so radio stations would retain their local to national scale on these digital systems. Far grander and international in scope, digital direct satellite delivery has taken some big steps forward recently, both for delivering a very wide choice of music radio channels across whole continents and as a way of serving the majority of the earth's radio listeners – those living in rural and impoverished urban areas – with some alternative listening than commerce or governments currently make available to them. Portable receivers are quite widely available and relatively inexpensive. Where it is laid, cable can deliver stations from any of the above, digital or analogue, but only for fixed point listening in the home, and therefore could only be an add-on to whichever form(s) of transmission take on analogue's mantle.

The last contender to arrive on the radio scene uses an altogether different delivery system, one that is already widely available across technologically advanced nations and is being spread with great speed and purpose into less prosperous nations. Wherever a personal computer is connected to the Internet, web radio is readily accessible today. The more you consider the Internet purely as a distribution system, in this case one for radio, the more potential advantages attach to it compared to those other digital routes I have just mentioned. Firstly, the spread and improvement of the infrastructure of the Internet is driven by far more powerful economic forces than merely the radio industry – important as it is. Secondly, the radio bit of the technology is one that's evolving as I write and can take its time to do so, whereas the other alternatives have to roll out as fully formed, self-contained systems in order to persuade us to adopt them *instead* of analogue. So their risk of failure must be higher. Thirdly, web radio has no need to supplant analogue radio and can live quite happily alongside any other broadcast system. The flexibility of the Internet means web radio can fulfil any one of a number of different roles: its reach can be both international and extremely local; its appeal can be anywhere on the spectrum between broad to highly specific. And fourthly (for now), its appearance coincides with the powerful social drift towards niche markets and smaller audiences in a multichannel media environment, towards individual consumerism and away from the minimum scale of audience broadcasters need to be viable. The trend is more advanced in the industrialized countries and there may be a reaction against it, or at least some stabilization of audience sizes, but there's nothing certain about that.

This is not to say there are no problems with web radio technology today. It's receivers are not really portable (yet), slower modems limit the sound quality (though for increasing numbers of listeners it is already as good as analogue FM) and signals can break up when demand exceeds capacity at certain points in the transmission chain – to name the commonest complaints. But in the six or so years of its existence, we have seen and heard the quality and stability of audio on the Web take enormous strides forward. Its rate of progress certainly bears comparison with any other advance in radio transmission technology. To quote from a recent Internet posting:

> 'It took until around 1980 before FM radio became a viable business, almost 20 years after the tech problems were surmounted. What does that say about webcasting's timetable?'

This observation was written (from the US perspective) in June 2001 by Bob Bellin, Chief Executive Officer of MP3Player.com and a radio industry manager of over 22 years' experience. It actually arose in an exchange of postings following an article Bellin had written for the admirable *Radio And Internet Newsletter* (*RAIN*) complaining not about technical issues, but about the twin problems of how to make web radio a commercially viable business and how music copyright should now be organized to make viability at least possible.

The period of about a year I've spent working on this book has, coincidentally, turned out to be something of a roller-coaster for Internet business in general and for web radio in particular. When I started in Spring 2000, the first Internet 'bubble' was about at its peak. The arrival of a critical mass of Web users – and perhaps a touch of millennial fever – had turned a cautious trickle of 'dotcom' investment into a deluge. New web radio stations were springing up everywhere and most established stations had by then decided they had to take the plunge into simulcasting their terrestrial output online. The US was well ahead of the rest of the world in the scale of its web radio operation. Its geography and history meant it had more terrestrial stations on air than any other country to begin with. Then it was the home of computing, then of the Internet and then of streaming technology. Its ICT infrastructure was better developed than anywhere and – crucially for web radio – its domestic tariffs for connection to the Internet were generally charged by subscription and not by the minute. Despite less favourable operating conditions elsewhere, much of the rest of the wired world had similarly caught on to web radio. The way ahead looked rosy.

It was important, I felt, for there to be a book written, from a radio practitioner's point of view, about what putting a radio station on the Internet meant. There were already several excellent technical books about how to get audio on the Web in general, plus the standard texts about getting a radio station on air, but I could find nothing specifically about the practicalities of setting up a radio station online.

In the early Summer of 2000 reality hit. The bubble burst and the money stopped flowing when creditors started asking how exactly the Web was going to turn their investments into profit. I began to read about individual Internet-only radio stations going to the wall, the major radio portal site BroadcastAmerica dramatically went into receivership and then – most seriously for web radio – at the very end of the year a series of Internet copyright bombs, which had quite quietly been ticking away since streaming began, started doing serious damage to American web stations' confidence in their future. The ruling on 11 December by the US Copyright Office that all US radio stations transmitting digitally (at that time, in practice this meant on the Web) would henceforth have to pay copyright fees to the record companies at a rate yet to be negotiated and backdated to 1998 was the first (I expand on the significance of this in Chapter 8). The repeated, high-profile, acrimonious court battles between the Recording Industry Association of America (RIAA) and Napster, while directed at MP3 file sharing not at web radio as such, cast doubt on the possibility that reasonable negotiations might take place about music royalties in relation to the size of the streaming audience. And then to cap it all, voice-over artists, represented by the American Federation of Television and Radio Artists (AFTRA), suddenly demanded substantial additional payments for the simulcasting of analogue radio ads they'd voiced onto the Web. As a result, on 12 April the companies behind most US terrestrial stations pulled their thousands of simulcasts, saying in effect that web radio had become too much trouble and they weren't prepared to be kicked around any more for offering a service that was costing them money to run (again, see Chapter 8).

Although these developments only directly affected web stations that were simulcasts of mainstream music stations based in the US, I was becoming concerned. Without such powerful radio players and the cross subsidy they brought to the advancement of streaming as a whole, might web radio after all be consigned to the (large) dustbin of technologies that just failed to happen? I needn't have worried. The rest of the web radio world carried on growing steadily. The one US-based case study I've been in contact with for this book, the independent RadioValve, who've negotiated their copyright arrangements independently and carry no audio ads, informed me that they noticed a rise in their audience figures following the 12 April shutdown. This effect was endorsed by many other reports coming out of America. In June Clear Channel, one of the majors who'd closed all 1200 of their US streaming stations, announced that they were beginning the process of getting them back online, not by settling with AFTRA, but by switching to an automated system for inserting different ad breaks into their online output (Snyder, 2001). This decision serves to emphasize that, despite the uncertainties of how it'll work for them in detail, in principle Clear Channel don't believe they can afford to be out of the web radio world and are ready to put further investment into their streaming operation. The technology has passed an important test of its value. The question of record company royalties has still not been settled in the US and is the subject of an appeal by the National Association of Broadcasters (NAB).

These events have brought some welcome realism to web radio's current situation in the Summer of 2001. It's not going to take over the radio world anytime soon and it doesn't yet have a persuasive business model to offer investors. On the other hand, it *is* a powerful medium that can lead the rest of the radio world in new directions – which I hope I have indicated sufficiently forcefully in this book. For many who are experimenting with web radio profitability is not the motive; communication between people is. Web radio can do this both on a very local level or globally in a way that broadcasting finds very difficult to do technically and has never made profitable. (I'm thinking of small-scale community radio and government-funded external services like the BBC World Service as comparisons here.) The traditionally profitable sector of music radio is about to undergo a profound reshaping, which looks increasingly to be out of the hands of the established terrestrial radio industry. One way or another the Internet will become – is already becoming – an extremely cost-efficient way for record companies or recording artists to promote and distribute their music: so cost efficient as to have already attracted huge investment. Web radio is much closer to the heart of that operation than the traditional driver of music sales, terrestrial radio. (This prospect, I speculate, explains Clear Channel's decision above and, perhaps incidentally, the increasingly hostile environment for web music radio that Bob Bellin and other American web radio insiders condemn. See also Ryan and Bingaman, 2001.)

Sobering developments for radio professionals; and we can be sure many more will follow in the next few years. And for non-professionals and those outside the established radio industry? The great excitement of web radio and a driving force behind its growth is that it is so easy to get your own programmes or stations online – and extremely cheap to do relative to setting up a licensed broadcast station. This book attempts to strike a balance between these two perspectives: on the one hand, it asks where web radio fits into the existing radio industry picture and on the other it suggests what web radio has to offer beyond those outside that frame. As I've said, although I am optimistic about what web radio can be, I hope I am realistic about the obstacles it faces before it reaches that potential: some are technical, some are legal, but the most important are the creative obstacles which will only be overcome by the imagination and passions of the new radio practitioners the Web invites into the previously select world of mass communications. Investors can pump as much money into the technology as they like, but to make this global experiment work we need the programme makers to generate the content that listeners will listen to and relate to.

The book takes a deliberately international approach. That's not to say all web radio stations have to have a global outlook, but that the ways of getting online are pretty much the same wherever you are and relatively free from the quirks of separate national radio broadcasting rules and regulations. It is a book both for potential practitioners and anyone interested in finding out what web radio is and where it fits into the new mosaic of digitally transmitted radio. I start from the premise that anyone interested in the content side of web radio (as opposed to the purely technical side of getting audio onto the Web) needs to understand what makes web radio different to the analogue radio we are all used to. Therefore, I see it as complementary to the many excellent books that explore techniques for communicating with an audience through radio and in no way a substitute. Indeed, I indicate those among them that I consider essential reading for anyone interested in any form of radio – past, present or future – in the 'Further reading' sections. It's a book that I hope encourages readers to think about what kind of radio we can build from the resource that streaming radio on the Internet gives us.

So I've organized the book roughly as five overlapping parts. Chapters 1 and 2 provide the context into which web radio has arrived. They attempt the tricky task of defining where the boundaries of what we can usefully call radio lie when it's put into the multimedia context of the Internet and other digital transmission technologies. One leading radio academic, Alan Beck, has recently argued in his intriguing monograph, *The Death of Radio?*, that the process of the digitalization of radio is much more than an upgrade of its transmission system: with the addition of its associated interactive services the very definition of the word 'radio' is in need of a major rethink. Chapter 2 in particular tackles that proposition so far as distribution on the Web is concerned. Chapters 3 and 4 are about the technical business of how web radio works, how to set it up and what new options it opens up both at the listener's end of the transmission 'pipe' and from the sender's end. In the middle of the book, Chapters 5 and 6 gather together a number of case studies from around the world which demonstrate how different radio organizations are applying the new flexibility web radio has to offer in a wide range of situations, from the very large to the very small. Chapters 7, 8 and 9 return to the other crucial practical dimensions of radio as a public medium, how to get noticed, how to avoid finding yourself on the wrong side of the copyright regulations I've alluded to above, or of the other kinds of legal pitfalls that may await the unaware webcaster. Although the Internet has had the reputation of being a 'rules-free zone', the reality is not quite as simple as that. Access to freedom of speech to a global public brings with it some serious ethical responsibilities and those who use it need to take an active interest in ensuring its survival. Chapters 10 and 11 then consider how the characteristics of the Internet transform the decisions to be taken about the all important radio content. I am all too aware that this is only the start of an evolving subject. As the technology and the practice move on, new forms of programme will emerge, more research will be accumulated and more books will need to be written about this vital dimension of radio. Finally, Chapter 12 offers a checklist of what has emerged in the preceding chapters about the ways in which web radio is different from the established uses of radio broadcasting: of where the two media overlap and where they diverge.

A note on sources

A further aim of the book is to act as a starting point for a good range of sources for further detail and lines of research on the subject, again both for the practitioner and the student of web radio. As well as books and articles, I point to many references I've found on pages on websites. But websites are more frequently updated than books, which can make precise referencing unreliable, so a brief explanation of my approach is called for.

In the body of the text I have consciously kept referencing to a minimum, except where quoting directly or indirectly from what someone has written or said. These I've bracketed and they can be picked up in the 'Bibliography' section (Appendix 3). Where they come from an article that's appeared on the Web there I give the file address in full, along with the publication date and also the date at which I found it there. Some of these articles I expect to stay at the same address for years, but others will be more transitory. It is quite often the case that older archive material on, for example, an online magazine site gets sifted and reclassified as time goes on. In the case of two leading online web radio magazines I have cited quite often, *RAIN* and *Radio Ink*, the alternative route is to check the publication date in my Bibliography and then to search their archived copies by date.

Otherwise, in the text I stick to referencing the URL of a home page, either for the whole site or the relevant sub-site, as the starting point for information that's more general in nature or else contained on several pages. These URLs are usually well established and I'd expect them to remain the same over time. These I have also collected together and categorized in the 'Useful websites' section of the Appendices at the end of the book.

Other unreferenced observations and information in the text I've judged to be sufficiently 'public knowledge' not to cite specific sources. The texts in the

'Further reading' at the end of the chapter provide more background and/or detail on those topics.

And finally, to try to keep pace with the phenomenal rate of change in the technologies and the availability of information on the Internet, this book has an accompanying website, which I will be updating regularly with significant developments in web radio as I become aware of them. That will include selected information or amendments suggested by readers, so your comments will be gratefully received. However, to keep up to date with the day to day news on the topics contained, I refer you to the various excellent online magazines listed under the appropriate 'Further reading'.

The address of the website is http://www.web-radio-book.com

Acknowledgements

I'm acutely aware that a single book cannot conceivably do justice to the scale of the global phenomenon of web radio. In the act of naming particular stations and sites and pointing them out as examples, I am neglecting many hundreds equally worthy of inclusion. So I would first like to acknowledge here the efforts of anyone who is expending their time and their enthusiasm for the medium of radio in this online experiment.

Equally, I take responsibility for the way I have represented the current state of the technology and its applications. I hope I have made sufficiently clear in the text that my descriptions and any conclusions are provisional: I have made every effort to check their accuracy at the time of writing, but the pace of progress means, I feel sure, that there are some relevant innovations I have already overlooked and others about to emerge as soon as this goes to press. I will endeavour to keep pace through the book's associated website.

For the present though, my thanks go to those companies and individuals who have given their permission to reproduce images from their websites on these pages. Among them, I would like to emphasize the key significance of the pioneering and continuing highly creative work being done by the employees of RealNetworks, Microsoft's Windows Media Player, of Apple's QuickTime, of Nullsoft and all the other software and hardware companies responsible for turning streaming from a promising idea into a technology that works so well for radio.

All rights associated with each of the illustrations reproduced in this book are reserved by the owners identified in each caption. Copyright details can be found on the respective websites. The 'Real' logo and the names RealNetworks, RealAudio, RealEncoder, RealGuide, RealPlayer, RealProducer, RealServer and RealSystem are trademarks or registered trademarks of RealNetworks, Inc. The names of all Windows products, Windows Media Player, Windows Media Encoder and Windows Server software are trademarks of Microsoft, Corp. The names of all QuickTime products are trademarks of Apple Computer, Inc.

Among the many people who've responded to my email inquiries, I owe a personal debt of gratitude to those who have so generously and enthusiastically spent time and effort in providing me with the case studies that illuminate the heart of the book. They are:

Steve Taylor, Group Enterprises Director, and David Jones, Head of IT, at Virgin Radio in London; Jonathan Marks, Director of Programmes at Radio Netherlands, Hilversum; Dean Schwind, the Station Manager, and his colleagues at

CFUV, University of Victoria, Canada; the guys who tirelessly run RadioValve from Boulder, Colorado – David Fodel, Brian Comerford, Brian Kane and Tony Middleton; Colin Kleyweg, Managing Director of Pulse Radio Pty Ltd in Sydney, Australia; Sruti Bala, colleagues at Amarc and the technical co-ordinators of the 2001 VSF project, Hermann Schwaersler and Roland Jankowski at Orange 94.0; Wijayananda Jayaweera, the UNESCO Regional Communication Advisor for Asia in Kuala Lumpur; Tanya Notley, formerly the volunteer worker at Kothmale Community Radio in Sri Lanka and the station manager there, Sunil Wijesinghe.

Beyond those specific illustrations I have also drawn widely on the fantastic wealth of information that is now so freely available on the Web. The generous spirit of those who contribute their knowledge to this world library deserve regular and fulsome thanks from all of us who benefit from it. For the purposes of this book I would like to acknowledge the insights I have derived from three excellent online publications in particular: Kurt Hanson's invaluable daily digest of industry news and opinion, the *Radio And Internet Newsletter* (*RAIN*), headlines from which have been delivered free to my desktop throughout my research; the packed website of *Radio Ink* for its detailed background and forthright discussion of current developments; and as a starting point for research into the labyrinthine questions of music copyright on the Web, I found the 'Kohn on Music Licensing' website a tremendous help. I am grateful too to the operators of all the other websites I have cited in the book and listed in Appendix 2.

Closer to home in the offline world, my thanks go to colleagues in the Field of Media, Journalism and Cultural Studies at Staffordshire University, who have supported, encouraged and enabled me to complete the book. In particular, I am indebted to John Herbert for being the catalyst and for his generous encouragement and feedback throughout. I am also grateful to Charlie Phillips at Capital Interactive and to Alan Beck of the University of Kent for making time to read the penultimate draft and for their very helpful feedback.

Working with Focal Press has been a genuine pleasure and I'm extremely grateful to the book's editor, Beth Howard, for her patient understanding and the calm efficiency with which she has nurtured this project from the outset. Thanks too to Beth's assistant, Christina Donaldson.

There are many others – radio professionals, teachers, academics and students – whose insights and influences I have absorbed over many years (since well before I'd ever heard of the Internet or streaming) and have now filtered and interpreted amongst these pages. Without their inspiration I would be in no position to broach the subject of radio in the new context of the Web.

Above all, though, I want to thank Meg, who has shared the twists and turns of my involvement in sound throughout those years, for putting up with my distracted attention and the unseemly number of evenings and weekends I've devoted to this computer in recent months.

July 2001

1 What is radio on the Web?

'Let us not forget that the value of this great system does not lie primarily in its extent or even in its efficiency. . . . Its worth depends on the use that is made of it. . . . For the first time in human history we have available to us the ability to communicate simultaneously with millions of our fellow men, to furnish entertainment, instruction, widening vision of national problems and national events.'

These words make a doubly appropriate introduction to a book about combining the first new medium of the twentieth century, radio, with the last, the Internet. They were spoken by Herbert Hoover, the then United States Secretary of Commerce, in 1924 about the uncertain beginnings of the technology by which humans learned to communicate with each other using radio waves (at the start of the third Washington Radio Conference). But they could equally be taken from one of the more restrained paeans of anticipation that greeted the emergence of the Internet into public consciousness almost exactly 70 years later.

In those early years on the frontier of wireless listening, the equipment was bulky and awkward to use, the sound quality was poor by today's standards and reception would often break up because, in America at least, too many people were trying to broadcast on the system at the same time: but nevertheless those who had receivers were captivated by the magic of the experience – and of course the novelty. If we take out the word 'wireless' from that sentence and substitute 'web radio' we have something very close to a description of the newest way of tuning in at the turn of the twenty-first century.

There are indeed many striking parallels to be drawn between the early assimilation of the two technologies into public life. Some are no more than incidental curiosities, but most arise from important characteristics they both share. So identifying these similarities – and also important differences –

between the 'use that is made' of radio transmitted on analogue waves and via the Internet forms the substance of this opening chapter. From the many parallels between the two – and those differences – we can get a useful sense of the trajectory of development we can expect for web radio.

Box 1.1   Parallel 1: Problems for listeners – by today's standards

In their early years, both technologies suffer from primitive sound quality, interrupted signals when their transmission systems become overloaded and from the immobility of receivers, in the form of the valve wireless and the desktop computer.

One crucial thing to recognize at the outset is that, whether we like it or not, the presence of the Internet forces us to reconsider what radio means to us as a medium. We have by now, most of us, taken it for granted all our lives: turn on the radio and there you have it. Radio needed no more definition than the transmission system by which we picked it up. All sound programming carried from a transmitter to our tuner using the properties of electromagnetic waves we called radio. What's more, the precise nature of the radio medium is determined by the available technology we use to hear it and that has changed over time. On a technological level the Internet is just another transmission system, but the fact that it is also a unified medium that can carry all the pre-existing mass media – in text, images and sound – separately or in combination means that for the first time we have to define what makes radio solely in terms of (a) the content and (b) how the listener distinguishes it from other sounds available through their multi-purpose receiver – the computer.

So, as this book is about putting radio *content* on the Internet, I intend to spend the first two chapters identifying the ways in which digitalization and the Internet are expanding the boundaries of radio and its relationship with the competing public media. In this first chapter, having offered some introductory definitions of the Internet and webcasting from the radio practitioner's perspective, I review the defining characteristics of traditional radio technology, emphasizing those characteristics it shares in common with the Internet. In the second chapter, I place web radio in the wider – much wider – context of all the other sounds to be found on the Internet. There are plenty of sounds out there and most of them are not radio.

The 'Further reading' at the end of this chapter gives a selection of more specialist texts that go into the kind of detail about the development of the two transmission systems that is beyond the scope of this book.

What's new about the New Medium?

The innumerable books and articles that have already been published about the Internet are testimony both to its importance as a new medium and to the power of suggestion over the human mind. Distinguishing between the real benefits and the hype is perhaps the most demanding challenge this combination of Information and Communications Technologies (ICT) presents us with. We are undoubtedly living through a major media revolution and that inevitably involves the violent collision of conflicting hopes and fears over how it will change our lives. But can we guess where this revolution is taking us? Some reference to the history of previous media technologies should provide some helpful, though not necessarily conclusive, perspectives; helpful because it offers a framework in which to decide what we can do with radio on the Web.

In the history of mass communication, no new medium has yet made an earlier one obsolete, despite the reiterated predictions at the time of each new arrival.

- Photography was supposed to mean the end of painting.
- Film was supposed to mean the end of the novel.
- Radio was supposed to mean the end of newspapers.
- Television was supposed to mean the end of film *and* radio.

What did happen, of course, was that the new medium changed its predecessor but did not replace it. Or, to put it another way, the older medium always adapted itself to fit into the new mix of competitors – redefining itself according to its intrinsic strengths. In the case of radio versus television, for example, one critical advantage that emerged for radio was that you can take it with you while you are doing something else. Before television, the old wireless had become the fixed centrepiece of domestic life across the industrialized nations and it commanded high levels of attention when it was on. At the same time as the TV was taking over that space, the technological switch from bulky, fragile valve to tiny, robust transistor freed the radio to accompany the individual, especially out into the car. We will need to bear these precedents in mind as we begin to assess the accuracy of early predictions about today's new technology:

- Now the Internet is supposed to mean the end of newspapers, television and radio.

Box 1.2   Parallel 2: The threat to competing media – or not

Early fears of the existing news and entertainment industries that analogue radio would 'steal' their audiences proved unfounded: in fact, the three industries soon become mutually interdependent. There are similar worries about the fallout from the convergence of text, sound and moving pictures onto digital platforms like the Internet, but the early signs are of an evolution of similar complementary relationships, for example, between web radio and analogue radio, as we shall see through this book.

Two key questions about newness

Returning to the quote at the start of the chapter, what the Internet proves to be 'worth' as a mass medium 'depends on the use that is made of it'. To be useful it must offer a new capability over and above the existing technology. In order to assess its usefulness to radio listeners there are two related questions I intend to take as recurrent themes throughout the subsequent chapters of the book. They are questions anyone intending to use the Internet to transmit radio must ask themselves:

1 What new strengths does web radio add to pre-Internet radio?
2 What established strengths of radio does web radio supplant?

But first, what is the Internet and what use is it to a well-established medium like radio?

The Internet on the phone system

The word 'Internet' – short for 'inter-network' – was first coined in the 1960s to describe a small network of research computers linked together via the US telephone system. It began as an experimental method of sending text messages (emails) between computers in such a way that they could not be blocked: if one telephone exchange or run of cable was out of action then the message would find an alternative route through the system to reach its destination address. The important characteristic of the phone infrastructure which this text-based inter-network exploited was that it had no centre, no single point of control. A single message could be sent to everyone connected to the network who knew how to use a computer to pick it up. Conversely, everyone on the network could post individual messages at a single computer location, known as a 'bulletin board', where they could all be read by anyone else any time they 'logged on'.

Back then, few people had access to a computer – they were still room-sized machines – but those whose employers ran one recognized the usefulness of a carrier which put one person into such a fluid dialogue with many people who shared the same interest. So word spread (via more established routes of personal and mass communication) and new text message networks sprang into being as different research institutions and university departments hooked their computers up to phone lines.

An important early move to standardize these disparate networks, so that one network could talk to another, was the creation of a common system of numbered addresses that would get a text message from any computer connected to the phone system on one network to any other computer on the phone system on another network. These were the Transmission Control Protocol (TCP) and the Internet Protocol (IP), devised and refined by Vint Cerf and Bob Kahn between 1974 and 1977, and still at the heart of the Internet to this day (see Naughton, 2000, for an excellent introduction).

The principle of inter-linked networks has since multiplied and evolved alongside the popularization of computer technology to inhabit the entire network of cables, exchanges, satellites and relay stations that make up the global telephone system, creating the Internet as we know it today. Any computer becomes part of the Internet when it goes 'online', with its own IP address: it is both sender and receiver. Disconnecting any computer or many computers from the phone system cannot stop the Internet working (although at its extremities, where there are fewer alternative routes, it becomes easier to slow down or isolate an individual connection). The Internet, then, is not a physical thing, designed for the purpose, but a medium that was discovered when the young computer technology met the established infrastructure of our oldest form of electronic voice communication, the telephone. Most importantly, it is a mass communications system whose infrastructure, unlike the fixed points of the radio transmitter network, is amorphous and decentralized.

A brief Internet disclaimer

In its short life, the word has come to mean many things to different people, which is a reflection of the many different uses people have found for the system it describes. So, very few general statements about the Internet, beyond the most basic of definitions, are likely to be accepted as 'true' by all or even a majority of Internet users. This is part of its mystique. In this book we are only interested in how the Internet can serve that older medium we know as radio. Otherwise, I will refer to the Internet only in the sense of a physical means of transmission or distribution, and I make no claims to do justice to any other uses it is put to. There are many excellent books and articles that explore the global Internet as a concept, a few of which I list at the end of this chapter.

The Web floats on the Internet

So why is this book called 'Web Radio' and not 'Internet Radio'? I certainly could have chosen the latter title: it is a term widely used in this context. But the World Wide Web (henceforth the Web) more accurately describes the international public experience of the Internet. Terms like website, web page and web address (which will usually begin 'www.') characterize by far the largest colony of Internet users, who have adopted the same set of agreed computer languages and standards to find and present information to each other.

The languages and standards of the Web were originated by Tim Berners-Lee and colleagues in 1990 for the European Laboratory for Particle Physics at CERN in Geneva, Switzerland. He was asked to provide that international community of experts with easy access to a common network of information sites – among the many that were being set up by other communities of Internet users in different computer languages. The two main standards he drew up were for Hyper Text Mark-up Language (HTML), the computer language in which text pages were encoded, and Hyper Text Transfer Protocol (HTTP), the standard form of address which enabled the HTML message to find its way from one computer, through the phone system, to other computers 'online' in the network. Because they worked so well, these standards were quickly taken up by other groups of users when making information generally available on the Internet. By the time the personal computer boom took off later in the 1990s, a critical mass of information was already sitting there on established websites in the tested and proven HTML, and so the lingua franca of the Web was the obvious one for most Internet novices to adopt. Tim Berners-Lee continues to orchestrate the development of Web standards through the World Wide Web Consortium. Their site at http://www.w3c.org/ contains a wealth of useful information on the history and current development of the Web.

A very important feature of the way the architecture of the Web was put together, to which I will return frequently, was its openness: the means to get onto it (the standards) and its millions of pages of content were made available as a free service to an international public.

Bringing radio to the Web

The original Web standards were not developed for transmitting sound or moving pictures. Anyone who has recorded a sound file onto their computer knows that it takes up a lot of digital 'space'. Digitally encoding or capturing the varying nuances of sound contained in a minute of speech for radio involves a lot more information (around 10 megabytes in CD quality stereo) than the same in 180 words or so of encoded text (around 420 times less at 24 kilobytes). The

Table 1.1 The important characteristics of the Internet and hence the Web

- Simultaneous two-way 'interactive' communication
- Open all hours, instantaneously across all time zones
- No centre and therefore not easily susceptible to overall control
- Signals automatically re-routed if physically blocked – though individual connections to the Internet can be legally constrained
- Designed originally to carry digitized text messages
- Based on computers which are designed chiefly to store, search and sort masses of digital data, as well as send it through the network
- An open resource, designed in principle for maximum access and the free exchange of information

analogy that is commonly used to help describe this problem of size is of the 'narrow pipe': the pipe-work of the domestic phone line was fine for relatively skinny text data, but squeezing much, much fatter audio data through such unsuitable plumbing would take a very long time – and far too long for it to emerge at the other end of the system sounding anything like its live original.

Nevertheless, in 1995, shortly after the birth of the Web, an American company called Progressive Networks made available a software package that stripped down the detail contained in digitized audio to such an extent that it could pass from one computer, through the phone network to another computer and emerge from a speaker as a (more or less) continuous stream of sound – at somewhat higher quality than an ordinary telephone conversation. They named the software RealAudio and the process became known as live 'streaming'. In radio terms, this was the equivalent moment to the first transmission of speech by R. A. Fessenden in place of Morse code on the 'radio telephone' in 1906: the quality was poor, but we could recognize what it was and envisage the possibilities.

Progressive Networks soon became RealNetworks (http://www.realnetworks-.com/) and went on to rapidly improve the capabilities of their RealAudio, closely followed by a number of competitors. Chapters 3 and 4 describe the details of how streaming audio works, but in order to introduce the relationship between terrestrial and web radio for now, given that sound can be sent across the Internet at reasonable quality, its important characteristics are defined by the above properties of the international phone network coupled with the computer's ability to search and store huge amounts of data at unimaginable speeds.

So, if the Internet is the medium through which data travel, then the Web is the agreed system of signals we use to 'tune in' to particular locations. How does this system compare with 'old-fashioned' radio broadcasting?

Radio *was* an interactive medium

Listeners to analogue radio are accustomed to thinking of themselves as strictly on the receiving end of a transmission medium. The path of a radio broadcast is in one direction only: from station to transmitter mast to radio receiver to our ear. Our scope for interacting with a programme is usually confined to the on/off switch or the tuning control. Occasionally we may phone, write or (now) email the broadcaster to contribute a dedication, question or opinion in response to their on-air invitation. Some of us may be moved to complain about (or, even more rarely, praise) something we have heard on the station. We *may* even step out of our listening role to lend our physical presence as a spectator at a live broadcast. But most listeners to mainstream radio do none of these things, they just expect to listen to radio.

This is the way the radio spectrum has proved most useful to most people. But radio waves are invisible and we easily forget how much the technology has in common with its more obviously connected cousin in sound, the telephone – that most personal, two-way talking, electronic medium. At their most basic, both pathways begin with a microphone and end with a loudspeaker; and the copper wire or the invisible radio wave can carry signals in either direction. The point is emphasized by the fact that, between Bell's invention of the telephone and the arrival of the wireless, telephone technology was used experimentally to 'broadcast' music and news live via local exchanges down the wires to domestic handsets (see Gilliams, 1925, and descriptions of the electrophone in Briggs, 1995, pp. 39–40 or in Crook, 1999, pp. 15–20). Radio on the domestic telephone proved impractical at the start of the century, when telecommunications networks were much smaller and private ownership was minuscule in comparison with today, so radio on the airwaves was quickly recognized as the more practical on every level. But now, by putting radio onto the Internet, we are returning to try out that same principle again, albeit with the addition of very much more advanced technology. As far as the domestic listener is concerned, though, the properties of the individual telephone connection have changed very little.

Box 1.3   Parallel 3: Radio's relationship with the telephone

In their early development, both analogue and web radio are extensions of the technology for carrying sound from point to point, the telephone network, but both quickly outgrow the capacity of its wires.

In the early days of radio technology, the apparatus was commonly called the 'radio telephone', a name which encapsulated the combination of the essentially 'private' uses of the telephone with the 'public' transmission of signals on radio waves. The quote from Herbert Hoover at the beginning of the chapter is taken from his address to the 1924 Washington Radio Conference, the third in a series he called to try to find a workable solution to the problems he was having as the US government's regulator of the airwaves. His Department of Commerce had failed to control the explosion of public, often interactive, transmissions being aired by radio enthusiasts to and fro across the country: as is commonly the case, the legislation was running to catch up with that astonishing technological leap forward.

Throughout this book we will encounter comparable problems on the 'wild frontier' of radio transmission on the Internet. So, in trying to understand how radio can make use of today's new transmission medium, we need to ask:

- What were the essentials of the technology that made analogue radio communication possible?
- What has the technology been used to communicate in practice?

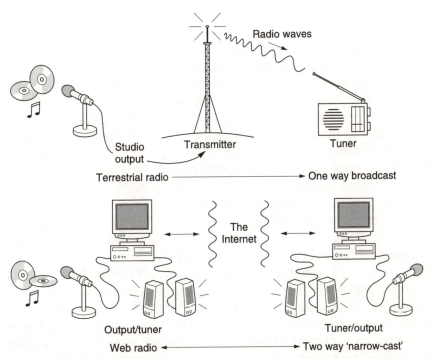

Figure 1.1 A simplified schematic comparison between the transmission characteristics of terrestrial radio (one-way) and web radio (two-way).

Some early utopian visions for radio

There are certainly some surprising and enlightening comparisons to be made between public perceptions of the possibilities of radio in the 1920s and of the Internet in the1990s. Although the intervening years of accelerating innovation have made us increasingly nonchalant about the 'next new technology', both of these particular innovations have been greeted with a sense of real expectation: each would be much more than a gadget for mere diversion or entertainment; it would be a force for good, for liberation, for unification and democratization.

Herbert Hoover's words at the start of the chapter give a flavour of some of the official rhetoric of the day. On the other side of the Atlantic, also in 1924, an idealistic young British radio pioneer wrote in more contemplative mood of our human sensory relationship with the world around us:

> 'We are missing infinitely more than we are receiving . . . Thought is probably permanent, and a means may be found to ally thought with ether direct and to broadcast and communicate thought without the intervention of the senses or any mechanical device, in the same manner as a receiving set is today tuned to the wave-length of a transmitter so that there may be a free passage between them.'

> (p. 224)

This remarkable image of inter-connected minds, conjured up by John Reith at the rhapsodic conclusion of his book *Broadcasting Over Britain*, contains precisely the same semi-mystical aspiration as many a description of the Internet in 1994. The three words 'free passage between', with all their overtones of unmediated, unfettered, universal communication, are all the more surprising when we think of the blueprint for radio broadcasting with which Reith became associated as the first Director General of the British Broadcasting Corporation: a highly centralized, tightly controlled monopoly. Nevertheless, within these words we can recognize an unmistakable yearning for a world *improved* by radio communication, which would help accentuate humanity's positive, co-operative potential by providing the means for facilitating mutual understanding. (Reith's horrific experiences during active service in World War One cannot have been far from his mind here.)

But it was the very power he saw in radio when it was still in its infancy that in fact created the need to tame it and eventually sideline its two-way, interactive potential as a public medium. In America, the pioneering chaos of too many private amateurs and would-be professional stations, sending and receiving on a limited spectrum of frequencies, eventually led to the establishment of a Federal Radio Commission (the predecessor of today's Federal Communications Commission, the FCC) under the Radio Act of 1927. Their remit was to organize the spectrum so that licensed broadcast stations across the country could be received without interference. This inevitably meant reining back small-scale and spontaneous transmissions to clean up the ether for more organized broadcasts with larger, purely *listening* audiences.

Box 1.4   Parallel 4: Amateur enthusiasm a driving force

Radio is an example of a simple technology that, once discovered, is never beyond the means of the committed amateur. And, once streaming software becomes available, the same is true of radio on the Web. So a great deal of the early impetus for the development and testing of both is done by non-professionals – to the bemusement of those who do not yet recognize the possibilities.

Over in Europe, by contrast, governments moved swiftly to curtail amateur experimentation early in the 1920s. Various models of partial or total radio broadcasting monopoly were imposed in each country, before the arrival of the affordable wireless set with internal loudspeaker created a truly mass *listener*ship. In effect, the ensuing build up to World War Two in Europe confirmed those wary politicians' fears as radio quickly proved to be an extremely potent tool for propaganda, disinformation and – the flip side of Reith's beneficent vision of mind expansion – thought control.

Words like propaganda and thought control, of course, imply a one-way flow of information, from an élite with power and authority downwards through a society, rather than a 'free passage' of communication through the ether. Two-way, interactive radio involves dialogue, many opportunities for public debate and, by definition, implies a counterweight to the centralization of the control of information and cultural expression which so characterized the rule of European states and their global colonies at that time. And, of course, it just would not have been manageable in practical terms because the spectrum of radio frequencies is so limited. As the playwright Bertold Brecht ruefully explained in 1930:

> 'Radio could be the most wonderful public communication system imaginable, a gigantic system of channels – could be, that is, if it were capable not only of transmitting but of receiving, of making listeners hear but also speak, not of isolating them but connecting them.'

(quoted in Lewis and Booth, 1989, p. 186)

Again, this sounds like a precise premonition of what radio could be on a decentralized system like the Internet. Brecht was himself an early radio enthusiast and he conducted his own amateur experiments with the medium. This was, after all, a relatively simple, cheap technology to master. His vision of a mass medium (or publicly accessible network) controlled at an individual, or at least a very local, level would be technically feasible if the development of the technological research were steered that way. But the application of any technology is always subject to the social context of its day, and in the political climate of 1930s Europe this was an utterly impossible dream.

Box 1.5   Parallel 5: Radio as a decentralizing, democratizing medium

Analogue radio emerges as a mass medium in the early 1920s before most adults in most countries have won the right to vote for their leaders. Many recognize its potential as a tool for pushing forward the cause of democracy because of its power to bring together audiences over vast distances and publicly to hold governments to account. And once again, the early champions of the Web in the mid-1990s promise that the new medium will empower the individual: this time through direct interaction within the 'global village', unmediated by government or corporate influence.

Vertical versus horizontal radio communication

The terms 'vertical' and 'horizontal' are useful in this context. They are borrowed from contrasting models of institutional organization, but they neatly encapsulate:

1 The contrast between this early utopian vision for analogue radio and the industry it became.
2 The differences inherent in the technologies of the phone-based Internet and of the traditional broadcast industries.

'Horizontal' describes the situation in which all the participants have an equal status, where communication passes freely between them and control is evenly dispersed: 'vertical' describes the opposite, where status is differentiated into a hierarchy in which information is controlled at the centre and communication flows not across, but upwards and mainly downwards from the few at the head of the hierarchy to the many at the bottom. Remembering the early utopian visions of radio, then, horizontal describes a strongly interactive, equal relationship between the listener and programme maker, while vertical describes the broadcast infrastructure that radio adopted, in which a small number of broadcasters disseminate to a mass audience. In this scheme, the commercial and public service sectors of the international radio industry (see below) are in the vertical category; their transmission systems are vertical and their organizational management vertical. Meanwhile, stations which aim to offer an alternative to the mainstream or dominant broadcast structures have, by definition, more horizontal characteristics.

Hence, vertical broadcast institutions:

- are large organizations reliant on economies of scale,
- are therefore hierarchical and 'top down',
- are managed centrally, at a distance from the listener,
- need large audiences, and
- must therefore appeal to majority tastes,

and horizontal broadcasters:

- are either small organizations or else operate as small decentralized units,
- are 'bottom up', involving listeners directly in policy making and programmes,
- need only attract small audiences (though they may incidentally gain wider popularity), and
- can serve minority interests, groups or communities.

Radio wave transmission began as an experiment in horizontal communication. But soon the technology and the broadcast infrastructure became organized into a much more manageable vertical system, as exemplified by the BBC's worldwide operation, centrally controlled from London.

Web radio, being based on the infrastructure of the one to one phone network, is inherently a horizontal technology. It is difficult (though not impossible, as we shall see later in Chapter 9) to envisage it in a vertical form. So, those who want to make use of web radio successfully need to understand and adapt their operations to this horizontal way of thinking (see Chapters 5 and 6).

Radio listening was shaped in the Broadcast Century

During the 30-year period between the 1930s and the 1960s, the vertical incarnation of the radio industry was consolidated and became woven into the fabric of societies all around the world. It was during this era of upheaval and strife that different countries developed their own radio industries, with their own traditions of broadcast style and programme content. These are the foundations of the infrastructure of analogue radio as each nation knows it today. And these foundations underlie the qualities and textures of the medium that we are about to transpose onto the Internet.

In terms of the wider social context, this brief but extraordinary span of years includes drastic global change in which radio played a central role, including:

- world war and reconstruction;
- widespread industrialization and rapidly accelerating urbanization;
- the start of the Age of Consumerism, individualism and the fragmentation of audiences.

Within each country, responding to these changes, there were the further indigenous layers of cultural, economic, political and legislative influence on what broadcasters chose and were allowed to air on national and local radio stations.

Radio transmission technology developed rapidly, mapped the world in transmission areas and set current expectations for accuracy or fidelity of its signals:

- initially Amplitude Modulated (AM) signals – travelled very long distances but gave relatively poor sound quality;
- from the 1960s the gradual adoption of Frequency Modulation (FM) – over shorter distances – gave much improved sound quality;
- most countries developed internal radio broadcasting infrastructures;
- strategic development of 'external' AM radio services, e.g. the Voice of America and the BBC's World Service (formerly known as the Empire Service, then the General Overseas Service).

The technology of radio receivers formed the experience of listening:

- from the 1930s the widely affordable, easy to tune, mains-powered valve radio with internal loudspeaker became a fragile fixture for the main communal living area of the house;
- from the mid-1950s TV took over the living rooms of the developed world;
- in the 1960s the transistorized radio – compact, robust and portable – changed listening patterns;
- especially when fitted in cars;
- the stereo high-fidelity music centre further improved the quality of home listening and the production values of broadcasters.

Changes in radio production technology, though less obvious to the listener, created the texture of the medium we now recognize as radio:

- microphones and electronic circuitry became more able to faithfully reproduce a wider range of sound frequencies;
- from 1945 cheap magnetic tape meant programmes no longer had to be transmitted live (though tape technology was developed in Germany from 1930);
- portable recorders made location news reporting and recording routine (although short recordings were previously possible, using extremely cumbersome disc-cutting equipment);
- editing and post-production changed the way programmes were put together and over time replaced the tyranny of the production script with spontaneous conversation and the voices of 'real people';
- tape gave birth to those attention-grabbing staples of modern popular music radio – the jingle, the station ident, the radio advert and the sting.

The complex interaction of all these (and doubtless many other) technological and societal factors created the foundations of radio broadcasting as we understand it today and moulded the experience we call 'listening to the radio'. While it is true that Internet technology allows us to tinker with this mould in all sorts of clever ways, the essentials of the vocabulary of radio communication, the way we understand what we hear, the way we decide what we want to listen to, our human relationship with a station, remain fundamentally the same.

Box 1.6   Listen to the world on the radio

One of the very useful ways in which web radio adds to our experience of analogue radio is that it makes it so much easier to study this elusive, transitory medium (of which more in later chapters). I include some addresses for websites of international examples of each of the three sectors below, from where you should be able to listen to and compare their typical output. A browse through the website illustrated in Figure 1.2, a major directory of stations you can hear on the Internet, reveals the number of radio stations available on the Web. Those who have not used streaming audio before may be helped by Chapter 3.

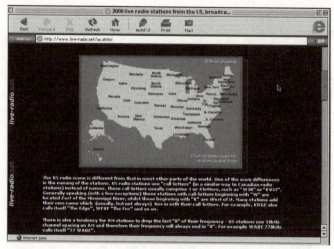

Figure 1.2 The web page at http://www.live-radio.net/us.shtml, which has links to over 2000 web radio stations in the US alone. The Live Radio site is a directory of web radio around the world (see also Chapter 7). Screen shot reproduced by permission of Brian Buckley.

The sectors of the radio industry

The texture of the listening experience is different from country to country according to its own history (quite apart from language). Nevertheless, those 30 years from 1930 to 1960 laid the foundations on which the present, still expanding, international industry was built. David Hendy (2000) provides a concise, comprehensive overview of today's international radio industry in the first chapter of *Radio in the Global Age*. He identifies five recognizable sectors or traditions: State Radio, Public Service Radio, Commercial Radio, Community Radio and Underground Radio. Since the nature of the Internet is already blurring the boundaries between some of these categories for radio on the Web (see Chapter 10), it will be useful here to identify their main attributes.

But, in terms of their finance, these five sectors can be simplified to three, along the lines used by Lewis and Booth (1989) throughout their pioneering history *The Invisible Medium*. They differentiate American style commercially financed radio from the publicly funded models preferred in Europe (whether 'arm's length' public service broadcasting or directly state controlled) and the largely voluntarily organized Alternative or Third Sector Radio.

When it became clear that radio was more than just a wireless method for point to point communication, the obvious question arose, 'How should it be paid for?' For, once the radio signal is 'in the ether', there was no technology for metering who is using how much of it: anyone within range of the transmitter who owned the right kind of receiver can pick it up. And the view quickly spread that everyone *should* become part of this audience – just as today international governments emphasize the importance of everyone getting online.

Whether transmission is terrestrial or on the Internet, obviously the source of a station's finance determines its characteristic content and style. So, combining Hendy's and Lewis and Booth's categorizations, we have:

• The early European model, based on the idea that radio was too important to be wasted in the hands of self-interested businessmen, made governments responsible for raising the money for services that were usually national, so that includes both public service and state radio.
• The American model, based on the reverse idea that radio was too important to be left in the control of self-promoting governments, gave it to commercial enterprise, who funded local stations through advertising.
• The alternative. Especially after World War Two, it became obvious that these two models were not successfully addressing substantial parts of increasingly fragmented national audiences. So alternative radio movements grew up, who had to find other financial means of supporting themselves on air. These relied heavily and characteristically on the enthusiasm of volunteers, both as participants and for fund raising.

The early European model – centrally funded radio

The concept of a medium deemed to exist exclusively for the benefit of a nation's public and not for profit was born with radio. The reasons why this should be the case are bound up in the coincidence of the social and technological histories sketched above. Again, we see a very significant parallel with the early years of the Internet as a publicly available information service and it is closely connected to the utopian hopes for both technologies discussed in the earlier sections.

Harnessing the range of enthusiasms and talents from the early experimenters to create a national public radio service needed a central organization and the mandate of governments. The possible financial options were:

1 Some kind of levy on sales of receivers, as the pioneer David Sarnoff originally suggested, unsuccessfully, for all radio broadcasting in the USA (see Barnouw, 1966, p. 157).
2 An annual licence fee on the ownership of a receiver, the arrangement developed originally for *public service radio* broadcasters, independent from the State, like the BBC in the UK.
3 Through government endowments which generate income through investment in the stock market, as eventually adopted in 1967 to support American public broadcasting (alongside charitable donations).

4 As an item of public expenditure paid directly out of general taxation, the solution especially favoured by authoritarian governments who wanted explicit, direct control over the content of *state radio* broadcasting.

These options are still entirely relevant in relation to the Internet today.

In countries that opted for (2) or (4), the public service or state radio broadcast organization typically began as a national monopoly or near-monopoly and grew quickly into a large hierarchical organization in a rigidly vertical mould (as defined above). Sooner or later though, under pressure from internal political lobbying or external broadcasters transmitting into its territory (and usually both), it lost its monopoly and had to compete with increasingly confident commercial broadcasters on increasingly commercial terms. Today's public service radio and even state radio stations must now fight for their places in the national media mix and regularly convince the majority of their nation's audience that they are worth the legally enforced payment (plus the freedom from adverts). Public service radio is typically seen as setting the standard against which the commercial competition must measure up. Ideally, it should also aim to reflect and represent the diversity of the national audience. Targeted web pages and associated webcasts of all sorts are now adding substantially to public service broadcasters' means of achieving that representation.

Box 1.7   Parallel 6: Web radio in the national public service mould

Established public service radio organizations see web radio as an obvious extension of their remit, e.g. by keeping their citizens overseas in touch with home. Listen to some examples of national public service radio stations 'simulcast' live on the Web: Minnesota Public Radio (http://www.mpr.org/) as an example of a station carrying programmes made by the US National Public Radio network (http://www.npr.org/); BBC Radio 4 (http://www.bbc.co.uk/radio4/); All India Radio (http://air.kode.net/live.html); South Africa FM (http://www.safm.co.za/); Australian Broadcasting Corporation's Radio National (http://www.abc.net.au/rn/). See Figure 1.3.

The American model – commercially funded radio

On-air advertising has become the commonest method for funding radio stations through most countries around the world. The transaction involved could not be more straightforward, hence its success. A station attracts a certain audience of listeners and sells air time to advertisers who want to reach that

Figure 1.3 The BBC Radio 4 web page at http://www.bbc.co.uk/radio4/. The BBC's main site is renowned as one of the most visited in the world. Notice that, as well as the live simulcast with the analogue broadcast, you can listen to archived copies of many of the week's programmes. Screen shot reproduced by permission of BBC Online.

audience: the cost of airing each advert is calculated on the size of audience that an independent research organization predicts will be listening to the station at that time of day.

The model, as developed in the US, has been so successful that just about everyone on the planet is by now familiar with the universal sound of 'format' pop music radio: a restricted playlist of tracks targeting a specific majority lifestyle and demographic; upbeat, friendly, almost invariably male host; 'strip' scheduling; hourly news headlines, sport and weather; regular traffic news; repetition of attention-grabbing station idents and fixed ad breaks. The globalization of the pop music industry has gone hand in hand with the spread of this format of commercial music station. Surfing between examples of the thousands of international commercial stations now simulcasting their terrestrial transmissions on the Web provides ample proof of the success and the honed precision of this formula.

The major complaint levelled at the commercial model is that, as it has evolved thus far, it has led to the homogenization of radio rather than true diversity. It turns radio stations into audience delivery businesses first and programme makers second. Consequently, their decisions follow the rules of business competition. The viability of the station depends on maintaining a consistent and predictable share of the potential audience; the higher the share, the better the return on investment. As with any other line of business, competitors congregate close together on the middle ground of mainstream taste, where experience shows they can expect to find the majority audience. In order to keep up with the nearest competitors, new variations in style and content are often closely imitated, while those differences that may lose audience are quickly jettisoned. And as with any other line of business, the history of commercial radio has been away from local ownership and towards increasingly vertical corporate consolidation. The extent of that consolidation is limited by national laws restricting the ownership of media outlets, but the largest media groups are now competing with each other for audiences across a global marketplace.

We'll see in the later chapters of this book that web radio is truly a double-edged sword in this world of commercial media giants. On the one side, it offers them cheap access to vast new international audiences and the advertising revenues that go with them, but on the other the Internet disperses audiences and hence their source of income. The arrival of 'narrow-casting' in place of 'broad-casting' allows an unlimited army of (relatively) tiny new competitors to offer listeners the kind of niche programming which mass broadcasters cannot provide. The Internet is not a conventional broadcast system which requires audiences in the thousands and millions to make a TV or radio station viable.

Audience size is completely scalable according to the financial means of the webcaster and the number of listeners they can attract. To begin transmitting on the Web, you only need a reasonably up to date computer connected to the Internet. As long as you have that you are never too small to be a radio station, capable of communicating with anywhere – down the road or on the other side of the world – and with an audience of one or thousands.

Box 1.8   Parallel 7: Web radio in the commercial mould

Established commercial radio groups tend to see the Web as a new commercial frontier through which to sell audience 'hits' to advertisers. Compare some examples of commercial radio stations 'simulcast' live on the Web: Jazz FM (UK) (http://www.jazzfm.com/); 95bFM (New Zealand) (http://www.95bfm.co.nz/bfm.php); Miki FM (Japan) (http://www.fm-miki.com/); Power FM (Canary Islands) (http://www.powerfm.com/). See Figure 1.4.

Alternative or third sector radio

Hilmes (2002) describes how the century's duel between the 'British Quality' model of broadcasting and 'American Chaos' has inhibited governments' consideration of other ways the technology could be used. The view that radio

Figure 1.4 The web page at http://www.jazzfm.com/. Notice the discrete banner advertising to appeal to an international web audience. The 'listen to jazz fm' stream is a simulcast of the analogue output, with the added visual dimension of a webcam in the studio. Screen shot reproduced by permission of Jazz FM.

can and should offer more choice than broadcasts 'from on high', whether from a national public service network or a commercially driven corporation, has been kept alive by the enthusiasm of supporters of a third category of stations, whose main shared characteristic is that they do not fit into the preceding two sectors. They are usually not-for-profit stations, which target a moderately or highly localized audience, operated on a small scale by radio enthusiasts, a high proportion of whom contribute on a part-time, voluntary basis. As the 'alternative' designation suggests, they survive outside of the mainstream and as such often find themselves at odds with the prevailing regulatory regime, to a lesser or a greater extent. So, the third sector spectrum stretches all the way from *community stations* with very long established broadcast licences, whose main struggle is raising enough money to support themselves, to unlicensed *underground stations* who operate entirely outside or even in direct conflict with their country's system for licensed transmission. Typically, they are organized as horizontal broadcasters, with listeners becoming involved as volunteer contributors, programme makers and administrators. The precise shape and size of this third sector varies enormously according to which national jurisdiction the stations, or at least their audiences, are bound by.

'Alternative', then, is a catch-all term which includes student radio, hospital radio, some forms of (not-for-profit) pirate radio and a category that is referred to variously as community radio, free radio or (somewhat confusingly) public radio, depending on where you live. Put the above criteria for inclusion in this sector together with the fact that the Internet is now *the* method for obtaining unrestricted access to a narrow-cast public medium and it is no surprise that many of these stations have become web radio's explorers and standard bearers.

Student or college radio

This is radio made by students for students, especially where universities and colleges are set out as campuses. The scale and sophistication of student radio varies enormously, but North America and Canada have the longest experience of college radio, subsidized within public education systems. There, they have been tremendously successful and often integrated into a region's mix of FM stations. In many other countries, attempts to follow this model have been constrained by (a) lack of external subsidy and (b) more restrictive licensing regimes – and usually both. Nevertheless, a very active tradition of student stations has established itself around the world. And now the Internet, with its central position as a global network for education, has transformed their potential to reach out, not only to interact with each other, but also to attract substantial international youth audiences as web radio stations in their own right. (Further background on European student radio can be found from the International Association of Student Radio, http://www.iastar.org/, and on North American college radio via http://www.collegelife.about.com/education/msub11.htm).

Hospital radio

Building on similar logic to student radio, that they bring very large potential audiences with time on their hands together into a single building or campus, many large hospitals (or regional groups of hospitals) have made space available for volunteers to operate their own small radio station, usually distributed not from a transmitter but hard wired to each ward. This is a strong tradition in the UK, among other countries, where it grew up alongside its National Health Service. The stations are typically run as registered charities and provide a musical request service. The benefits of the Internet to the transmission of hospital radio are not immediately obvious, but as an avenue for taking dedications, publicizing their role and fund-raising, the website is proving a useful addition to their service (see, for example, the directory at http://www.hospitalradio.co.uk/).

Pirate radio

The last 30 years of the twentieth century have been characterized by the accelerating fragmentation of audiences and demand for more choice of listening. Radio piracy has been used increasingly over that time to challenge the regulators to allow space on the frequency spectrum for stations that more proportionately reflect the diversity of ethnic and cultural expression of a geographical area or the latest musical form that is growing up on its streets. The typical pirate station today is either appealing to a city's minority ethnic population, perhaps in their own native or cultural language. Or else it is a focus for fans of a particular type of 'underground' music (i.e. not mainstream) and the culture that goes with that. And, of course, there is often an overlap between the two.

Web radio now poses an interesting choice to this generation of radio pirates, to which I will return through this book: is getting 'on air' on the Web a reasonable substitute for being a pirate of the airwaves? For the fans and evangelists of new categories of music the answer seems, at the moment, to be yes (see Chapter 2). But for a pirate station targeting a local community in any broader sense with words and conversation, the answer is more likely to be no, or not yet. This is precisely where their audience, for example a disadvantaged inner-city ethnic community, do not, as yet, have access to the Internet and web radio. And here we are starting to talk about pirate radio in the same breath as community radio. There is indeed a very large overlap between this and the next category, wherever the aim of the pirate broadcast is to demonstrate that there is a section of audience whose interests are not being served by the licensed stations in their area.

Community, free or public radio

In Australia it's called public radio, in much of Europe it's called free radio and in the UK, North America and Canada it's often called community radio, but sometimes public or free as well. Whatever the overtones of the nomenclature, these are all stations which spring from the grass roots to serve the interests of a particular sub-section of the total radio audience, either for a short time or over many years. The oft-cited grand-daddy of community stations is KPFA, which has run more or less continuously from Berkeley, California, since 1949. Its founder, Lewis Hill, also set up the Pacifica Foundation to support a network of like-minded 'alternative' stations across the US (see Box 1.9). But, since radio became such a portable medium, community stations have sprung up all around the world at different times to talk to and support a vast range of interest groups. It is all too easy for casual listeners to mainstream radio in the developed world to forget the very different importance radio has in poorer parts of the world. For an isolated, rural community in South America or Sub-Saharan Africa, the radio is likely to be the major source of up to date local news, information, education and (to reuse Hoover's phrase from the start of the chapter) 'widening vision of national problems and national events'. In such cases, it is much easier to recognize radio as an instrument of democratic empowerment.

The best guide to the range of such stations is through the national affiliates of the World Association of Community Broadcasters or Association Mondiale des Radiodiffuseurs Communautaires – Amarc for short. Established in 1986, they now represent around 3000 members and associates in 106 countries. Their website is http://www.amarc.org/.

Web radio might be seen as a natural home for this kind of narrow-casting to communities of interest – because it sidesteps any problems with licensing and availability of frequencies – but for the problem of the receivers: many users of community radio are the very people who are least likely to have access to the Internet. I will return to this important consideration in Chapter 3 and look at some interesting case studies in Chapter 6. But pursuing the idea of 'communities of interest' does lead to a very important new set of possibilities that web radio presents right now: on the Internet such a term need have no geographical boundaries. So, to take one small example, a station aimed at the Vietnamese population in Sydney might now attract listeners and contributors from other Vietnamese communities in Paris or Hanoi.

Box 1.9   Parallel 8: Web radio as an alternative to the mainstream

Visit some sites for community and pirate radio: Radio Free Quebec (http://www.radiofreedom.com/); 4ZZZ (Australia) (http://www.4zzzfm. org.au/); and links from Pirate Radio Central (http://www.blackcat systems.com/radio/pirate.htm/).

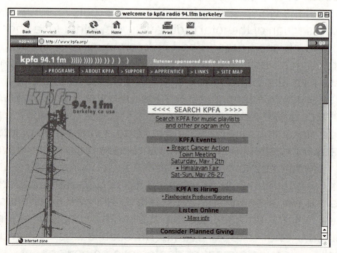

Figure 1.5 The home page of KPFA, originally the famous Berkeley community station and part of the influential Pacifica network, now in search of a wider, like-minded online audience at http://www.kpfa.org/. Pacifica's new appeal to more mainstream and therefore larger audiences is opposed by many long-time supporters who see its programmes as losing their alternative status. Screen shot reproduced by permission of KPFA.

The forgotten sector – amateur or 'ham' radio

The tradition of amateur radio is often left to one side in books about broadcast radio – because it is not, strictly speaking, broadcasting in the mass audience sense. But it certainly falls within the scope of a book like this one, which is about the partial return of radio to its roots as a means of point to point or 'one to few' communication. Ham radio is horizontal radio as it was before the industry went vertical: individuals caught up in the magic of sending and receiving conversation through the ether, often between continents. When the radio spectrum was being parcelled out between public broadcasters and government users (military, shipping, emergency services and the like), a section of the international short waveband was retained for use by the amateur pioneers of radio. Winning a licence to transmit on one of these frequencies involves passing your country's test of technical competence and proving that you are a responsible citizen. So the 'hams' never learned to take radio for granted in the same way as the rest of us, because they were actively engaged in the process of electronic communication and had to search each other out by surfing the short wave spectrum. Whether web radio embodies the same romance as the radio wave, invisibly undulating over land and sea, is a separate question, but audio streaming on the Internet now allows exactly the same possibilities for this form of communication – without the licensing. Whichever the route of transmission, it is not surprising that amateur radio enthusiasts should have been quick to spot the potential of the Internet as an addition to their traditional means of communication. See, for example, http://www.ham-links.org/ or http://www.arnewsline.org/ and Chapter 12 in Douglas (1999).

A note on DAB

Web radio has been made possible by the process of encoding analogue sound into digital code. It is catching up fast with another form of digital radio which has had a much slower development phase, Digital Audio Broadcasting (DAB), but which is planned to replace the traditional analogue radio signal over the coming 10–20 years. We will return to the contrasts and possible relationships between web radio and DAB later on in the book, but the two are very different systems, both in their transmission and their reception by the listener. But, to complete this discussion of the vertical/horizontal models of radio for a moment, we should simply note here that inherent in DAB technology is an increase in the vertical character of broadcasting. This is because it is transmitted in 'multiplexes' – bundles of seven or so stations, which are then unscrambled by the receiver. So each individual station needs to bid to the operator of the multiplex for transmission space. It is the operator of the multiplex that wins the

Table 1.2 Some established characteristics of analogue radio technology

- Although an interactive, horizontal medium in its early experimental days, radio became most effective as a vertical model of distribution
- But inherent in listening to radio remains the *sense* or illusion of a one-to-one, conversational (i.e. horizontal) relationship between presenter and listener
- The technology that made radio portable meant listening to it became an increasingly individual activity, which has emphasized the central importance of its personal, intimate qualities
- Listening is a secondary activity which means that, along with listening to music, radio has become an accompaniment to the routine activities of daily life in a way that the more demanding visual media cannot be
- The international industry divides into three sectors, which are readily defined both by their source of finance and the aims of their content: all in different ways can benefit from the supplementary strengths of web radio
- In many parts of the world, competition between and within the sectors has led to a rapid proliferation of stations, trying to attract increasingly fragmentary audiences: the social trends towards consumer choice are pushing towards the limits of the radio spectrum governments make available

licence from the regulator to transmit. The significance of this is that small stations have to align themselves with the interests of the corporations who run the multiplexes. In other words, they are yet one stage further removed from the horizontal roots of radio technology. A real strength of web radio, for the small station, is that it is much closer to that horizontal model.

Summary

This chapter has assembled many of the basic ingredients that will be involved when we think about putting together the century-old medium of radio and the newest medium of mass communication, the Internet. The point to emphasize is that web radio is still a very young, imperfect technology. We do not know yet what kind of a medium it will settle into. There is nothing automatic or predestined about that. It will depend on how listeners use it and above all on how enthusiasts shape its content. We can only compare this early stage in the evolution of web radio to its analogue parent. Terrestrial radio has evolved a set of characteristics which make it a unique form of communication, quite distinct in its uses from the competition, TV and the printed media. The Internet brings a whole range of supplementary facilities, some of which make it extremely attractive to radio practitioners. Most important among these are that it makes getting a station 'on air' very easy, that it does not require a licence to transmit, that its range is local to global and that it has an inherently interactive, horizontal infrastructure. But the Internet is also very confusing in the wealth of media uses it brings together. This is a time for radio practitioners and fans to pause for reflection. It is vitally important for us to understand radio if we are to make a success of web radio. The next chapter places web radio in the context of the other closely related, even overlapping, applications of recorded sound on the Web.

Further reading

Barnouw, E. (1966). *A Tower of Babel: A History of Broadcasting in the United States*, Vol. 1. Oxford University Press.

Briggs, A. (1995). *The Birth of Broadcasting 1896–1927*. Oxford University Press.

Douglas, S. J. (1999). *Listening In. Radio and the American Imagination*. Random House.

Hendy, D. (2000). *Radio in the Global Age*. Polity Press.

Hilmes, M. (2002). Who We Are, Who We Are Not: Battle of the Global Paradigms. In *Planet Television* (L. Parks and S. Kumar, eds). New York University Press.

Lewis, P. M. and Booth, J. (1989). *The Invisible Medium*. MacMillan.

Naughton, J. (2000). *A Brief History of the Future. The Origins of the Internet*. Phoenix.

Tracey, M. (1998). *The Decline and Fall of Public Service Broadcasting*. Oxford University Press.

Winston, B. (1998). *Media Technology and Society: A History*. Routledge.

2 . . .And what web radio isn't

'A few years ago I was at a technology conference and I was
approached by three different people in turn, one from music, one from
publishing and one from broadcasting, and they each asked me, rather
nervously, how the coming of the computer was going to affect their
industries . . . I knew from the mere way they asked the question that
they weren't ready for the answer. It would be like a bunch of rivers, the
Amazon, the Mississippi and the Congo, asking how the Atlantic might
affect them. And the answer of course is that they won't be rivers any
more, just currents in the ocean.'

Douglas Adams (2000)

It is not yet possible to conceive of the sum total of ways in which our public
media will be changed by digital communications technology in general and the
Internet in particular. In these early days there are almost as many predictions
about their power to transform our lives – or some say not – as there are media
analysts. Time will tell which among them have read today's evidence correctly.
What we can say for certain is that digitalization does dissolve the boundaries
between our traditional media of print, radio and television in terms of their
transmission. It is at either end of the transmission 'pipe' that the uncertainty
lies: how much will people choose, or be persuaded, to make use of this
technological convergence, as practitioners and as audiences? This chapter
surveys in brief where web radio sits in relation to its nearest neighbours'
activities on and around the Internet and sketches this author's interpretation of
where its boundaries currently lie. Again, time will tell which of those boundaries
endure and which disappear; time and the explorations of today's practitioners
of web radio.

In the first half of the chapter I look at the crossover between radio and the
promotion and selling of music. There follows a short diversion to define web
radio's boundaries with some other competing routes for broadcasting radio in
digital form. The second half of the chapter concerns radio's relationship with

the visual media. All of the themes introduced here are developed in more detail throughout the book and I cross-refer to the relevant chapters as the connections crop up.

Convergence of digitalized media technologies

The whole complex technological edifice of information and communications technology (ICT) is built on a terribly simple principle which has been with us since 1844, when Samuel Morse figured out how to 'encode', as a series of electronic dots and dashes, the prophetic words 'What hath God wrought?' and send them down a copper telegraph wire. The principle of digitalization, the modern echo of Morse's dots and dashes, is nothing more elaborate than the translation of a complex form of information into the simplest possible signal so that an electronic circuit board can 'process' it in an instant. The simplest electrical signal you can send is to turn a current 'on' or 'off', which are the two instructions carried by the ones and zeros of the digital binary code.

As far as radio practitioners were aware, digitalization started to have its real impact in the early 1990s, when familiar analogue equipment and quarter-inch tape began to be replaced by 'digital audio workstations' (DAWs), by digital portable recorders – first DAT, then MiniDisc – and by computerized playout systems in their broadcast studios. Something very similar was going on in television production at the same time, and of course many newspapers and the publishing industries had undergone their conversion to digital methods through the preceding decade. So the dawning realization that all three media could happily be contained on a single desktop computer and sent together through the new global communications systems led many to the initial deduction that a convergence of the technologies inevitably meant a convergence of use: we would all become consumers of a single 'multimedium', a seamless mix of text, graphics, sound and moving images.

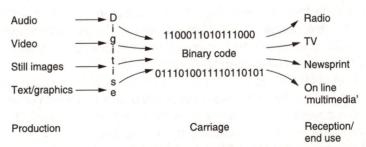

Figure 2.1 Digital production allows the separate branches of the mass media to interact and shift their relationships: encoding (production), converged common carriage and end use.

Now, we can find plenty of examples of multimedia sites on the World Wide Web, but the enduring question is how will people decide to use each element the multimedium makes available to them *at any one time*? Will this, generally speaking, be separately or in combination? The fact that radio and television have both been transmitted on radio waves for most of the twentieth century and could theoretically be received on the same instrument did not lead to them becoming one, because each medium is defined by its end use. In particular, 'primary' media like newspapers and TV, which demand our full visual attention, by definition cannot compete on the same territory as a 'secondary' medium like radio or CDs, which allow us to do something else at the same time as we listen (Shingler and Wieringa, 1998, pp. x–xi).

Divergence of media uses

In attempting to understand the Internet in this early stage of its evolution we tend, inevitably, to rely on preconceptions formed through our experiences of the traditional media or while sitting in front of a personal computer. As Marshall McCluhan observed in his studies of the media in 1967: 'We look at the present through a rear-view mirror. We march backwards into the future.' (Discussed in today's context in Levinson, 1999, p. 173.) We cannot fully recognize what we've got in such a radical, new technology. Instead, we have to explore it, step by step, through the uses we already know. So radio practitioners of every description need to explore the Internet in the present to find out what it can do specifically for radio: what weaknesses of the existing medium it can improve on and what new strengths it can add? Some new uses for radio will come and go as fads and gimmicks, others will endure.

As noted early in Chapter 1, for the first time radio has the challenge of defining itself by the nature of its content rather than the receiver we use to hear it. Douglas Adams' vivid image of broadcasting and publishing as currents in an ICT ocean neatly emphasizes for us the absolute fluidity of the medium through which web radio reaches the listener. So any boundaries radio does manage to define for itself on the Web are likely to be leaky ones. There are now many more ways for exchange to take place along those boundaries between individual media currents, which mix up the definitions and blur the edges between our familiar, self-evidently discrete radio, TV and print media. This fluidity could be taken to imply that radio might eventually become swamped by the dominance of the visual on this converged platform. However, fluidity is not the same as convergence in the sense of merging the uses of the media. Convergence does not mean reducing three into one.

So, set against predictions of the inevitable rise of a single multimedium – which would equally inevitably be dominated by pictures and text – is the view that the ICT ocean represents a vast new evolutionary opportunity for each of the established media to escape their, by now, inbred lineage and grow into their complementary uses more completely. Switching metaphors for a moment, a certain amount of cross-fertilization (or out-breeding) tends to induce new vigour in the offspring. Hence, by challenging customary boundaries and absorbing new parameters, radio on the Web can become more useful to more listeners. This view envisages a *divergence* of uses among the media which make up the Internet. There is a growing body of evidence to support such an interpretation. To take two examples of surveys in America, a UCLA study (2000, p. 18) found that Internet users watched 28 per cent less television and that they were more likely to listen to radio and recorded music than non-Internet users. And in 2001, the leading US radio audience research company, Arbitron, with Edison Media Research, conducted a poll which found (p. 5) a correlation between the proportion of the population expecting to spend more time using both the radio (34 per cent said more) and the Internet (30 per cent) over the following year and those expecting to spend less time with TV (33 per cent). These are tentative projections at the moment, but they offer evidence for a conclusion which we would intuitively expect: if you are occupied visually working or surfing on a computer screen, you are also likely to be listening to the radio and/or music at the same time – just as you would be driving a car or doing household chores.

Radio's relationship with the music industry

The music industry quickly learned to embrace radio as a most generous benefactor, but only after an initial reaction of deep suspicion in the 1920s. For almost a century thereafter, radio has provided the international shop window which has made music recording among the world's most profitable industries – with an annual turnover $38.5 billion in 1999 (IFPI, 2000).

It was David Sarnoff, while he was contracts manager for the American Marconi company in 1916 or 1917 (sources differ), who is credited with coining the term 'radio music box'. In so doing, he envisaged the new technology as a universally available entertainment device which would bring live and recorded music into every home. The business of creating a mass market for the shellac 78 rpm music disc was no more than 15 years old at the time and a marriage between the two technologies looked potentially fruitful: radio needed records as a cheap means of drawing audiences and filling air time as much as the recording industry needed radio to promote its music sales. But the record companies, songwriters and musicians balked at the idea of 'giving away' performances of their music over the ether – free promotion or no free promotion. Radio had created a fresh legal paradigm for the copyright lawyers to get their teeth into. The result was a new set of rights agreements which allowed radio stations to broadcast recorded or live performances of music in return for payment (a) of royalties to the songwriters per play or performance and (b) for licence from the record company to broadcast their product. (The fact that the US agreement only involved radio stations paying royalties for (a) and not (b) has assumed major significance today, to which we'll return in Chapter 8.)

The Internet and the music industry

Now the Internet has turned music copyright upside down once more and created yet another rights paradigm. At issue for the artists is still the ownership of their work and whether they can earn any income from it. The record companies' position, their need for financial protection, looks very different now compared to the uncertainty of the 1920s: their industry has turned out to be an immensely profitable winner during the Broadcast Century, not least because music licensing has in most territories guaranteed them an income stream both from the promotion of their records *and* from the sales which arise from that promotion. This is a rare legal privilege in business terms, which the existence of the Internet is now in the process of undermining. The Internet is self-evidently an extremely useful medium for the music industry to connect with its audience (once again), but it does not suit the existing revenue collection model at all. Digitalization of music allows the end product, the officially released recording, to be translated into too many different forms for the companies to keep effective tabs on (see the 'Streaming' and 'Downloading' sections below). Its point to point, interactive, on-demand characteristics, and the potential for everyone online to send and receive music across it make enforcement of individual payments utterly impractical. There is little or no technical distinction to be made any more between the means of promoting a record (radio airplay) and the means of owning a copy.

The progress of the Napster case through the US courts during 2000 and 2001 has demonstrated how big a copyright headache the widespread downloading of music at near CD quality over the Internet is giving the music industry. This collective act of 'free exchange' or 'music piracy' – depending on your point of view – also neatly encapsulates the depth of the ideological division, mentioned in Chapter 1, between the two competing ideas of what the World Wide Web is for: on the one side are the supporters of the exploratory, unregulated, open exchange 'wild frontier' spirit that gave birth to the Internet, and on the other those who regard the Web as a new business environment to be tamed and controlled along existing commercial lines. Both, we will see, are highly relevant to web radio.

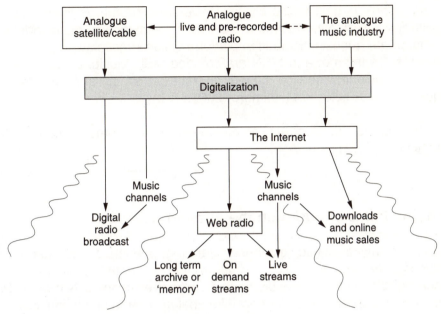

Figure 2.2 Web radio in relation to other audio activities on the Web.

Chapter 8 discusses the extremely tough questions these technological developments are posing for all concerned. The whole symbiotic relationship between the music industry and the radio industry has suddenly got a whole lot more complicated. And there are now increasingly strong signs that substantial parts of the commercial radio industry will soon be fully united, through the Web, with the distribution arm of the record industry. At this edge of radio the integration between record promotion and sales is looking increasingly seamless (see Box 2.1).

Box 2.1 Increasing integration between record promotion and sales

Three significant public announcements in April 2001 point the way:

1 Three of the major record companies, Warner Music Group (AOL Time Warner), BMG (Bertelsmann) and EMI, have agreed a deal with RealNetworks to launch MusicNet to distribute music recordings directly to the global public using – of course – Real software, which is also the most widespread format for web radio.

2 The world's largest music group, Universal (Vivendi), is joining forces with Sony Music Entertainment and Yahoo – a major web radio portal site – to create a music distribution platform called Pressplay.

3 Microsoft's Internet arm MSN are creating MSN Music, a free, personalized, radio-like service based on musical styles and moods, not jukebox track selection (Helmore, 2001a & b).

Whether or not these particular distribution plans come to fruition, the intention is obvious.

The many forms of audio on the Internet

In order to make sense of these alarming scenarios, we need some definitions.

Once digitized, audio can be distributed on the Web in one of two ways. Either we listen to it in a continuous 'stream' like analogue radio or we can 'download' it as an audio file. Downloading does not take place in real time and the file can only be listened to once the transfer is complete. So it's more like storing a CD on your shelf to listen to whenever you choose. Within each of these two categories there are further subdivisions which allow different possible uses.

Streaming

Audio streaming is the Internet application which makes web radio possible. Visit a web radio site and the chances are you will be offered both a 'live' stream and a choice of 'archived' streams (for example, those suggested in Chapter 1).

The *live stream* is truly the Web equivalent of an analogue radio broadcast: it carries the output from the broadcast studio or an outside broadcast (OB) unit in real time. (In fact, for most established stations it is still often exactly the same output as the analogue broadcast, delayed by the few seconds it takes to process the signal at either end of the transmission path.)

Typically, selected programmes or items from the live output are stored on the site's *archive* so that visitors can listen to them 'on demand', again as a continuous stream and at the same sound quality as the original live webcast (in contrast to downloading; see next section). This 'time-shifted' listening is a very significant new departure for the majority of radio audiences. Most of us have not had access to the radio equivalent of the time programmable video recorder. We are used to missing favourite programmes when we go out – or else we carefully arrange our lives to fit around the radio schedules. Time shifting has major implications for programme makers and web station schedulers which deserve much fuller consideration – see Chapter 11.

Like a video recorder, the listener can also pause, fast forward or replay an archived stream.

Some smaller, 'Internet-only' stations exist solely as archived streams: they may not have the personnel to run live output or they may expect their niche audiences to 'find' them over a period of days, weeks or months. Conversely, a typical mainstream, speech-orientated station is likely to make most of their archived programmes available on demand for a week, or an hour in the case of an hourly news bulletin.

Downloading and shopping for music online

Shopping for music is, of course, a different kind of activity to listening on terrestrial radio and here's our first important definitional boundary for web radio. The Internet can certainly bring the listening and the decision to buy what we've heard very, very much closer together (see Figure 2.2). Many websites run as online music shops and it makes sense for them to borrow presentation methods that have been tried and tested over decades of music radio. So the distinction can be difficult to spot at first. But if, after you have got past the streamed audio ads and promotions, the site is offering to sell or give you audio files of your favourite music to *download*, typically in MP3 format, or to burn tracks to order onto a CD for you, then – for the purposes of this book at least – it's not really a web radio site, it's a music shop.

For traditional radio programme makers, there is no confusion. The relationship between the DJ, the listener and the sale of the music product remains the same as it ever was: the possibility of prompting spontaneous *e*-purchases may influence the way a station plans its playlists, or indeed how a programme is paid for, but the job of the radio station is to talk to its listeners, communicate with them and nurture their long-term interest and/or affection. It is for the record company and especially the music retailer to accommodate the changes in how we buy the CD, the download or other format of our choice.

For example, a site like http://www.peoplesound.com/ may offer streamed sample tracks to listen to, but it remains a virtual shop in which the experience is one of browsing, using visual cues as well as listening. The decision to download (or order the CD) is active. It requires us to suspend whatever else we were doing and give it our full attention, for seconds or minutes. It is likely to entail further decisions: which computer file to download to, whether it's worth the time it takes to download, perhaps entering our customer or credit card details. Of course, as with high street music shopping, you are not obliged to buy and you can spend many happy hours listening to tracks of your choice. This does not make the experience radio.

Music channels and the automated web 'jukebox'

Somewhere between the online music shop and the DJ presented web radio station, though, yet another offspring of digitalization can be found: the automated web 'jukebox'. This is altogether a more contradictory phenomenon to define in radio terms, since it is quite clearly an extension of music format radio but, in doing away with any form of presenter or news or indeed any kind of radio studio at all, it removes the essential element of broadcast communication: one human person talking directly to another or sharing with them some form of entertainment.

Many terrestrial music format stations began storing their 'playlisted' music on computer hard drives and accessing them through software applications, such as RCS *Selector*, in the mid-1990s. One important feature of such programmes is that they can either play out tracks in the order you specify or they can be set to 'random play', just like a domestic CD player. The level of automation can further be set either for 'live assist', in which case a DJ is present to drive the show, or 'fully automated', with or without DJ links recorded onto the hard drive. (For more discussion of the impact of automation on format radio see, for example, Douglas, 1999, pp. 347–53.)

This kind of computer-based automation transfers very readily from terrestrial music station into the interactive environment of the Internet. A live stream comprising no more than a regularly updated playlist of fewer than 50 tracks set to random play and with a minimum separation between repeats is all it takes. Not very inspiring, but easy to do. Whereas commercial pressures restrict terrestrial stations to variations on the most popular formats (such as Contemporary Hit Radio, Classic Rock or Country), on the Internet a much wider range of faster moving, minority markets can be served in similar fully automated fashion as well (such as, in 2000 parlance, Hip-Hop, Garage or Trance music). Alternatively, 'lifestyle' channels define themselves by mood and pace, combining music from across genres. A high proportion of sites that describe themselves as web radio stations are made possible by such jukebox technology because it means a single small enterprise can offer multiple formatted streams across a wide spectrum of musical genres and sub-genres with minimal staff costs. Information about artist and track is accessible in text form somewhere on the receiver's screen, where there is also often a click-through option to buy or download.

Figure 2.3 A montage of screen shots showing the many music streams offered by NetRadio!. From the http://www.netradio.com/ home page, the 'jazz' channels page reveals a number of sub-categories. Screen shot reproduced by permission of NetRadio!.

Box 2.2

At April 2001 the NetRadio browser at http://www.netradio.com/listen/ index.html is arranged in 15 music genres – plus a comedy and a news/ information heading. Within each genre are up to 32 music channels each representing a sub-genre (some of which appear under more than one main genre heading). Figure 2.3 shows the browser open at Jazz (left) with its 15 music channels plus three links to text info (right). The click-through to buy the CD is to Amazon.com.

Music sites like NetRadio.com illustrated in Box 2.2 are also referred to as 'web music channels', which perhaps more accurately describes what their listeners expect from them. This form of access to new or favourite music without doubt represents the future of a significant sector of the Web and I do not underestimate its appeal, nor its origin in one branch of analogue radio, nor indeed its importance for the music industry of the future. In fact, I would go so far as to suggest that the evolution of a Web-based music channel sector is already beginning to radically reshape the whole of the radio industry – online and offline. This is an area of radio that is going to demand a good deal of research in the near future to map the changes. If music channels and online jukeboxes work for enough listeners, why employ a disc jockey? (See Chapter 10.)

For the purposes of this book though, I will define music channels as being on the periphery of web radio, neither fully in nor fully out. I will return to this debate in Chapter 10 and so some aspects of this book are relevant to someone planning a web music channel or site. The 'Further reading' at the end of Chapter 4 includes some other books specifically about how to stream music on the Web that are more obviously geared towards the music channel.

Downloading radio programmes at high sound quality

There are a number of reasons why it might be an advantage to download a complete radio programme, as opposed to going to a streamed archive. They are likely to be 'unique' programmes, for example a live concert or a well-produced radio drama.

- It might be a programme you want to keep indefinitely, or perhaps send to a friend, in the same way as you would buy an audio cassette or CD copy.
- A compressed archive stream may not give the quality necessary to appreciate the full tonal range of the original recording, for example in a highly crafted radio drama.
- As a radio station you may be taking advantage of an invitation to download a programme from another station or programme maker's website at full audio quality, specifically for rebroadcast.
- Similarly, sending and receiving full quality audio files via the Internet as email attachments (which also involves downloading) is merely the newest, more convenient equivalent to sending pre-recorded radio material via the mail or 'down the line' via an ISDN or satellite link. In conventional broadcasting terms, downloads like this are private, not public transfers. On the Web, however, they may be offered publicly as supplementary listening.

Downloading *programmes* is no more than a by-product of radio *programming*, which means to say that it is a separate, supplementary activity to radio listening. In the public sphere it is analogous to home taping off air, that long-established method of capturing radio for reuse. In both cases the recordings are still experienced as radio programmes with their own integrity once they are playing through your speaker(s): they cannot be mistaken for anything else. A treasure trove of an example is the Are You Sitting Comfortably archive site (http://www.rusc.com/), on which Ned Norris has gathered together thousands of historic American radio shows, which, for a token subscription, you can download for personal use at any time. We can also look on this as a form of time shifting (see Chapter 11) similar to the use of the home video.

However, in the web radio world of scalable, niche audiences, such downloads do open a new set of possibilities for those interested in experimenting with the forms of the crafted radio programme. Most mainstream radio broadcasters have traditionally been reluctant to give air time to such experiments which, by definition, risk losing audiences. But web radio does open a widely available public 'laboratory' in which creative exploration can take place, especially involving new techniques made possible by advances in digital production methods. In time, such a laboratory should enrich radio listening as a whole. Today's radio experiment *may* become tomorrow's commonplace mainstream technique.

Web radio's relationship to other radio transmission routes

Once encoded in digital form, radio output is now capable of being transmitted by several different routes, of which web radio is but one. This can be confusing as the 'digital radio' tag may be used to describe all these routes collectively or else in a variety of quite specific individual meanings. (Even more confusingly, the description 'digital radio' is also applied to radios that pick up conventional analogue signals but which employ a digital tuning mechanism.) So I'll avoid the phrase in this book and stick to the industry terminology as defined in this section.

These digital transmission routes are, of course, additional to the conventional analogue technologies which use Amplitude Modulation (AM) or Frequency Modulation (FM) of radio waves. As we've seen, web radio travels a point to point route, whereas the other competing digital systems use one-way, 'one to many', broadcast routes. As such, they reproduce the broadcast characteristics of analogue terrestrial transmission plus some unique additions of their own.

So, the principle of technological convergence remains in force here *within* the medium of radio. Although the digital transmission routes remain distinct and confer their own characteristics to the content, as far as the listener is concerned they all have the potential to come out of the same listening device because they all need to be decoded by a computer chip. The chip may live inside a dedicated radio receiver or it may live in a desktop computer. So looking into the future of radio we must get used to the idea that retuning between stations may in fact involve switching from one of these transmission routes to another. To this extent, web radio does (already) overlap with other forms of radio transmission. I'll return to the implications of that overlap when I discuss the reception of web radio in Chapter 3, but the rest of this section offers a very brief summary introduction.

Digital Audio Broadcasting (DAB)

Literally, the term digital audio broadcasting describes the whole principle of encoding and transmitting radio in digital form using the electromagnetic radio spectrum. But in its title form, the DAB banner (and associated logo) is the trade name for the particular standard (Eureka-147) that has become the world leader and is now well established across Northern Europe, Canada, Australia and South Africa. However in the USA the Eureka-147 standard was initially seen as neither suitable nor necessary. Because of the absence of US backing, 4 and 5 years after its official launch in Europe and elsewhere, manufacturers of receivers have been very slow to respond and provide DAB radio sets that are (a) affordable by most people and (b) as portable as we are used to. There's plenty of information on DAB at http://www.worlddab.com/, the official website of the international consortium behind developing the standard.

Instead of transmitting radio as a continuous FM or AM analogue signal, DAB conserves bandwidth by only transmitting a stream of pulses, the ones and noughts which encode the sound. It is transmitted on a dedicated section at the top of the radio wave spectrum in the form of several bundles or 'multiplexes' of between eight and 12 stations each. (In the UK, this is at frequencies between 217.5 and 230 MHz.) DAB is also, at the moment, free to air – though it is designed to accommodate encryption and subscription options.

Some other aspects of DAB that are relevant in competition with web radio are:

- One of DAB's selling points is that it can also bring you scrolling text and/or pictures – for example, to provide background information on what you're listening to, advanced traffic news or website URLs. Web radio can, of course, offer much more in that visual department (see later sections in this chapter).
- At the moment, DAB gives very much better sound quality than web radio as long as most people connect to the Web using a domestic modem. DAB car radios don't need to be retuned as you travel between reception areas, which was always a problem with FM, but . . .
- DAB coverage is largely dependent on the extent of renewal of the transmitter network (though see 'satellite broadcasting' section below). This is an expensive process so it favours centres of high population. In the UK, for example, at the start of 2001 the BBC's network DAB transmissions covered

60 per cent of the population and Digital One, the national commercial multiplex, covered 75 per cent.

- The licensing of multiplexes by consortia and 'sub-letting' to stations makes DAB an even more inherently vertical broadcast system than analogue became. So it is the polar opposite of web radio in terms of the potential for interactivity, third sector stations or niche content.

More recently in the US the iBiquity company has won the backing of the NAB in the development of their IBOC system. (The trademarked name is iDAB, but IBOC, short for In Band On Channel, is the more widely used abbreviation. The website is at http://www.ibiquity.com/.) This system is designed not to bundle up multiplexes but to place a digital channel on either an FM or an AM frequency *alongside* the analogue transmission band of an existing station – hence the descriptive name. It therefore sits somewhere in-between the FM-based Eureka-147 standard and another standard being developed to digitalize AM frequencies.

Digital Radio Mondiale (DRM)

This is a later arrival in the field, but a close competitor with DAB. Whereas DAB uses the VHF frequencies traditionally associated with conventional FM transmission (i.e. above 30 MHz), DRM is designed to use the lower frequencies of the old AM short, medium and long wavebands. Pilot transmissions are scheduled to begin in 2002. The official website of the DRM consortium at http://www.drm.org/ shows, perhaps significantly, that there is worldwide support for this system, including in the US where the need for improving their extensive network of AM analogue stations is more apparent than it is for FM. The most attractive features of DRM are:

- DRM is being designed to replace poor to moderate quality AM transmissions with clean digital (though mono) signals, so the listener will hear a much greater improvement than the relatively smaller step up from FM stereo to DAB. For geographical and historical reasons the AM radio tradition has remained particularly strong in the US, where it supports many hundreds of local and regional stations.
- DRM is aiming to be 'low tech' in comparison to DAB, while achieving these gains in quality plus text and data streams. This means the transition to DRM promises to be a much less expensive proposition for individual station operators. AM transmitters can cover relatively larger areas more effectively than can FM, which means (a) that fewer transmitters are involved in converting a complete national or regional network to DRM and (b) that it is significantly more cost effective for regions of lower population density.

● Unlike the DAB multiplexes – but like IBOC – DRM technology does not so far appear to necessitate a different pattern of licensing to that which exists for analogue frequencies.

Bearing in mind the United States' strong lead in web radio, these characteristics of DRM – and perhaps IBOC – suggest a greater potential synergy between these digital routes than between web radio and DAB – especially when we remember the global reach of short wave transmissions.

(See also Rudin, 1999, for a discussion of the development of terrestrial digital radio.)

Digital Direct Satellite Broadcasting

In the first 10–15 years of its public availability, satellite broadcasting was associated in most people's minds with analogue TV transmissions. But many analogue radio stations looking to extend their reach and avoid terrestrial interference have quietly been arriving on satellite. Now a truly global phenomenon like digital WorldSpace has taken this form of radio broadcasting a dramatic step forward (see Box 2.3). And it is the prompt availability of relatively cheap, versatile, portable receivers that shows us the potential of this method of transmission (in contrast to DAB's slow start). WorldSpace is not the only satellite radio network, but to date it is the most ambitious and so demonstrates how important satellite broadcasts of radio may well become in the near future.

Similarly, two services, the Sirius Satellite Radio service (formerly the CD Radio project) and XM Radio, go on air across mainland USA in 2001, aimed specifically at in-car listeners. This is a subscription service (at around $9 a month) which supplies a choice of 100 commercial free music, news and entertainment channels. Again, the company has worked successfully to get the support of many major car manufacturers ahead of the service's launch (http://www.siriusradio.com/ and http://www.xmradio.com/).

Box 2.3

WorldSpace achieves near complete global coverage with three satellites, the first of which, AfriStar, began broadcasting in October 1999 across a 'footprint' stretching from Western India, across Africa and into Europe. In September 2000 Hitachi, among other manufacturers, had produced a portable radio (the KH-WS1), much like any other portable radio and in a comparable price bracket, which could receive the 39 digital AfriStar stations as well as the usual spectrum of terrestrial analogue FM, MW and SW stations. The AfriStar stations are a mixture of music-based and speech-based stations in a range of different languages; some are rebroadcast from conventional stations and some are made specifically for WorldSpace. Visit their website at http://www.worldspace.com/ for more detailed information.

Figure 2.4 The WorldSpace Corporation home page at http://www.worldspace.com/. Screen shot reproduced by permission of WorldSpace Corp.

The crucial overlap between a service like this and the benefits web radio offer to established radio networks lies in its universal global reach – with the additional benefit that it is independent of phone networks or desktop computers and so more likely to be accessible to a target listener who, in WorldSpace's case, lives in a developing country. The important difference between the two is that satellite is once again an inherently vertical broadcast system: individual stations have to negotiate terms with a large private owner (WorldSpace Corporation) to gain access to the airwaves and the possibilities for audience interaction are even less than on an analogue station.

Radio in the visual world of multimedia

Radio's success in adapting itself to the rise of television lay in the fact that, once turned on and tuned in, it makes no visual demands on its audience. The unique point of radio is that it is the 'eyes free' medium, which enables the visual

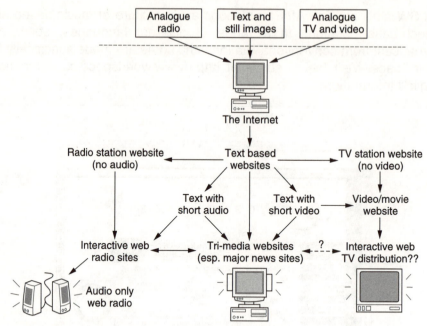

Figure 2.5 Web radio in relation to the visual dimension of the Web.

cortex of the listener's brain to attend to other tasks or else to conjure its own images in 'the mind's eye'. The Internet, on the other hand, originated as a visual, text medium, accessed through a screen. Most of its users experience it as an activity which demands even more visual concentration than watching television.

One temptation in such a visually orientated world is to think that the most beneficial thing this technology can do for radio is to supply it with images or text. Visits to the websites of many existing radio broadcasters show that their managers are excited by this new dimension to radio, for example through the addition of 'webcams' in the studios (e.g. BBC Radio 4's *Today* programme at http://www.bbc.co.uk/radio4/today/view/view.shtml). Indeed, this is the very reason why many radio enthusiasts are suspicious of web radio, because they fear that the requirement to interact visually weakens radio's unique identity and heralds its take-over by TV. On the other hand, studio webcams may be a bit of a curiosity and they do support the idea that radio is about presenters working live in real studios, though it is difficult to imagine actively watching one for any length of time.

The following sections pick out the main ways in which web radio overlaps with the visual on the Internet. In each case I indicate later sections in the book where the theme is discussed in practice and in more detail.

The website is the web radio station's 'front door'

The World Wide Web is a collection of web pages and web pages are by definition to be looked at. On the first visit we are likely to find our way to a web radio station via its URL, which is the address of a web page (see Chapter 3). *En route*, we may go via a search engine, web directory or portal site and here again our navigation is likely to be a visual process. Chapter 7 looks at the question of how stations can let listeners know they have a front door and how to help them find it. This involves careful use of the visual dimension of the Internet.

The station's website can also give us text and graphic displays of the programme schedule for the day's live stream or options to search for a particular archive stream. It can offer us selected background to programmes and links to other (visual) websites should we want more detail.

The website is our means of interacting with programmes, for example by emailing comments or requests. But once I have the address to a station's stream stored on my web radio tuner (which might be a desktop PC or something far more mobile), I can go directly to the station at the click of an icon, just as on my old push-button tuner. As we shall see in the next chapter, there are also dedicated web radio tuners on the market which look and behave like a conventional radio and tune directly to the audio stream.

So the well-designed, visually appealing website is a crucially important part of web radio, just as the well-targeted poster and newspaper ad campaigns are crucial at the launch of a new analogue station. But in either case, once the listener has found you, it is the content of what they hear that keeps them coming back and it is the content which may make them decide to build their relationship by interacting with your station (see Chapter 7).

Websites with additional audio

Sound is used to support the visuals of many websites. From the 'swoosh' behind the 30-second moving graphic on an e-commerce front page to the welcome address spoken by the company director to the online lecture, there is a wide spectrum of sound techniques to make your visual content more 'compelling', as the web jargon puts it. They may use the same software as web radio, but their purpose – as with online music shopping – is very unlike radio. In most cases, this branch of webcasting owes more to the conventions of TV and so the sound is supplementary. They are designed to win our full attention so that we focus our eyes on the visual content on the computer screen.

Sites like these fall into two categories:

1 Commercial, for whom these pages represent the public face of a company on the Web. They need to find dramatic ways of exploiting the latest multimedia technology to grab and then hold the attention of the 'passing' potential customer, to stand out in the virtual market square. Sound is a powerful element within that, but the distinction from radio is easy to draw – the site is essentially visual and the sound clips are brief.
2 Educational or informative, for example a lecture at an online university site or a recorded interview at a newspaper site offered as background to a story in print. These archived presentations clearly do have a lot more in common with the conventions of speech radio. Indeed, here is an instance where the skills of an experienced radio programme maker will benefit the creation of the presentation. But the distinction again comes with the fact that the visuals – whether text, graphics or video – dominate the site and are essential or integral to its purpose. The lecture in this form is therefore designed to be watched and not simply listened to.

There are many 'how to' books on webcasting available which give excellent advice on this kind of application of audio as a tool of web design. I list some of them at the end of Chapter 4. They offer other interesting perspectives on this area of overlap with web radio.

Interactivity and the visual

A recurrent theme throughout this book is that web radio is distinctively an interactive form. Exactly how a station should best exploit that interactivity is a creative decision for the programme makers: some radio content invites or suggests more interaction, some less. The challenge is judging where to draw the line between adding to it or detracting from it. Chapters 7, 10 and 11 examine different forms of interactivity in more detail, but the fact that many of the options involve full visual attention, even if temporarily, deserves mention here. Some typical examples of visual interaction might be:

● To find supporting text information on, for example:

  – title or background of a piece of music being played;
  – details of the performer's next concert dates;
  – sources of factual information behind a current affairs programme;
  – programme schedules and/or credits.

- To see pictures of, for example:

    - presenters in action – stills or video;
    - musicians during a track – i.e. promotional material or on their own website;
    - advertisers' products or links to their websites.

- Entering on-air or off-air competitions.
- Participating in audience polls or votes initiated by a programme.
- Corresponding via email, maybe directly with the station or else with other listeners via a chat room or bulletin board.

Any one of the examples can become more or less complicated and demand more or less attention from the listener. Many of them also imply a balance between offering the listener more to engage them (so winning their ongoing support) and tempting them with too much distraction (OK if they're still listening to you following a link you've given them, but also risks losing them for good to discoveries they find more interesting).

There are obviously plenty of new possibilities for web radio makers to experiment with. And this is a difficult area in which to try to draw hard and fast boundaries – the multimedia currents swirl powerfully together here. I'd suggest there are at least two aspects of visual interactivity that the programme maker needs to be clear about when planning this side of a site (see, for example, the virginradio.co.uk case study in Chapter 5).

1 Visuals are a supplementary or additional service, an optional extra to the core activity of listening – because many listeners won't want or be able to interact with a screen. Visuals may be helpful to the station, for example in building an identity or 'brand' (see Chapter 7) but, as such, they should be designed to complement the type of listening: any interaction with the screen should be easily done while listening; it should be judged in relation to the level of concentration the radio content demands.

2 There is a spectrum or continuum of visual attention. It runs from radio only (no visuals supplied, except those in the listener's mind's eye) all the way to full immersion in the stimuli from the screen (web TV or, at the extreme, a fully interactive computer game). Somewhere in between, towards the radio-only end, are text or email interactions, which are the more instantaneous versions of familiar activities of consulting schedules in the press, sending off for a fact sheet, entering a competition or in some way writing in response to what we hear – all more or less visual activities that have become part of the experience of radio.

When a new station sets up its website it is crucial for them to really understand what their core service is: and therefore where it should be on that spectrum of visual attention. A pertinent question might be, are you sure you don't really want to be doing web TV?

Web TV

At this end of the visual spectrum we have obviously strayed into the territory of another book. Moving video pictures can be streamed and archived on the Web in more or less exactly the same way as audio, therefore much that we can say about web radio has some relevance to web TV – for example in relation to the horizontal, point to point strengths of the Internet. However, the precise relationship between the screens of a computer and a TV has yet to be widely tested in practice, and any future relationship between web TV and its parent medium looks a lot more complicated than that between web radio and its forebears.

But it is the overlap between audio and video on the Web that is of interest to us here. Take the example of a special event like a live music concert. Such events are now regularly streamed over the Web, especially where an international star is involved (see, for example, the QT TV channel, http://www.apple.com/quicktime/qtv/ or Real's Live Events http://realguide.real.com/live/ or the pay per view http://www.livemusic.com). Broadcasting such concerts has been a staple of radio since its inception. However, the web radio producer now faces an interesting challenge (if the Internet rights to such an event are available; see Chapter 8). Because convergence now means that technically she can, should the producer stream video of the event on the station's website as well as the audio?

If, knowing the expectations of her audience, she decides yes, then she has certainly crossed over into web TV – with all the expense of additional technical expertise and resources that entails. The obvious, though crucial, point to remember in this case is that, in the joined up world of the Internet, the video stream is the optional extra: she can't stream the concert without the audio and expect an audience. So this new era of converged media gives the web radio producer the opportunity to revisit the question that was first posed when TV was a novelty: 'What do pictures add to the radio?'

It's a question every web radio maker is now faced with more or less daily. The more it is asked, the clearer the answer is likely to become. Radio – no visuals needed – has its place competing with TV and print on the Internet, just as it has done so successfully in the Broadcast Century. The challenge of 'multimedia' should not cause us to lose faith in radio, just as long as there are people out there who can make distinctive web radio programmes and enough niche audiences to listen and respond.

A summary of intersections for web radio

This chapter has offered a brief tour of the perimeters of radio on the Web as it exists today – in its infancy. It will certainly grow and mature, shaped by the people who make the programmes and the people who engage with them. There are two important points to emphasize in this attempt at defining its boundaries.

Firstly, it is the integrity of the live experience of listening to the radio that lies at the heart of web radio, even where the listener hears it as an archived stream. But, secondly, because digital convergence allows us to add on all sorts of peripheral, non-radio options onto a station's website, we need to evaluate each of them very carefully to assess how far each supports or detracts from the station's communication with its listeners. Station X may target an audience who are listening at a personal computer with time to attend to visually demanding activities on its website. That route has its consequences in terms of expertise and personnel to design and maintain a dynamic website (see Chapter 5). Station Y, by contrast, may target an audience who are listening rather than looking and would only occasionally refer to its website. Their staff could devote most of their resources to making distinctive radio, to which a busy website would be more a distraction than an addition to the service (see Chapter 6).

To avoid confusion in these areas of overlap, it will be most helpful to define the 'web radio station' as only the streaming audio part of a website, as described earlier under 'Streaming'. It may well be that the front page of the website leads to a range of options, including ones we have mentioned in this section – perhaps a music buying area, some web video archive, a games area, a chat room or a music-on-demand jukebox-type stream, where the listener chooses all the tracks.

All these options are part of the overall identity of the web radio station, but the job of the person in charge is what the substance of this book is about. That person will certainly have to understand how the station interacts with neighbouring activities on a mixed site and think about, perhaps experiment with, how to make use of some of the overlaps the technology makes possible.

One of the delightful perils of logging on to the Web is that it tempts you in all sorts of unexpected directions. Putting your radio station on the Web is no exception. So, while I'll endeavour for the rest of the book to steer a course in the middle of the ocean current of web radio, there will be points at which I drift towards its edges to look in more detail at the mixing taking place there.

But before considering content in more detail, it's time to familiarize ourselves with the nuts and bolts of the streaming process.

Further reading

Arbitron/Edison Media Research (2001). *Internet VI: Streaming at a Crossroads – Executive Summary.* Published as PDF file from http://www.arbitron.com/ (as at February 2001).

Covell, A. (1999). *Digital Convergence: How the Merging of Computers, Communications and Multimedia is Transforming Our Lives.* Aegis Publishing.

Douglas, S. J. (1999). *Listening In: Radio and the American Imagination, from Amos 'n' Andy and Ed Murrow to Wolfman Jack and Howard Stern.* Random House.

Gauntlett, D. (ed.) (2000). *Web.Studies.* Arnold.

Hendy, D. (2000). *Radio in the Global Age.* Polity Press.

Levinson, P. (1999). *Digital McLuhan. A Guide to the Information Millennium.* Routledge.

Merriden, T. (2001). *Irresistible Forces: The Business Legacy of Napster and the Growth of the Underground Internet.* Capstone.

UCLA (2000). *The UCLA Internet Report: Surveying the Digital Future.* Published as a PDF file on http://www.ccp.ucla.edu/ (as at February 2001).

3 Stream receivers and how the listener listens

Among the many imponderables of the Internet, one thing is certain: the technology for picking it up will continue to improve and adapt itself to the ways in which people want to use it. The Web will not remain trapped within the desktop computer for long – many of its applications quite evidently cannot wait to get out. The ICT companies have at their disposal huge investment capital sums with which to finance the research and development of the 'killer applications' that will really set it free. The combination of the pace and forward momentum behind this technological revolution is unprecedented.

The number of web radio stations online is difficult to keep track of precisely, but at the time of writing is commonly estimated at around 5000 (e.g. by http://www.penguinradio.com/ in March 2001). Twenty-two per cent of Americans, the most researched audience, are estimated to have tuned into some streaming audio on the Web (radio plus music channels) by the end of the year 2000 (Arbitron/Edison, 2001, p. 17). The potential global listening audience can be gauged very approximately from estimates of the numbers of people who so far have access to the Internet (Table 3.1).

Table 3.1 NUA Internet survey of published surveys at November 2000

	Numbers of Internet connections in millions
World	407.10
Africa	3.11
Asia Pacific	104.88
Europe	113.14
Middle East	2.40
Canada/USA	167.12
Latin America	16.45

Source: http://www.nua.ie/surveys/how_many_online/index.html

Remember web radio has only been with us for 6 years. For the vast majority of its listeners it remains something they do while working or playing in front of a computer. But this immobility is a temporary state of affairs, just as in its early years listening to analogue radio was awkward and for most users meant giving their full concentration to a crackling signal in a set of headphones or a horn speaker. Or just as for the following 40 years the common 'wireless set' was tied to a mains socket. So in thinking about how we receive web radio today we need to regard the first few years of the twenty-first century as a transitional phase for this technology.

Hence this chapter begins with a look at the commonest, basic streaming technology most of us in the developed world have access to now. We then move on to consider where we are going with radio delivered via the Web. From where I sit in 2001, the journey ahead appears to begin with four related, technological steps forward:

1 Faster domestic connections to an 'always-on' service as the norm.
2 End to end improvements to the infrastructure of the Internet to reduce reception problems arising from 'net congestion'.
3 More efficient methods of streaming at smaller file sizes.
4 The development of more mobile access to the Internet.

We should certainly plan for significant advances in these areas within the next 5 years and I'll come on to their expected impact on web radio reception later in the chapter. But to begin where the majority of web listeners are today, I will assume a low bandwidth connection via a domestic, earthbound phone line in this introduction to the principles of streaming.

How streaming works – an overview

For now I will further assume the listener is tuning into a web radio station using a domestic computer. The basic requirements in this case are:

- a computer with an Internet browser installed (e.g. Netscape Communicator or Internet Explorer) and a streaming software package, or player, that corresponds to the one being used by the radio station to transmit;
- a connection to the Internet, which might be via a modem with a nominal connection speed of 14.4, 28.8 or 56 kilobits per second (kbps), it might be via ISDN (Integrated Services Digital Network), via DSL (Digital Subscriber Line) or some other 'broadband' connection;
- some form of subscription to an Internet Service Provider (ISP).

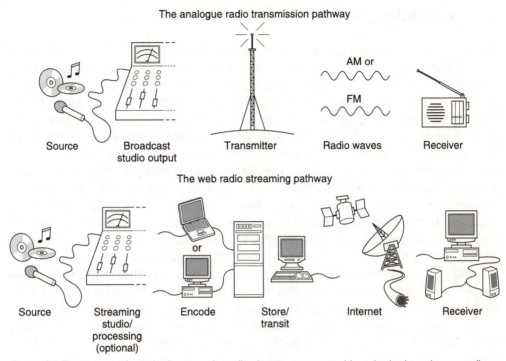

Figure 3.1 The stages of producing a web radio stream, compared to a typical analogue radio transmission pathway.

We can break the streaming pathway into six main steps between the studio microphone at one end and the listener's ears at the other. Figure 3.1 shows how they approximate to the traditional analogue pathway.

The programme maker for an analogue station needs to understand comparatively little of the technology beyond the transmitter. By now the radio receiver is assumed to be a universal piece of technology and usable more or less wherever the listener takes it, within range of a transmitter. But to understand web radio we need to go back to basics and plan programme content around the variety of ways the listener can tune in. Therefore, we need to know about the limitations of the transmission system (as well as its possibilities) and work backwards to make sense of what the server needs to do to get the audio data out to the audience.

So we'll trace the streaming pathway in the above diagram backwards, from right to left: this chapter looks mainly at the receiving end and the next chapter then fits into place everything to the left of that.

'Packet switching' technology

Although, as we've seen, the Internet is superimposed on the infrastructure of the phone system – an international agglomeration of old copper wire, new fibre optic cable, telecommunications dishes and satellite links – it is actually easier to envisage as a bizarre form of electronic postal delivery. Placing a phone call, at least via a traditional exchange, means switching open a continuous electrical pathway right the way through the system so that the caller talks to the receiver in real time – similar to the continuous real-time pathway of the analogue broadcast shown in Figure 3.1. But sending anything on the Internet – text, graphics, video or sound – involves chopping it up into standard sized, tiny segments or 'packets', addressing each of them individually to their destination and sending them off to find their own way through the network, then to be reassembled in the right order by the computer at the receiving end. The network's automatic 'packet switching' only takes notice of the address on the packet: the route travelled to get there is immaterial, but this does mean that some packets can take (milliseconds) longer to arrive than others which have run into heavier traffic. This is clearly not a real-time operation. To overcome the problem that in any transmission the odd packet is liable to get lost along the way, the receiving computer returns an electronic receipt for each separate packet as it arrives. Any packets that are not acknowledged within a few milliseconds the sending computer sends again, until both computers have accounted for all the packets. Hence the jerky way in which web pages assemble themselves on the screen as you watch.

Sending text and graphics in this way is not a problem because we don't use them in real time anyway (although we may get bored with waiting for them to arrive). Downloading even very large sound or video files is fine as well, because we expect them to take a long time to download and the odd few seconds here or there make no difference, just as long as we get the complete version in the end. In a time-based medium like radio, though, even fractional delays in reception soon destroy their meaning for the listener. So the inventors of audio streaming technology had to find some way of getting the packets to arrive at the receiving computer sooner than they are needed.

It may seem incredible that such a system delivers anything at all (and indeed as John Naughton (2000, pp. 102–9) explains, for years telecoms engineers doubted it would), but it turns out that it's amazingly efficient at handling high volumes of traffic between millions of simultaneous connections. And remember that the Internet's chief *raison d'être* in the first place was that it should work, in effect, on its own with no centre. That technological prize entails some key costs, which follow, for sending sound data through this packet-switched system.

Buffering

Arranging for the packets to arrive at the receiving computer before they are needed means building in a short delay between the arrival of the first packet and the time when it is decoded back into analogue sound. Thus, a roughly 10-second 'buffer' allows enough sound data to be assembled in the correct order to begin recreating the first second of the transmission. Subsequent packets continue to arrive and get sorted as the sound 'streams' uninterrupted from the speakers. (That's the theory, but see below for more on buffering.)

Scaled bandwidth

Bandwidth is a key concept for practitioners of web radio. It refers to the effective capacity or 'bore' of a 'pipe' in the Internet. At the centre of the network bandwidth is high (because it is designed to carry multiple connections), but at the periphery, the domestic end, it is much smaller. For the individual tuning in to a web radio station at home, small bandwidth is not too much of a limitation (although it does to some extent determine audio quality). For anyone transmitting web radio, though, *their* bandwidth needs to be able to cope with multiple requests for streams, one for each simultaneous user. Bandwidth is a precious commodity and so (unlike terrestrial broadcasting) the cost of transmission goes up with the size of their audience (though see Chapter 4 for details of alternative webcast modes). For terrestrial transmission the limited commodity is broadcast spectrum – which restricts the number of *stations* – whereas for web radio it is bandwidth – which limits the number of concurrent *listeners*. Conversely, for niche stations serving small audiences the cost of getting on air is comparatively small. This is what is meant by the 'scalable' nature of web radio. If more listeners try to take streams than a server's bandwidth can accommodate, individual receiver connections start to fail.

The need to compress data

We already know that raw digitized sound data occupy a lot of computer memory. Or, to use the image of standard sized packets passing through the 'pipes' (wires) of the phone system, either all the pipes need to be extremely wide or else the duration of the buffering needs to extend towards a complete download for the full information contained in a CD quality sound file (e.g. a *WAV* or *AIFF* file) to stream effectively. But most pipes are narrow at the receiving end, so streaming involves sacrificing data to bring the files down to a transferable size. How much data are sacrificed depends on a number of technical factors as we'll see later, but typically streaming software needs to make a sound file around 50 times smaller than a CD quality original to fit it comfortably through a 28.8 kbps domestic modem. However, as we'll also see later, this does not mean what our ears perceive is 50 times 'worse' quality sound.

A note on 'embedded' audio files

In the last chapter, we established the difference between streaming and downloading sound files. As a receiver of sound you have probably, consciously or not, encountered a third type of sound file, which arrives 'embedded' in a web page. Embedded sound is only really useful for web radio as a way of adding short trails, stings or station idents to a station's web pages (see Chapter 7), but the distinction is worth mentioning here to avoid possible confusion. For future reference, embedding does become a more powerful method for streaming where receivers have very fast connections.

Embedded audio files are sent in a single step as complete, compressed files along with all the text and images that make up a web page. Therefore, they have to be short – typically less than 30 seconds – or else they start to seriously retard the opening of the web page on a typical modem connection. But embedded audio can be encoded using one of the same proprietary brands of software as we use for streaming, RealSystem G2, Windows Media or QuickTime (or some others not currently used for streaming, such as Shockwave). In order to decode an *embedded* sound file your computer needs to have installed the appropriate *Plug-In* for the system. In order to decode an audio *stream* you need the appropriate *Helper Application.* So if your new computer comes out of the box with Windows Media Player installed (as is most likely if it's a PC), that means it has both the plug-in and the helper application. Similarly, if you download RealPlayer G2 both parts are installed (unless you override the standard install default). For streaming purposes, then, we are interested in the helper application of the given player.

Starting the stream

Clicking to request a web radio stream from a website sets in train an ongoing dialogue across the Internet between your receiving computer and the server holding the streaming audio files (see Figure 3.1). The 'listen' or 'play' icon on the station's website is a hyperlink which instructs their web page server to send your computer a small text file, often called a 'Metafile', which contains (a) instructions to your computer to launch the appropriate helper application and (b) directions to the location of the stream you have requested on its streaming server. (Note here that the web page may be located on the same server as the streams or a different one.) The metafile is usually automatically stored on your computer's desktop (for example, as a '*real*' icon with a short name that ends with the suffix *.ram*). From there, it (should) automatically trigger your computer to send its request back to the right location on the server to begin sending the stream. Meanwhile, the interactive window of the helper application, the 'player', has opened on your desktop, where it shows a sequence that goes something like 'connecting' followed by 'buffering' with a countdown of the seconds until the stream starts playing. If you keep hold of that metafile you can use it again to go directly to the server for that particular stream for as long as it's stored there, bypassing the website. So the metafile becomes your equivalent of a push button on a radio tuner. That's obviously a very handy function, which is exploited by the dedicated web radio tuners we'll meet later.

ISP connections, bandwidth and connection speeds

One powerful asset of web radio is its international reach. On the other hand, the provision of Internet services around the world is patchy – from the very high concentration of ISPs in affluent and densely populated regions to their complete absence in the poorest regions (see Table 3.1). What is more, the pricing strategy of each region's ISPs is determined by the very different charging regimes operated by the private or state-owned telephone companies. As far as line quality is concerned, the core infrastructure between the administrative centres of most countries is relatively up to date, but at the local level the age and condition of the lines between an ISP and their clients may (a) restrict the maximum connection speed they can achieve and (b) create large variations in those speeds minute by minute at busy times of day. And finally, there is variation between different ISPs in terms of their size (maximum capacities during peak times), their experience of maintaining services under pressure and their ability to solve individual customers' connection problems.

Once online, two of those variables most influence how people use web radio:

- the cost of listening (i.e. of connection); and
- reception quality.

The cost of listening

Listeners the world over are accustomed to tuning into their favourite analogue stations for free – once they have invested in a radio and the batteries or trickle of electricity to power it. (We can ignore for now the ways those stations cover their costs of providing that service.) So any model that expects anyone to pay simply for listening to the radio is going to be a hard one to sell. The two means of paying for a connection to the Internet at the moment are either pay as you go or a flat rate subscription. Some ISPs employ a combination of both; for example – like mine as I write – charging a modest monthly subscription with a toll charge for going online during business hours, but no toll during evenings and weekends. Payment by the minute is obviously a powerful inhibitor of web radio listening – to which we'll need to return later.

Strength of streams and connection speeds

The quality of reception you hear when you tune to a web radio station is essentially a reflection of the connection speed at three or four points in the streaming chain:

- Firstly, it depends on the strength of the stream when it leaves the server.
- Secondly, 'net congestion' may mean some or all packets in the stream taking a circuitous route to your ISP.
- Thirdly, the actual speed at which your ISP streams to you varies according to how busy its lines are.
- And finally, all the preceding connections being sufficient, the speed of your modem (or other connection) imposes the maximum sound quality you'll hear.

Bandwidth, the width of the Internet pipe, is referred to in several different ways, which are all interchangeable. It is measured according to the maximum 'connection speed' it permits – so many kilobits or megabits per second (kbps or Mbps). Thus, connection speed is also commonly abbreviated to 'bit rate' or 'data rate'.

In comparison with some other planned uses of the Internet as a delivery medium, web radio's data rate ambitions are modest. Table 3.2 gives some comparisons for different streaming requirements.

So a consistent bit rate of 128 kbps will give a sound quality above the best FM stereo radio, provided that speed is maintained from end to end of the transmission. In other words, even a very fast modem cannot give better web reception than the slowest connection in the chain between the originating server and itself. An ADSL modem requesting a stereo MP3 stream will still experience loss in quality and eventually break up if any part of the path between them is less than 128 kbps. Local cable suppliers, where they are available and offering an Internet service, can offer a big improvement over a telephone modem, but on the downside these networks are vulnerable to their own form of localized congestion, which can slow individual connections down

Table 3.2 Comparative connection speeds

40–60 Mbps	Digital High Definition TV
10 Mbps	10-Base T Ethernet LAN
6–10 Mbps	Digital TV DVD (NTSC)
1.54 Mbps	T1 phone line
1.54 Mbps	WAV audio uncompressed (at 44.1 kHz, 16-bit, stereo)
1.5 Mbps	Cable modem (typically)
1.14 Mbps	Compact Disc uncompressed (at 44.1 kHz, 16-bit, stereo)
1.0 Mbps	ADSL high speed modem
512 kbps	ADSL adapted phone line
128 kbps	MPEG-2 Layer 3 (MP3) stereo uncompressed
128 kbps	Dual ISDN
14.4–56 kbps	Telephone (analogue) modem

Source: adapted from EBU Webcasting Group (1999, p. 51).

dramatically when peak demand for their combined services, including TV, approaches its capacity.

The common nominal connection speeds of analogue modems are 14.4, 28.8 and 56 kbps. As far as streaming audio is concerned, those maxima include a 'headroom' of around 25 per cent for other data involved in supporting the connection, so those nominal speeds equate to streams delivered at around 10, 20 and 32 kbps. Ten kilobits per second is adequate for simple speech-only content. Twenty kilobits per second provides quite a reasonable threshold for AM quality sound for mixed speech and music. But as the streaming software writers keep refining their codes, the perceived quality at 20 kbps and above continues to improve in leaps and bounds.

When you visit a web radio site you are often given a choice of two or more of these nominal modem speeds. (If there is no choice and no speed specified the stream is usually around 10 kbps.) However, this practice is likely to die out as the newer versions of the streaming software automatically detect connection speeds as part of the hidden dialogue with the receiving computer and adjust themselves continuously, to make fullest use of the maximum bit rate available.

The common tools of compression – streaming software products

The software products required for compressing the audio data at the sender's end and decompressing them for the receiver are collectively referred to as 'streaming software'. Competing brands of streaming software continue to be created around different 'algorithms', which are the complex mathematical formulae that automate the compression and decompression processes (from which the sub-classification 'CODEC' is derived). As in Figure 3.1, each software 'suite' usually comprises three separate parts, the encoding software, the server software and the client software. Once encoded, the sound is stored or travels in the proprietary, compressed file format until it is decompressed and decoded by the client software in the receiver's computer.

The web radio listener of 2001 is most likely to be familiar with two or three of the brands of client software which dominate the streaming media market: RealNetworks' RealPlayer and Microsoft's Windows Media Player (WMP) are the most widespread, with Apple's QuickTime Player in third place. (All of them stream video as well, though QuickTime's strengths are better established in that medium.) A fast growing fourth method of streaming sound only uses MP3, which is of course not a proprietary format, but an open 'standard' format. Many different factors contribute to each player's market share, of which sound quality for the listener has thus far been a relatively insignificant one.

Box 3.1 Individual use of client software

In their January 2001 'SoftUsage' report, leading industry analysts Jupiter Media Metrix (http://www.jmm.com/) surveyed the use of the various proprietary media players in the US home and workplace. Among their detailed findings were the following comparisons. They measured 'Unique Users' as the number of Americans using the standalone media player client application at least once in the given month, January 2001. Bear in mind that the players are not only used for web radio and that many Unique Users would use more than one of them.

At home: of a total of 81 547 000 Internet users, 51 per cent used a media player of some kind, an increase in streaming use of 33 per cent over January 2000. RealPlayer continued to lead the field with 30.7 per cent of total Internet users having used it via an AOL connection (the dominant ISP in the US). During the same period, 26.4 per cent had used Windows Media Player and 8.9 per cent QuickTime.

At work: of a total of 29 575 000 Internet users, 48.3 per cent used a media player of some kind, an increase in streaming use of 34.9 per cent over January 2000. RealPlayer registered 34.6 per cent of total Internet users via an AOL connection. During the same period, 30.4 per cent had used Windows Media Player and 8.5 per cent QuickTime.

Steve Coffey, executive vice president and chief development officer at Media Metrix commented:

> 'While aggressive bundling campaigns have long since pushed ownership of multimedia players to nearly 100 per cent, usage over the past year has been driven by the increasing quality of the user experience. . . .Greater connection speeds, more efficient content delivery, as well as better and more content are among the key factors that will continue to move this trend forward.'

Source: Jupiter Media Metrix January 2001 SoftUsage Report as reported on *PR Newswire*, 3 April 2001.

Real

For web radio, the RealSystem G2 continues to be the most popular choice. As Progressive Networks, the company launched the first RealAudio compression format (denoted by the file extension *.ra*) and the RealPlayer in 1995. Ever since, now as RealNetworks, it has led the field in streaming products for the Web. Streaming is the company's sole focus. Their home page is http://www.realnetworks.com/, which is the place to begin searching both for their streaming products and their extensive and very helpful technical information and tutorials. RealPlayer does support an increasing range of file types, including MP3 streams, QuickTime and Microsoft WMP's ASF files.

Figure 3.2 The RealPlayer as it appears on the desktop. Screen shot reproduced by permission of RealNetworks®.

If you haven't already got RealPlayer installed on your computer you can either download from their site a free copy of a less advanced version or pay for the most recent improved version (which in 2001 costs $29.99). There are versions available both for PC and Mac platforms from http://www.real.com/.

Windows Media Player

It has been well recorded that Microsoft were late getting into the Internet. And consequently RealNetworks had a head start of at least 3 years on Windows in the field of streaming. However, Microsoft have since caught up very rapidly by developing their own proprietary file format (ASF) and integrating Media Player (often shortened to WMP) into every new Windows operating system they've sold since Windows 98. With the absolute guarantee of such a large number of players ready to receive out there it has proved relatively straightforward to persuade many web radio stations to stream using WMP software. The ASF format claims a sound quality close to MP3, but at roughly half the file size. Once a PC-only format, more recently WMP has been available as a free beta download for Mac platforms. The WMP player supports MP3 streams, QuickTime and RealAudio. It also allows you to change its appearance on the desktop to your own preference, through customizable 'skins'. Downloads and further details are available from http://www.microsoft.com/windows/windows media/en/download/default.asp.

Figure 3.3 The Windows Media Player as it appears on the desktop – undisguised, with no 'skin'. Screen shot reproduced by permission of Microsoft Corporation.

QuickTime

QuickTime (QT) was developed by Apple for Macintosh, but it is available both for creating and listening (and viewing) across platforms. Its product are organized and offered in a slightly different way than the two PC specialists, but the end use is very similar in practice to RealPlayer and WMP. It can store audio or video as a QuickTime 'movie' (with the .mov suffix) or receive a live QT stream. The files are sent and read using the open standard Real-time Transport Protocol (RTP), which adds to its flexibility in customized development. The request side of a unicast RTP set-up travels in Real-time Streaming Protocol (RTSP). The QT player comes pre-installed in all recent Mac computers and can be downloaded for PCs from http://www.apple.com/quicktime/download/.

Figure 3.4 The QuickTime Player as it appears on the desktop – here tuned to dasWebradio. Screen shot reproduced by permission of Apple Computer, Inc.

Other formats – streaming MP3

The infamous MP3 CODEC, both in its original conception and its widest use, is most associated with the compression of music files at close to CD quality – for downloading and storage – but into only one twelfth the size of a WAV file. However, a number of streaming companies have developed ways of streaming in MP3 which take advantage of the fact that, despite the resulting files' small size, they manage to preserve such remarkable sound quality. Whereas RealProducer needs to achieve a compression ratio of 50:1 to get CD quality stereo down to a bit rate of 30 kbps, an MP3 stream only needs a further compression of 5:1 to get 'near CD' quality stereo down to 30 kbps – and half of that can be achieved by combining stereo into mono. So travelling across the Web does not demand another whole new compression format; the MP3s travel as they are, but the trick is to get the server intelligently to 'thin' the data according to the connection it detects from the receiving end.

The comparatively high sound quality of this format and its relative stability mean that it is steadily gaining ground among web radio stations. Some offer it alongside Real G2 as an alternative stream. (It's often signed as 'm3u', which is the file format of a sequence of MP3 files assembled into a playlist for archived or live output.) The format has been built up as a streaming medium by music enthusiasts for whom 'reception' quality was an overriding consideration. At present it is no harder to use by stations or listeners than its competitors and its only significant disadvantage is that it arrived late so has limited audience reach.

The importance of MP3 streaming has recently been recognized by Real, MSN and QT, whose players are all now capable of decoding it. However – once again for the time being – many variables come into play between server and player which can introduce bugs and minor incompatibilities, so it is advisable to reckon that each system works best within the compression format for which it was devised. So these are the best known specialists in streaming MP3 for web radio purposes.

A company called Nullsoft has been a driving force here with their '**SHOUTcast**' software (http://www.shoutcast.com/). There's a choice of software for listening to streaming MP3 on PC, Mac or Unix, for example the specialist players Winamp on PCs, Audion 2 for Mac or XMMS for Unix or MusicMatch for all three platforms. The appearance of all of these players can be camouflaged on the desktop using a range of different downloadable or customizable 'skins'. Recent versions of RealPlayer, WMP and QT now also support streaming MP3 (see Appendix 2 for more MP3 streaming software sites).

Figure 3.5 Panic's web page for Audion 2 at http://www.panic.com/audion/, with the player (upper right) and an example of their copyright panel (lower left) superimposed. Screen shot reproduced by permission of Panic.

StreamWorks is a streaming MP3 application that was originally devised by Xing Technologies, again, back in the early days of the Web. Xing is now part of RealNetworks, but StreamWorks' server and player software continues in its own right (http://www.xingtech.com/).

Another, frequently mentioned source of streaming MP3 is Liquid Audio, but their applications are not suitable for web radio. They're geared very specifically to high quality, secure distribution of music for downloading over the Web.

Different Internet companies continue to develop their own media players and you will occasionally be invited to download them to access their streams – often as a form of membership of their service; for example, 'Spinner Plus' for users of the Spinner music radio cum sales site, http://www.spinner.com/.

A significant aside on formats

The Internet Streaming Media Alliance (ISMA) are a collection of major players who are working to promote the MPEG standard (of which MP3 is the best known at the moment) as *the* future format for streaming. There is a persuasive logic about this view. Firstly, broadband technology, which is gaining an ever stronger presence on the Internet, can handle the distribution of MPEG quality stereo sound with ease and no compromise on sound quality. But, secondly, it is also a format which streams very effectively down to connection speeds of 28.8 kbps (see, for example, EBU Webcasting Group, 1999, p. 59). ISMA includes Apple, Cisco and Sun Microsystems, but RealNetworks and Microsoft remain, for the moment, outside as they attempt to dominate web streaming with their proprietary CODECs. You can find out more about ISMA at http://www.isma.tv/html/about/index_about.html.

Desktops and laptops as radios

For many users, web radio is and will remain something they listen to while they are at a computer for some other visual activity. Most PCs, all Macs and many laptops now come equipped with at least a basic sound card – essential for the final decoding stage of streaming. The speaker arrangement may be anything from inexpensive headphones, a pair of active speakers or a cable connection to the stereo hi-fi all the way up to full 5.1 surround sound.

At home, this may be while surfing visual pages or playing games on the Internet – with provisos: on a phone modem each request for a new page steals bandwidth from the stream and is liable to interrupt the connection; and if the computer's sound card is receiving web audio the games need to be visual only. On the other hand, true to its nature as a secondary medium, if you are online anyway on a toll charged line, you may as well also be tuned in to web radio as

Table 3.3 Modem connectivity in US households in November 2000

Modem speed	Percentage of net users
14.4 kbps	5.5
28.2 and 33.6 kbps	23.3
56 kbps	59.2
High speed = ISDN, LAN, Cable Modem and DSL	12.0

Source: Nielsen NetRatings November 2000, reported in *The Standard* (http://www.thestandard.com/), 26 February 2001.

it won't cost you any more. Similarly, if your online activity is confined to toll-free evenings, web radio becomes a more attractive accompaniment. We'll return in the next chapter to the relevance of these restrictions to the organization of programme material on the web radio station.

But web radio really comes into its own – in fact, so does much of the Internet – when the listener is able to get a so-called 'broadband' connection, typically in the form of some kind of DSL service (Digital Subscriber Line). The spread of this technology across the world is sadly going to take time. In 2001, it is already well advanced in the US, with about 12–13 per cent of online homes having a broadband connection – or, as 53 per cent of all the country's homes are online, 7 per cent of all US households (Arbitron/Edison, 2001, p. 12; and see Table 3.3) – while in the UK, for example, 'Asymmetric' DSL (ADSL) only became available for domestic users at the start of this year and take up is so far very slow. In less developed countries, a good deal of modernization and further development of the infrastructure will be needed before the service can become widespread.

DSL brings the packet-switched network direct to your computer without upgrading your existing copper phone cable. (The last leg from ISP through an analogue modem is circuit switched.) This explains the much higher connection speeds, but it also brings the added advantage that such connections remain permanently open: they are designed to be 'on all the time'. It further means they cannot be metered like a circuit-switched line, which the caller 'occupies' for as long as they are connected. Instead, you pay a monthly subscription for a DSL connection, which has sufficient bandwidth to supply several concurrent uses (for example, two or three high quality audio streams, plus phone, plus multiple html connections). As DSL becomes the 'norm', the initially rather off-putting subscription charges should fall into a more affordable price bracket and web radio in the home takes another very significant step forward.

DSL subscribers with older computers may need to consider upgrading, because streaming at these faster bit rates demands higher processing speeds. And, of course, the quality of sound *from* a DSL connection remains dependent on the strength of the stream leaving the server, the capacity of the routers along the transmission path and the reliability of the ISP's hardware.

Many people listen to the radio *at work* or at an institution like a college or university. In the US at least, the consensus is that web radio is used more at work than in the home (MeasureCast, 2001). ICT connections at work are typically broadband and on all the time, so this is another important point of access for web radio, whether for background entertainment or educational content. On the other hand, many office buildings have physical barriers which make it hard to receive a clear AM or FM signal inside – for example because their steel structure deflects the signal or through the interference generated by busy computer networks. In these circumstances, web radio provides the only viable way for people to tune in to their favourite terrestrial station, with the additional benefit that the choice of station is completely individual for each person in front of their computer.

In addition to the vast range of stations out there on the Web, the technology is ideally suited to running an in-house radio station. Reception can be kept purely internal if it is streamed over an Intranet or Local Area Network (LAN), where connection speeds are likely to be high and the sound quality excellent. Or the station output can be split into two streams, one for internal consumption and one for global access on the Web. Unsurprisingly therefore, educational institutions are well represented on directories of international web radio stations.

Off the shelf dedicated web radio devices

One of the earlier promises made by Internet futurologists was that it would soon become an invisible technology, seamlessly absorbed into everyday life: that familiar domestic appliances would increasingly be designed to exploit the powers of the global network in ways that didn't involve us endlessly 'logging on' and interacting through browsers and search engines. Web radio has been among the first uses to begin to fulfil this promise. Boxes 3.2 and 3.3 introduce the first generation of dedicated web radio devices. In the second half of 2000, the electronics giants started showing an interest in this brand new technology – as indicated by 3Com's take-over of Kerbango – and in 2001 several others are starting to become more widely available.

Broadly speaking, they demonstrate two different approaches to bridging the desktop/radio gap. One harks back to the early days of the wireless radio set by creating a standalone device which hides all its computer hardware inside the casing of a radio. The other adds a dedicated tuning device on to any existing Internet-enabled computer – which still does the decoding work – and links it via wireless remote control to a conventional listening unit, like a hi-fi or portable radio. Note the two converging meanings of wireless here. In its original usage, the 'wireless' radio did away with the wires connecting the tuning device and the listening apparatus by combining both functions into one set – though it still needed wires to connect to the mains and usually an external aerial. The tuner received electromagnetic radio frequency (RF) signals sent from a distant transmitter. In the world of computers, though, contemporary 'wireless technology' is all about physically separating functions and substituting low powered (RF) signals for wires between devices.

Box 3.2 Standalone devices

The prototype Kerbango Radio was the first on the scene in the US. It is a standalone AM/FM/Internet radio tuner with an outward appearance suggestive of a 1950s Bakelite wireless set. Like a wireless set it needs a mains power supply and an external aerial. Sadly, in March 2001, 3Com announced they would not, after all, be bringing the Kerbango radio to market and were looking for a buyer for the project. The beta versions did work and the concept remains a strong one. The (now suspended) website is at http://www.kerbango.com/.

Figure 3.6 The Kerbango AM/FM/Internet radio. Screen shot reproduced by permission of 3Com.

Like Kerbango, Penguin Radio is both an online radio tuner website and a prototype self-contained hardware FM/AM/Internet radio tuner to connect into a domestic amplifier and speakers (http://www.penguinradio.com/).

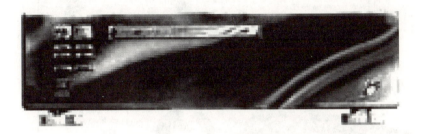

Figure 3.7 The Penguin Radio hardware tuner plugs into a hi-fi amp. Screen shot reproduced by permission of Penguin Radio.

Box 3.3 RF wireless devices

These two devices are inexpensive ways of listening to web radio away from an online computer by using remote control – low powered radio frequency (RF) transmission. Because there are different national RF standards, both of these are on sale to the North Americas and parts of Asia Pacific, but not yet to the UK.

The iM Radio (formerly Sonic Box) Remote Tuner consists of a base unit transmitter that links to an online PC, a small receiver that plugs into the amplifier of a domestic sound system and remote (no wires) software tuner which stays with the listener. The remote tuner comes with hundreds of pre-set web stations and the option to programme in others you choose. As its appearance suggests, it then works very much like a traditional radio tuning dial. The company also make other variations on this model (see http://www.sonicbox.com/).

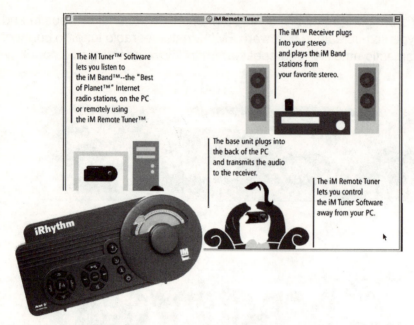

Figure 3.8 The iM Radio Remote Tuner. Images courtesy of iM Networks.

The Akoo 'Kima' KS-110 Internet radio device also works on RF and simply has a base station to connect to an online computer and a remote receiver/speaker, which is portable around the house and up to a range of 300 metres. The listener has to go back to the computer to retune though. More details are available at http://www.akoo.com/site/products.cfm.

Figure 3.9 The Akoo 'Kima' KS-110 base unit and receiver. Image supplied by Akoo.

Footnote: in March 2001, the European mobile phone company Ericsson announced they were launching a similar remote, portable radio tuner, which linked to a base computer using 'Bluetooth' wireless technology (see also below).

However, at this stage in the game, as these dedicated web radio tuners reveal, whichever unit actually receives and processes the streaming audio still needs to run off mains electricity. This is because streaming demands a lot of continuous energetic activity of the microprocessor at the heart of the computer, the so-called Central Processing Unit (CPU). The higher the bit rate, the harder the CPU has to work. As a result, the battery life of a fully remote unit would be too short to be practical for the way we use a portable transistor radio today. And hence also palmtop computers, powerful though they are, cannot yet realistically be adapted to receive web radio streams for any length of time. They are restricted to data rates that are too slow for that.

In fact, the same technological hurdle stands in the way of the development of lightweight, battery powered DAB tuners, though of course the details of reception differ. So how come MP3 players can read music for hours on a modest battery? It's streaming that eats the processing power. Once audio has been *downloaded* via a desktop computer onto some form of hard disk, as an MP3 file, the processing power needed simply to read back the stored data as sound is no more than for other portable storage media like MiniDisc or the drive of a palmtop. But as we've noted in Chapter 2, downloading MP3s (as opposed to streaming them) is a separate activity. Web radio reception requires a CPU fast enough to deal with streaming.

So the race is on to find the truly low powered, high speed microchip technology. That may prove to be one way forward.

Portable radio around the house

But we should take one step back here and look again at the wireless principle employed by iM Radio and Kima. I just said that it is the unit receiving the stream from the Internet that is too power hungry to work like a battery driven radio. What if we accepted that limitation but thought of the desktop computer as a base unit not only to drive a set of remote speakers, but integrating several other remote functions around the house as well? In other words, it becomes a kind of Internet utility box instead of a workstation. Now if that utility box has a broadband connection to the Internet, we can start to envisage the set-up where, for the monthly subscription to DSL or cable, we can run a home wireless network comprising a number of individual laptops, maybe a couple of web radio tuners, phones and a fax, and that's before we get on to TV services.

We know that devices that receive and decode radio waves can happily run on batteries for many hours. 'Wireless technology', based on high frequency radio waves transferring data across short distances, is in fact a major new field of research at the user end of ICT.

Three well-advanced examples of wireless networking standards are Blue-tooth (http://www.bluetooth.com/) – which is now being incorporated into the new Ericsson internet radio above – Wireless LAN (http://www.wirelesslan .com/) and Apple's Airport (http://www.apple.com/airport/). Different hardware manufacturers are looking to add these wireless standards into a whole range of household and office products. At the time of writing, they do not yet include the next generation of web radio tuners, but it can only be a matter of time.

Web radio back in the ether?

In this short section, we take a step into the sphere of technological speculation. It is worth mentioning here because it is speculation in which many international telecoms companies are currently investing very large sums of real money. They are betting on full mobile access to the Internet, either via networks of land-based transmitters or via direct satellite links – or some combination of both. Instead of our Internet streams arriving on phone lines, the dream is that one day soon they'll come, like good old radio signals, through the ether.

There are many questions to be asked about such a reconfiguring of the Internet which lie well beyond the scope of this book (though the companion website will carry updates on the issues that affect web radio as they crystallize). For example, could a mobile Internet be interactive in the present one to one sense, or would it be more suited to something closer to a conventional broadcast model? (See Chapter 4.) Or could a purpose-built network ever be as decentralized and uncontrollable as the present one which evolved ahead of any business model or legislative framework? Will the financiers and vested interests allow it to be, now they know more about what the Internet is? (See Chapter 9.) Whatever the answers, they will certainly impact directly on the future development of web radio.

The prospects for streaming via mobile phones

The distribution of mobile phone networks around the world is uneven. They are particularly suited to areas of high population density and relative affluence, hence parts of Europe and the Far East have pioneered their early develop-ment. The different networks at first grew up independently of each other, using different protocols to achieve the extreme compression needed to send the human voice in a recognizable form but at the smallest possible bandwidth through a busy system. The challenge in 2001 is (a) to unify these networks under an agreed protocol or standard – the more universal the standard, the more people will use it so the higher the value – and (b) to add further value by hooking them into the global world of ICT so that, for example, they can receive streamed audio from the Web.

For a while, when it was launched in 1999, the European **Wireless Application Protocol (WAP)** appeared to promise literally to bring the Internet to the mobile phone – and so it did in part. WAP is a standard that is shared by the major European mobile phone manufacturers. A WAP phone can be used for email and to download text and basic graphic information from the websites which offer themselves in WAP format. But the network is too slow and subject to congestion to cope with streaming as it works today. The bit rate is typically only 9.6 kbps, but more important, like the dial up modem, connection to the system is circuit switched and so it doesn't take much WAP Internet traffic converging on one transmitter to exceed its capacity.

Similar limitations face the Japanese equivalent of WAP, **i-mode**, which is the proprietary protocol of the NTT DoCoMo corporation. Although it is efficient at dealing with text over the Internet, it also connects at 9.6 kbps and in its current form is too slow for streaming.

If the answer lies in a faster, more efficient switching system, then a packet-based standard like **General Packet Radio Service (GPRS)** would seem to provide just that. In Europe it is being promoted as a major step up from WAP when it is finally launched sometime in 2001. Industry analysts are more cautious, predicting connection speeds of no more than 26–56 kbps (see, for example, Dennis, 2000), albeit with a much more efficient use of each transmitter's bandwidth. Being packet switched also means the connection is continuously available (within range of a transmitter, of course). However, there are further hurdles to overcome before GPRS becomes a viable web radio delivery system. It will, for example, take some time (and money) to develop a comprehensive transmitter network and, more importantly for streaming, the handsets will need to be able to cope with much faster processing speeds than current models. As mentioned above, with today's chip technology, that presents difficulties in terms of how long a listen you can expect from each charge of the battery. Faster CPUs also generate more heat, which in a hand-held device presents a further challenge for the manufacturers to overcome.

The GPRS standard is often referred to as '2.5G', because it is half way between the second generation of (European) mobile phone technology, WAP, and the third generation (hence '3G'). This network is planned for worldwide launch in 2003 using the **Universal Mobile Telecommunications System (UMTS)**. It would be reckless to try to predict how this much faster system will work in practice for streaming, or even whether competing standards might have changed the whole mobile landscape by then. In principle though, the predicted bit rates of up to 2 Mbps should be more than adequate for receiving web radio at high quality – as long as bottlenecks in the network do not become overloaded. However, if in the meantime battery capacity for handsets has not significantly increased, we should expect mobile phones at best to be suitable for receiving short news bulletins or sports reports and not as a realistic means of tuning in to a favourite music station.

In-car web radio?

Within reason, battery charging and bulky receivers are not such a problem in cars, though. And motor manufacturers are becoming interested in building mobile Internet services into their cars. We can expect to see a variety of web-based systems on the market in the next 5 years, although, despite the obvious potential compatibility, it is not clear that web radio will find a place among them in the short term, purely because the market to deliver other radio services into vehicles is so well established. To take one example, the most widely available in-car Internet service at the moment is General Motors' OnStar service (http://www.onstar.com/), which is delivered partly through land-based analogue GSM cellphone transmitters and partly via satellite. It's a subscription service that combines a wide range of functions, from vehicle tracking and security, to routine Internet services like email, news services and stock market information. The data it receives at the moment though are downloaded text, which 'talks' to the driver using voice recognition and emulation software. On the radio side though, there is a somewhat mixed picture at the time of writing. GM is now gearing up to add XM's imminent direct satellite broadcast of 100 or so fixed radio channels to the OnStar package in the US (http://www.xmradio.com/).

In other words, the focus is on established broadcasters and those with substantial financial resources supplying their stations through digital satellite broadcast or digital terrestrial broadcast rather than via the Web. It may well be that small Internet-only stations should not expect to penetrate the mobile or in-car markets any time soon.

Summary

So what are we, the web radio listeners, to conclude from this tangle of transmission routes and ways to tune in to web radio? It's not exactly consumer friendly, is it? Not yet, at least.

The first generation of dedicated web radios gives us an important clue to the potential: sets can already today be made reasonably cheaply to function in recognizably radio-like ways. (In this web radio is giving other digital transmission formats like DAB, which had a head start, a run for their money.) For the foreseeable future, however, the desktop computer will remain at the heart of the medium, whether as a listening device in its own right or as the hub of a wireless network which enables listening around the house and garden. Those who want to make use of the interactive dimension of web radio of course also need more than a receiver. Finding and requesting newly available streams – for example a particular archived programme – will continue to require some form of networked desktop or laptop. Similarly, referring to any more elaborate, supplementary visual information than basic text or images will be much easier and satisfying on a larger screen. And those wanting to send audio streams as well as receiving will need to do so through something with the power of at least a modest computer (see Chapter 4).

For the listener, then, in the short term the next phase in the evolution of web radio will be determined by factors within the limits of the existing infrastructure:

- The availability and take up of broadband (DSL) connections.
- In many other parts of the world the availability of *any* ICT infrastructure is the limiting factor.
- The more efficient use of bandwidth (see Chapter 4).

The medium-term prospects for the technology are much more speculative. We surely will have much more radio being delivered via satellite. We may well have some kind of news-orientated radio being delivered in short bulletins via descendants of today's mobile phones or car radios. How much of that content will be produced as web radio is open to question (and we'll return to consider the possibilities in the final chapter).

What the present diversification of delivery systems for radio does suggest is that we, the listeners, should be getting used to the idea of going to different transmission routes for different kinds of radio. The programmes themselves are, after all, already moving quite freely from one platform to another. The current thinking among governments in the developed world is that, for existing national and local radio, terrestrial transmission will be switching from analogue to some form of digital broadcasting by around 2010–2015 (on current very rough estimates). This is already supplemented by direct digital satellite radio broadcasting on an international or continent-wide scale. But both of these are, as we have seen, inherently vertical systems, which cater efficiently to larger, mainstream audiences. The place for web radio is to provide the horizontal dimension. It can cater uniquely to niche audiences, to those who are likely to take a more active or selective approach to their listening. It allows them to interact and participate in radio independently and on their own terms. Perhaps most significantly for the longer term health of all radio, web radio offers a low cost point of entry to this mixed economy for new programme makers and fresh ideas about what radio can do. The next chapter assembles the essential components of this laboratory.

Further reading

General web radio news and information websites – in addition to those cited in the
    text:
Radio And Internet Newsletter (*RAIN*) http://www.kurthanson.com/
Radio Ink http://www.radioink.com/
Streaming magazine http://www.streamingmagazine.net/
Zdnet http://www.zdnet.co.uk/
The website for this book at http://www.web-radio-book. com
And see the end of Chapter 4 for more technical texts on streaming.

4 Streaming radio output

Web radio's equivalent of a radio mast is the computer. Anyone with a phone connection can set one up to send their radio programmes out to the online world. There are many specialist sites on the Web which tell you how to go about doing this (several are suggested at the end of this chapter as 'Further reading'), but for those approaching web radio for the first time there are a number of important basic principles to be aware of before diving in.

Perhaps the first point to emphasize is just what a vast resource the Internet is in its own right. Not only are there the websites of companies who provide the software for streaming – stacked with as much technical detail as you can absorb – there is also an entire international community of radio people out there who collectively have amassed a vast amount of experience with streaming in a short space of time. And if they're streaming successfully they're likely to be up to date in the extraordinarily fast moving world of Internet technology. Most of them have email addresses displayed on their websites, so find a station that's doing something similar to what you're thinking of (see Chapter 7) and see if their webmaster has any tips or recommendations about streaming. Of course, some won't reply, but many will: that's the spirit of the Internet.

So, this chapter gives an essential introductory guide for the uninitiated or the curious and points to a range of sources that will enable you to build your understanding of the technical side of serving streams for web radio. Websites are (most of them) kept up to date in a way a book can never be, so this book has its own companion web address (see 'Further reading'), where I can regularly post new information and amend links as they change or fall out of use over time. At the end of Chapter 3 I also listed a number of online magazines, newsletters and information sites which are dedicated to reporting new developments in streaming.

Scalability

The concept of scalable transmission is central for anyone wanting to stream a web radio station. In broad principle, scalability is a big plus when you are a small station with a small maximum audience because it allows you to get on air without too much expense. For a popular station though, it can be seen as a real weakness of the technology because it means your costs rise in direct proportion to the number of simultaneous streams you are trying to support. We'll see in this chapter that the picture is not quite as black and white as that: there are some options for keeping the cost of additional listeners down.

A novice station expecting only a few tens of concurrent listeners can manage on a fast domestic modem or ISDN connection with a reasonably fast computer (permanently online), but any station expecting larger numbers will need to think in terms of a dedicated server (a powerful computer designed for multiple distribution) and paying for increased bandwidth. The cost of renting additional bandwidth from the line owners or holders is likely to be a major part of the small station's budget – compared, for example, with the computer hardware – so one of the first things to consider is . . .

Who runs the server?

There are costs and benefits to be compared in order to answer this question, and the sums are changing all the time as the technologies move forward. The alternative to running the server yourself is to take advantage of one of a range of host services that are increasingly available.

Host streaming services

Once you have created the content for your station, these services take care of handling the streaming and maintaining the output onto the Web on a 24-hour basis. They work on the principle that they are situated closer to the centre of the Internet and so have direct access to very high bandwidth. A significant point about this kind of service is that you can choose a host from anywhere in the world, which means you needn't be constrained by limitations of infrastructure or curbs on free speech within your own country, which might apply if you ran the server yourself. Host services fall into three approximate, overlapping categories.

Your domestic *Internet Service Provider (ISP)* may well host a small number of streams on your behalf from one of their servers. They charge a set rate per stream, which is in addition to any free or charged space they may offer for your own web pages when you join. Each stream represents a single listener's connection to the server and the total number of streams is the total number of listeners connected at the same time. So this kind of service is most suitable for hosting shorter archived programmes which, say, less than 100 people are likely to link to at the same time – though you may plan for thousands to visit over a period of days or weeks. As a UK-based example, in early 2001 the Demon ISP were offering to host 100 streams for £5 per month per stream (http://www.demon.net/), which adds up to £6000 per year.

So-called '*edge services*' are companies who specialize in professional website provision, and many organizations use them to design and manage their entire web presence. Like ISPs, their servers have access to huge bandwidth because they are situated on the main arteries of the Internet. They tend to offer flexible services to meet a wide range of different needs, but the larger ones will handle streaming output and web pages for a radio station. The cost would be by negotiation according to the kind of output and audience size a station planned. This kind of company can be particularly useful when a smaller web radio station is hosting a one-off live webcast event for which they expect larger numbers of concurrent listeners than the station's modest bandwidth can handle. A base price for hosting a 2-hour live event with a capacity of 1000+ streams might start in the region of the equivalent of £500 at 2001 prices. A visit to one of the following sites (among other 'edge services' or 'web host services' you can find through any search engine) will give some idea of what they have to offer:

Akamai	US based	http://www.akamai.com/
Coollink	US only	http://www.clbn.com/
Digital Island	US based	http://www.digitalisland.com/
Level 3	offices worldwide	http://www.level3.co.uk/
Perfect Technologies	French based	http://www.perfect.fr/
Madge.web	offices worldwide	http://www.madgeweb.com/

In return for your money you get a guaranteed streaming service and full control over your website and brand image.

At the opposite end of the price spectrum there are a number of specialist *webcasting host sites*. Prominent among them in web radio today is Live365 (http://www.live365.com/), which bills itself as a 'radio revolution' (see Box 4.1). It is based in the US, but now acts as host to very large numbers of smaller web radio feeds from around the world. (The site claimed it hosted 25 000 online 'stations' at the start of 2001.) The majority of the stations are in the form of archived MP3s and so accessed on demand, but Live365 also has facilities to host live transmissions. There are some very real advantages to using a site like this to get started which any intending, first-time web radio broadcaster should consider before investing in server hardware and software. Firstly, Live365 is a beacon site for anyone interested in radio on the Web and so they help their subscribers find listeners (see Chapter 7). Secondly, they charge nothing to keep what they call a 'personal' radio stream operation on air 24 hours a day and 365 days a year (see Box 4.1). Alternatively, they offer more advanced services charged on monthly rates. StreamAudio (http://www.streamaudio.com/) work on a similar principle, though all stations are currently restricted to Windows Media Player format and each is now charged an inclusive monthly fee ($395 in January 2001). Whether they charge a little or nothing, sites like these depend on covering their not inconsiderable costs through advertising, which means you may not be in control of the adverts associated with your page(s) and/or streams.

Box 4.1

Live365 have developed a strong presence as a web radio host because they offer a range of low cost or free hosting services plus a very comprehensive global network of servers to relay streams efficiently around

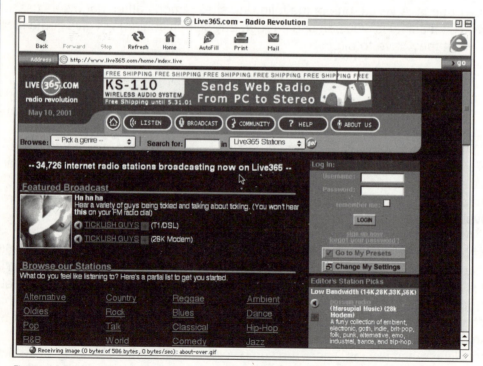

Figure 4.1 The Live365 home page. Screen shot reproduced by permission of Live365.

the world. They work on the principle that 'you supply the audio and we'll do everything else'. For the beginner, this means they supply you with their software which you use to encode your audio and then send it to them. Their streams are in MP3 and usually at lower bandwidths. The illustrated home page shows that they also offer a massive tuner of their clients' streams which listeners can personalize to their own tastes.

Stations who use a host can safely ignore the challenge of . . .

Running your own server

The alternative to having someone else host your web radio content is to operate the streaming yourself by running your own server. Technically a modest, reasonably up to date domestic computer – at a minimum with a 286 MHz, Pentium 2 or equivalent G3 processor and 64 MB of RAM – connected to the Internet via a fast domestic connection like dual ISDN can act as server for up to 10–20 concurrent streams, though there are many technical factors both in the computer and on the phone line which are likely to reduce that capacity. And of course a server needs to be permanently online to be effective. So the cost of your domestic connection will be a significant factor if it's charged by the minute. More important, being permanently online makes a domestic computer extremely vulnerable to unwanted probing and tampering by others on the Net unless you install an up to date firewall (and this in turn can create its own problems with the streaming process, which you need to check before you install firewall or any other security software).

The usual and safest starting configuration is to have one computer (often called the encoding computer) for capturing the content and/or getting it into the right form linked to a dedicated server which stores and manages the streams. We'll come back to deciding on the specifications of the server later.

So in this set-up (see Figure 3.1) the stages from microphone to server are:

- *Capture the sound*. The sound inputs are likely to originate in several different forms, some analogue (e.g. microphone, analogue tape, vinyl) and some in various digital formats (e.g. CD, MiniDisc, DAT). 'Capture' describes the stage of getting them all into the same digital format as sound files on a computer (e.g. WAV or AIFF files). In a live transmission, the capture and the next operation, encoding, are likely to be a single step.

- *Encode the sound files*. This, as we've seen, is the process of compressing the large sound files into much smaller ones. Each proprietary streaming software has its own 'algorithm' or 'CODEC' for achieving this while compromising the sound quality; we eventually hear as little as possible (see next section).

  (Note that the words 'encode' and 'compress', which are interchangeable in this particular context, can be confusing because each has more than one meaning in radio. Here 'encode' does not have the general meaning of 'convert analogue sound into digital code' or 'digitize'; instead it refers to the translation of a large generic digital file format into a very much smaller proprietary or standard format used by the streaming software supplier. Similarly, this process involves a very different order of 'compression' than is commonly applied in studio recording and broadcasting.)
- *Store on or pass though the server*. The encoded files are then passed on to the server. Either they sit there as archived files waiting for on-demand requests or they pass straight through as the feed for a live output. It is also possible to automate the conversion of the live stream, clip by clip, into stored archive files. Some different software, known appropriately as 'server' software, then recognizes a request from an online receiver and starts chopping up and addressing the stream of packets and pushing them out onto the network. This third step is the part a host service would take care of.

This principle is the same whether you are a small or a large station, the main difference being at the third step, where the choice of server hardware and software is determined by the number of simultaneous streams the station anticipates.

The receiver requesting the stream must, of course, have the requisite 'client' software (the 'player'), which is capable of accepting the packets and decoding or decompressing them in order for their sound card to convert the digital data back into analogue sound (see Chapter 3).

Selecting your audience

Practitioners in terrestrial radio are used to thinking in terms of their station having an indiscriminate area of coverage, which is governed only by the power and position of their transmitter(s). From the potential audience within that area, the only direct influence a station manager has over who listens is through the choice of the content and its scheduling (plus perhaps a little marketing as well – see Chapter 7).

In web radio there are many more decisions to be made about the nature of the audience, which determine the technical planning for transmission from the server:

Content versus size of audience

An obvious first consideration, but sometimes forgotten in the excitement of getting on air. The content of programmes must be well targeted to a particular audience: on the Web there's no shortage of alternative listening. Chief among the causes for losing listeners are: (a) content that's indistinguishable from what is already available, especially if it's already on FM locally; (b) overloaded connections where the signal breaks down to produce distortion or drop out; and (c) web pages that take an age to open and/or make it difficult to find the 'listen' icon (Lake, 2001). I'll come back to content in much more detail in Chapters 5 and 6, and to creating the right 'front end' in Chapter 7, but for the moment there are two important technical considerations that follow from any decisions about content.

Is it live or archived or both?

Many web radio stations offer both a live output and a collection of archived clips or longer programmes. Either affect the number of streams and therefore the station's bandwidth requirements. For a live output, the number of streams must be chosen according to the most popular period of the daily schedule. If your server can't cope with demand and the streams start breaking up, the programme is unlikely to remain popular for long. Generally speaking, archive-only stations need fewer streams (a) because listening will spread out over time according to people's own schedules, not the station's, and (b) because if lines are busy the keen listener is more likely to try again later, especially if they have a particular interest in a particular archive clip. Opting for a mixture of live and archive may even out the peaks of demand, though then you need to calculate for sufficient streams to cope with both. Maintaining an up to date archive clipped from a live output can also have considerable implications for staff time.

Twenty-four-hour schedules and the selection of clips

The Internet is a 24-hour medium and scheduling live content across time zones poses all sorts of tricky questions about your audience's patterns of listening. One solution, especially suitable where you don't have 24 hours of daily live programming, is to operate more than one duplication of the schedule in parallel, staggering their starts to fit different time zones. Unlike offering archives on demand, this is treating recorded copies of the schedule of programmes 'as live'. (Like the earliest days of analogue radio, many web stations start life with only a few hours of programming and build up their presence as they find their audience.) Stations who do build an archive must also consider how many clips they can store on their server as against their time sensitivity and relevance to a non-local or international audience, if that's who they are targeting (see Chapter 11).

Receivers and connection speeds

There are two distinct website strategies on show on today's Internet: the inclusive and the exclusive. The exclusive sites tell the mystified user 'you can't access this site because you haven't got the right plug-in' or 'your helper application needs updating' or 'you need to access more memory' – in other words, the site's owner is on a higher technological plain than you are. The inclusive ones open on almost any old post-1995 machine. We'll meet the exclusive website design again in Chapter 7, but setting up a streaming server is no different. It is very easy to inadvertently exclude large sections of potential audience by imagining they're as up to date as you are. Put the other way round, it is entirely possible to deliberately exclude audiences you're not interested in by the way you set your server up, either through your choice of software or by the connection speed you expect them to have at their end. Whichever server software you elect to use (see below), you will need to decide whether to offer your listeners more than one connection speed. Remember the listener's connection speed, or 'bit rate', is measured in kilobits per second (kbps) and is the maximum rate at which data are transferred through the modem they use to connect to the Internet. (In practice, server streams are sent approximately 25 per cent slower than the nominal connection speed to allow for supporting data and congestion on the way.)

- 14.4 kbps – the usual speed of early analogue modems, which a surprising (though steadily falling) number of people still use. The most inclusive option, copes with speech alone reasonably but sacrifices sound quality, so you'll probably want to offer a higher alternative as well. Sometimes described misleadingly as 'AM quality', though it's rarely as clear as a strong AM signal to a radio with an average quality speaker.
- 28.8 kbps – for the time being still (just about) the commonest safe speed to use in practice, given the current reliability of ISP connections when their lines are busy. A 56k modem may well be connecting at speeds that fluctuate from 45 to below 30 (depending on ISP, age of the local line and any networking on the user side).
- 56 kbps – in practice the receiver will get better results if this is a 56k ISDN connection as opposed to a 56k analogue phone modem. Single ISDN will give something closer to average FM stereo quality, depending on the sound card and speakers used.

- 80–112 kbps – speeds in this region usually require a more expensive dual ISDN connection or equivalent and, so long as they are sustained, can give something approximating to CD quality sound, which is the eventual goal for web radio. By choosing these speeds on your server you would, in 2001 at least, be selecting for people listening via a T1 or better connection at work or those at home with above average connections only.
- 128+ kbps – for web radio this looks a likely optimum data rate to work towards in the future, being the rate of an uncompressed stereo MP3 stream. (Or at least at the time of writing: further improvements in the design of CODECs may well achieve the same quality at lower bit rates before long.) It preserves something close to realistic CD sound quality for music and elaborate radio productions, it is comfortably contained within the capacity of a DSL adapted phone line, but doesn't overdo the demand for bandwidth on the streaming server (see below).

The technology continues to move forward rapidly, and increasingly servers are able to detect and respond automatically to the connection speed of the receiver and similarly the players are able to adjust to fluctuations in the speed at which data arrive, using so-called Variable Bit Rate (VBR) software. But the important point here is not to forget the unsophisticated user when setting up server streams – unless you actively decide not to compromise on sound quality for the content you plan.

Location of audience and alternative webcast modes

There are many different reasons to put a radio station on the Web, but anyone who does so needs to think very carefully about the likely global location of their audience. There are several ways you can control that through a server if you want to.

As mentioned in the previous chapter, a very straightforward decision may be made by a university or other institution to exclude an outside audience and conserve bandwidth by running a web radio station internally on their Intranet or LAN. Alternatively, they might run two separate streams, one on their Intranet comprising the institutionally orientated live output and the other offering archived content of wider interest on the Internet.

There are also a number of different *modes of webcasting* which can be achieved by more complex modifications to the server arrangement. The value in investigating which best suits the audience you want to reach lies in the fact that some make much more efficient use of the available bandwidth than others.

Up to now, the streaming I've described is the *'unicast'* mode – and indeed that is the default mode for the rest of this book unless stated otherwise. That's

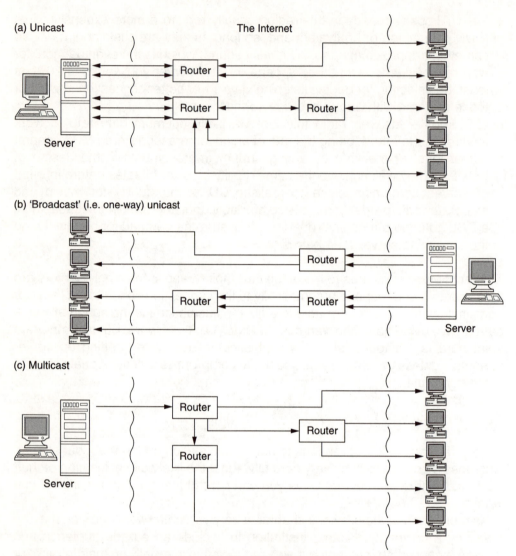

Figure 4.2 Schematic diagrams comparing the different modes of webcasting: (a) unicast; (b) 'broadcast' unicast; (c) multicast via 'multicast-enabled' routers.

because, at this time, it is the dominant mode for web radio, whatever the network it's on. As the name suggests, unicast means one to one webcasting: each listener requests their own single stream from the server for the duration of the transmission. It is very hungry for bandwidth, but it retains the very significant point to point characteristics discussed in Chapter 1 – which of course includes on-demand access to archived streams (see Figure 4.2a).

For radio users the term '*broadcast*' mode is a confusing one in the context of streaming – because it is not broadcasting in the 'through the ether' sense. However, it is used to describe a type of live, listen-only transmission on the Internet, stripped of its two-way, on-demand capabilities (see Figure 4.2b). It is possible to operate in 'broadcast unicast', but this doesn't really add any advantage in the context of web radio. Where it does come into its own is if you can use the fact that the connection is outwards only to save on bandwidth – at the cost of losing the on-demand streams.

This you can do in '*multicast*' mode – one to many (sometimes called 'broadcast multicast', but again in the present context it will avoid possible confusion if we drop the 'broadcast' bit altogether). Multicast is increasingly being engineered on the Internet as a means of conserving bandwidth and making more efficient use of this highly valuable commodity. Here a single live stream is distributed down a spine of designated 'replicating servers', but not across the whole of the Web. Each request for a stream is picked up on the nearest replicating server on that spine and the stream is relayed onwards to the client from there instead of from the originating server – which makes the operation much cheaper. As far as a web radio station is concerned, it is more of a one-way system which precludes individual requests for archive programmes. However, it is possible to see such a system evolving to facilitate repeating 'as live' loops of programming for different time zones or the exploration of simultaneous live 'conferencing' between web radio creators. The major technological obstacle is that the firewalls which protect the infrastructure of the Internet from online tampering were put in place before streaming made the whole thing more complicated. Your ISP should be able to advise on the suitability of multicast for particular situations. Multicast is also an especially useful option to consider for transmissions across an Intranet, where of course it can stay within a firewall.

Finally, there is the option of setting up a system of '*relay servers*'. This is a miniaturized version of multicasting in which the originating server (say in Manchester, UK) streams to a small number of remote servers (e.g. in Boston, Ankara, Delhi and Sydney), which are enabled to receive a unicast stream and relay it as multicast to listeners in each geographical region, or perhaps on a series of smaller LANs. Again, this saves dramatically on bandwidth for the originating station but precludes many of unicast's interactive, on-demand possibilities.

Clearly, these options have to be considered in the light of your station's resources, intended content and target audience. However, in one sense or another each of the modes is capable of delivering its own form of web radio.

Measuring your audience

Already then, we have a quite bewildering range of options to think about before we start putting together our radio programmes. But then in web radio we can always start small and test the water – beginning with the unicast model. Fortunately, one of the things computers do especially well is store and search through reams of information, so the web radio server is able to give the station very precise feedback about its listeners. I'll return to this later in the section 'Managing the server' and again in the case studies in Chapters 5 and 6, but typically this might include:

- which country or region they tuned in from;
- which programme(s) they listened to and for how long;
- which archive clips they requested most and which not at all;
- which connection speed they selected or was detected;
- any transmission errors they encountered.

All extremely useful for tailoring content to audience, eliminating (inevitable) teething problems and – if it's relevant – letting advertisers and sponsors know how many listeners you attract at which times of day. This, albeit indirectly, is another aspect of the interactive power of web radio: after all, this is information which terrestrial broadcasters spend a great deal of time and money trying to estimate through far less direct audience research methods.

But, on the technical side, it is a crucial tool for the station to decide how to match streams to audience size and so avoid wasting money. It is very easy to overestimate how many concurrent streams your station needs – perhaps partly wishful thinking, but mainly because we are used to estimating even small terrestrial radio audiences in the thousands. A web radio station starting from scratch, on the other hand, should think in terms of fewer than 60 streams (unless of course they have specific knowledge to the contrary) and an established terrestrial station just launching onto the Web would be well advised to start experimentally with no more than 60 – which for some of the software providers is currently a significant pricing point.

Encoding and streaming server software products

In the following sections, I summarize the factors which might influence a station's choice of streaming software. The picture is changing all the time, so research is essential: have a look at each of the brands' websites; take a trip around an independent directory of web radio stations, like http://www.live-radio.net/, to get a sense of what similar stations are using; and ask around.

You'll notice that some stations offer more than one format to maximize their potential audience. However, this does entail additional set-up and running costs. At present, there is no authoritative, independent, scientific study that gives a measure of sound quality for each format against stability and consistency of signal so, as in earlier 'format wars' (like VHS versus Betamax video), it is factors like easy availability and market dominance that become far more significant when a station makes its choice.

Real

For web radio the RealSystem G2 continues to be the most popular choice. It offers an inexpensive entry level for a small station, but its prices rise steeply above 60 streams, where it has the reputation of being the most rugged and stable in situations where thousands of simultaneous unicast streams are running on a 24-hour basis. At this top end it is aimed at ISPs and streaming hosts who can recover their costs from their clients.

RealNetworks' encoding software is currently called **RealProducer** (formerly RealEncoder). The basic, starter version is a free download available for any platform (e.g. Windows, Unix or Mac). The same CODEC is also licensed to Syntrillium as an output option within their audio editing package CoolEdit Pro (from http://www.syntrillium.com/). The more advanced version, **RealProducer Plus**, is $200 (March 2001 prices) and once you've piloted your output that's the one you'll need. Both support bit rates from 14.4 kbps up to broadband, with the option to use Real's SureStream technology to optimize the connection between upper and lower bit rates according to the amount of congestion on the line. Both have on-screen 'wizards' which take you through the encoding step by step, plus additional comprehensive instructions. Both allow you to embed short sound clips as html files into a web page or else stream via RealPlayer G2. You can get an overview of what to expect from RealProducer by following links from http://www.realnetworks.com/getstarted/index.html and specifications and system requirements via http://www.realnetworks.com/products/.

From the encoder, the streaming files can either be sent on to be loaded onto a host's server, or else to your own.

RealServer software is only available for PC (e.g. for Windows NT, Unix, Linux, Solaris operating systems). RealNetworks offer a **Basic RealServer** as a free download. This is a useful introduction to their larger server packages as – depending on your set-up – it will handle a maximum of about 25 streams. Above that, they have an ascending scale of packages which are priced according to the number of streams (the following at early 2000 prices are a guide). The **RealServer Plus** is aimed at small scale operators with a maximum of 60 streams (around $2000). The **RealServer Professional** range starts at

100 streams (for around $6000 plus $2400 annual upgrade and support service) and goes up to 2000 streams (around $80 000 plus $32 000 annual upgrade and support).

The RealServer software can be mounted on a range of PC operating systems, including Linux, Windows and the specialist heavy duty systems like Solaris and Unix, so it is a more flexible package than its nearest rival . . .

Media Player

Microsoft Windows Media has its own proprietary file format, which it calls Active Streaming Format (ASF). As well as bundling the **Windows Media Player** within the cost of the post-Windows 98 software, the company also now incorporates the streaming server capability within its **Windows 2000 Server** software. (The earlier server software ran on Windows NT Server 4.0.) The third essential piece in the suite is **Windows Media Encoder**, which is available as a free download (from http://www.microsoft.com/windows/windowsmedia/en/download/). So for those (the majority on the Net) already operating Windows software, this is a very easy route to take.

For pre-produced on-demand files, several Windows-based sound editing software packages now also save into the ASF file format (for example, Sonic Foundry's Sound Forge, details from http://www.sonicfoundry.com/).

Like RealEncoder, Windows Media Encoder offers the choice of step by step on-screen wizards – to take beginners through the process – or else your own manual settings. As of version 7, this system doesn't offer the possibility of embedding audio as html in a website, but, for a web station starting out, it offers similar features to RealProducer, including the choice of bit rates from 14.4 kbps up to broadband. The latest Encoder allows you to run 50 simultaneous live streams directly from the encoding computer (if it is networked with sufficient bandwidth). As suggested earlier, this method of streaming should be approached with caution, unless you are operating within a safe Intranet or LAN.

Microsoft also provide a very helpful set of pages to guide the beginner through streaming using Windows Media Player, at http://msdn.microsoft.com/training/roadmaps/roadmap3.asp.

Windows Media Player is competing with Real in the middle of the streaming market, and seems to be particularly aimed at internal use within company networks, where the Windows server software is already in place. The WMP server allows both unicast and multicast transmission, so the latter can be used to save on bandwidth on live streams. Perhaps due to the fact that the server software can only run on the Windows operating system, WMP has not yet made serious inroads into the specialist high bandwidth, 24-hour unicast market that Real continues to dominate.

QuickTime

The principles of the QuickTime system are slightly different to the previous two formats. The encoding stage involves two pieces of software running on a Mac (PowerMac, G3 or G4) or on a PC: **QuickTime 5** (the basic version, which will encode a live stream, is free) plus the recommended transmitter software, **Sorenson Broadcaster** (currently v. 1.1 at around $190 at early 2001 prices) or Live Channel. The output from here is a single stream which can either be sent as single unicast or across a small LAN as a broadcast. The live stream can also be archived in clips for later use. This set-up constitutes the first half of the streaming process, which then needs additional QuickTime Streaming Server software to multiply and control the streams in unicast or multicast mode.

The audio being streamed can either be pre-recorded as a QT 'movie' (so called even if it's only sound), which is a QT file with the suffix .*mov*, or else as a live feed. The **QuickTime Pro** software for creating these movie files – among other editing facilities over the basic – costs around $25 to download. So the encoding computer captures the input sound in QT format and then Sorenson Broadcaster is the interface you use to compress it and choose from a range of processing and output options.

QuickTime Streaming Server software can then be specified on a range of different server hardware. At the cheaper end, a Mac OSX Server running on a fast G4 can be perfectly adequate for a multicast or small unicast operation, but other suppliers of specialist heavy duty (expensive) Unix-based servers, like SGI, IBM, Sun or Cisco – running Darwin Streaming Media Server or RealServer 8.0 – will also serve QuickTime streams. The server software cost does not in this case rise with the number of streams, so overall prices are determined by the hardware you choose and how much bandwidth is needed for on-demand (unicast) streams. As a start-up proposition though, prices tend to be lower than for Real and closer to WMP.

QuickTime streams use a non-proprietary protocol, Real-time Transport Protocol (RTP) for the outgoing stream and Real-Time Streaming Protocol (RTSP) for interactive requests from the receiver. You may need to configure any firewalls or security software to take account of this.

Apple's useful streaming tutorials are at http://www.apple.com/quicktime/products/tutorials/ and further information about Sorenson Broadcaster is at http://www.sorenson.com/. Live Channel details are at http://www.channelstorm.com.

Other formats – streaming MP3

There is nothing proprietary about the MP3 standard. So there are many audio software products which encode sound files in that format – including many

DAWs like CoolEdit Pro or ProTools. The trick in streaming them across the Web is to get the server to 'thin' the data intelligently according to the connection speed it detects from the receiving end. This is becoming an increasingly popular method of streaming, especially for on-demand streams, because the sound quality through moderate connection speeds is usually better. (Remember too that the software developers in this format are focused only on sound and not also trying to make their players work for streaming video pictures.)

Nullsoft has been a driving force here with their 'SHOUTcast' software (http://www.shoutcast.com/). The encoding software is **SHOUTcast Source**, which comes as a plug-in for Winamp. More recently, Panic have introduced their Audion 2 player/encoder, so you can originate your MP3 stream from PC or Mac. **SHOUTcast Server** software needs to be run on a server with plenty of bandwidth and, once installed, it links it into a Distributed Network of Audio Servers (DNAS) – which acts as a sort of quality control for this SHOUTcast streaming because of the minimum system requirements it demands. SHOUTcast Source can be operated from a Windows operating system, or else a Unix variant like Linux or Solaris.

Another interesting feature of the SHOUTcast streaming software is that you can cap the maximum number of simultaneous streams you serve and display on your site the number of listeners connected as compared to the cap. This helps preserve a minimum quality rather than the alternative of stretching the bit rate according to demand until streaming connections start to break down arbitrarily.

StreamWorks is the streaming MP3 application originally devised by Xing Technologies and now part of RealNetworks. However, StreamWorks' server software continues in its own right (http://www.xingtech.com/). It is a sophisticated system, geared more towards publicizing music demos, but nevertheless usable for web radio – particularly on an archive site. Again, you can preserve audio quality by setting a limit on the number of requests for streams your server will accept.

Server hardware configuration

The server hardware you use depends entirely on the scale of the streaming operation you have in mind. On the small scale, this can be very inexpensive as I've noted and so it makes sense to experiment first if you are planning to run your own server. The important thing to emphasize here is not to overestimate the number of streams you will need – hence bandwidth – and to think carefully about how much you want to archive.

Most of the advice websites recommend that to run a basic audio streaming pilot the minimum spec for the server is nothing exceptional in terms of today's computers. The processor speed should be at least 266 MHz, with 128 or

256 MB of RAM (depending on the format) and as much memory on the hard drive as you can afford.

A simple calculation of data rate of the stream multiplied by the number of streams gives the *bandwidth* you'll need. So if you are streaming at 20 kbps and expect 60 simultaneous connections the total bandwidth is 1200 kbps, or 1.2 Mbps, which will fit comfortably through a T1 phone line. Conversely, on a T1 line, if you want to offer uncompressed MP3 streams at 128 kbps, you would only be able to run 11 simultaneous streams (bandwidth divided by bit rate). This scale of pilot will give a reasonable indication of where your next step up should be, remembering that multicast or a mixture is always an option within this range of bandwidth.

If you are seriously planning on launching with hundreds or thousands of simultaneous streams or indeed want to offer higher connection speeds, you will clearly need to carry out much more research and discuss the options directly with each of the software companies – who will be only too keen to advise on that scale of ambition.

The other factor to consider in choosing the server is the amount of storage memory you will need. Obviously, for live streams this is no more than the standard hard drive that comes with the above type of server. If you want to archive clips the calculation is again simple:

$$\frac{\text{bit rate the clips are encoded at (kbps)} \times \text{total length of clips (seconds)}}{8}$$

(to convert kilo*bits* to kilo*bytes*).

This returns us to the question of what you want the archive to be doing. Do you really need to make the whole of your 2-hour breakfast show available all day at 20 kbps? That one show will occupy 18 MB on your hard drive for as long as it's there. And how many listeners do you expect to listen to the whole 2 hours? Shorter clips of highlights might be more cost effective.

Managing the server

It is important not to underestimate the time that can be involved in managing your own server – which may be one more reason to consider using a host. How much time exactly depends on what you are asking the server to do for you.

- *Setting up*. Obviously, the most labour intensive part of the operation. Even if you are not an expert, a day should be enough to get a basic stream running. However, you will need to keep a close eye on it until you know it's stable.

Budget time for problems to arise in the early weeks. Most server software will give you detailed fault reports, so that even if it doesn't crash you will know if requests for streams are failing to connect and then you can set about finding why.

● *Live streams.* Once you have a live stream up and running smoothly it should look after itself. Keep a close watch on the maximum number of simultaneous streams though. The closer you run either to the bandwidth capacity of your Internet connection or your software, the more crashes you will experience. In other words, a system running at capacity will demand more of your time, so if that's the regular situation it may be time to upgrade.

● *Archiving from a live stream.* Depending on the amount of what you are archiving this can be more time consuming. Again, your server software will probably automatically store a copy of your live stream as on demand when you ask it to. What takes the time is organizing that storage in useful sized clips. It is possible to write your own operating 'scripts' dictating how long you want clips to be, but tying that in with programme junctions is less straightforward – for example if the schedule varies day by day.

● *Monitoring requests and server management information.* You can decide to use the server's metrics data as little or as much as you like. However, it's there because it is all potentially extremely useful to a web station operator. If you are not interested in the size of your audience, or when they tune in and out, or which part of the world they come from, or what the commonest connection speeds are, then this part of the operation need take no time at all. On the other hand, as we'll see throughout the book, the option to respond directly and immediately to your audience (through this kind of data and/or through email feedback if you encourage it) is one major way web radio differs from broadcasting.

The above pointers are of course for the streaming side of the operation. You may also house your station's website on the same server, although there's no need to: it can live on a computer on the other side of the world if you want it to. So I have not mentioned here the management of emails, chat rooms or bulletin boards. I'll say more about those options as they crop up through the book.

The case studies in Chapters 5 and 6 give some useful indications about how much of their time different types of server operation take up.

The streaming studio

So what about the first part of the webcasting chain, the all important production of the content? From Chapter 5 on, we'll return to the nature of web radio content, so this section is only concerned with technical considerations.

The web radio production studio is, in its own way, just as scalable as the streaming capacity of your server. At the minimum, the inputs might be no more than a single microphone and some means of playing in some other audio material – digital or analogue – plugged into the sound card of your encoding computer. At the maximum, it is the full output of a terrestrial national network station. The purpose of this section is to suggest the key considerations to be aware of if you are planning to assemble a studio specifically for the purpose of creating a web radio station from scratch. There are many other excellent books on radio production and studio techniques – a few of which are included under 'Further reading' – so here we are interested in bolting web radio on to that body of knowledge.

The most important rule to remember is *keep your input as clean and crisp as you know how.* Just because it's about to be so heavily shorn in the process of compression, this does not mean sound quality on the input side is unimportant. Quite the reverse. The decompression at the receiver's end *magnifies* many of the imperfections in a careless recording.

A few words on some basics of *digital sound production*, which should be followed up through the 'Further reading' at the end of the chapter. There are, of course, a wide range of fully digital studio tools available now which should help keep your sound clean – so long as it goes in cleanly: digital mixing desks for live work and DAWs for post-produced programmes. However, there's no reason why a good analogue desk shouldn't do just as well for web radio – and even well-recorded analogue tape. Both systems can give rise to their own particular sound problems if not set up correctly or used carelessly. Digital 'clipping' due to over-recording maximum levels can be at least as awful as analogue tape hiss due to under-recording by the time it gets to the web radio listener.

Transferring from good old vinyl via a mixer straight into the encoder can present problems because the surface noise of the record is magnified somewhat through the streaming CODECs. If you are using a lot of vinyl records, especially well used ones, they should be 'cleaned up' first. Your mixer's filter pots may offer a crude solution, but there's a wide choice of increasingly effective 'de-clicking' or 'de-scratching' filtering software either as a plug-in or built into most of today's generation of digital editors that will do a far better job. Once you've found the cleanest settings, automated batch processing of a collection of files can save a lot of time.

Digital distortion can be a particular problem recording out of a DAW via the sound card. For this reason, it is advisable to organize any post-production work on computers that are networked with your encoding computer. Work throughout on the DAW using an uncompressed standard file format like WAV or AIFF. When it's finished, transfer the file onto the encoding computer on the network and only compress it into the streaming format as the very last stage.

This relates to another hidden 'trap' of the wonders of digital sound recording. It may be easy to imagine that once sound has been digitized it is immune from the kind of *generational degradation* we associate with copying analogue recordings. The way we combine different digital equipment in radio – CD, DAT, MD, plus all the computer file formats – it is not.

Although digitization is all about simplifying sound into binary digits, the processes of recording, storing, retrieving, editing and compressing digital sound all involve different forms of digital language, devised by different manufacturers according to different technical protocols. On the face of it, they are compatible and seem to talk quite happily to one another: we can do a fully digital transfer from CD to MD or from MD onto a hard disk editor with no apparent loss of quality. But each successive digital generation can overlay small variations which can subtly shift qualities in the sound, such as losses within some frequency ranges and exaggeration of others. In the compression and decompression of streaming, some of these changes can be greatly and unpredictably magnified.

So, keep count of the number of copying generations (= digital formats) you introduce between the original sound source (raw recording, CD, etc.) and the encoding. As a rule of thumb, try and keep it to no more than three. That means, for example,

raw MD recording → computer editing file format → encoding format

is three digital generations. So, bouncing back and forth between a hard disk and an MD, even if it's all done through digital connections, is not risk free as far as eventual sound quality for the receiver is concerned. Obviously, there are many circumstances in which the risk is worth taking, but this is a useful rule to be aware of in the breaking.

Digitization is a balancing act between fidelity of sound and quantity of data. The two parameters that govern both are *sample rate* (sample points per second in kHz) and *bit depth* (depth of resolution or precision of each sample). In radio, we are typically asked to work at a sample rate of 48 kHz at 16 bits (for example, in setting up a DAW or DAT recording). This is in excess of 'CD quality' (44.1 kHz, 16 bits), but has less risk of losing details which may become noticeable once the sound has been through the transmission chain. Similarly, to be on the safe side before you start compressing, CDs should be ripped onto your DAW at 48 rather than 44.1 kHz.

The job of the streaming CODECs is to minimize the quantity of data while preserving the best fidelity under the circumstances, so what sample rate and bit depth should our standard file be saved at to go into the streaming format? If the – clean – sound is more detailed than the web radio listener can possibly hear, can we save on data in a controlled way *before* handing it over to the streaming

CODEC for more drastic pruning? The advice from the technical experts seems to be, again as the final step before encoding:

1 Halve your data by saving in mono, unless stereo is *really* important.
2 Halve it again by cutting the sample rate down to 22.05 kHz for streams of 28.8 kbps or less.
3 Preserve detail across the tonal range by keeping to 16 bits, unless for speech at slower than 16 kbps.
4 Lose the very top of the hearing range, which will barely be missed by most listeners, by applying a low-pass filter to remove sound frequencies above 10 kHz.

(See, for example, the NPR experience recounted by Holt and Mandra, 2000.)

A note on 'archiving'

In the streaming world, the word archive is used interchangeably with 'on demand'. However, if you intend to keep copies of programmes in a permanent archive, it's best to preserve the full original audio quality and to store them in uncompressed form. You can then take advantage of improvements in later generations of CODECs when you stream them next time.

Summary

Streaming appears, then, quite a complex business, with very many variables to take into consideration: no more technical variables, in fact, than the end to end system of transmitting analogue sound, but web radio does give you the chance to manage them all – if you want to.

If you are not running the server, getting started is really very straightforward and the only thing you really need to worry about technically is the connection you use to get your output to your host. There are various ways of doing this which the host will advise you on. Beyond that, you are free to concentrate on getting the content and studio quality right – the traditional skills of radio.

If you decide to run your own server, allow plenty of time for early experiments. The scalability of the technology is your ally in this. You can find out whether this route is for you for no more than the cost of two modest computers, one to encode, one to serve. When you have that right, then you can start investing a step at a time and learning through your own particular experiences. The following two chapters illustrate how a range of different web radio operators have done that – and survived to tell the tale.

Further reading

Beggs, J., Thede, D. and Koman, R. (eds) (2001). *Designing Web Audio*. O'Reilly & Associates.

Dean, D. (1997). *Web Channel Development for Dummies*. Foster City, CA: IDG Books.

Holt, R. and Mandra, C. (2000). How NPR webifies its programming – and you can, too. In *Current*, 30 October and published at http://www.current.org/stream/stream020npr.html as at Feb 2001.

McLeish, R. (1999). *Radio Production* (4th edn). Focal Press.

Miles, P. (1997). '*Internet World''s Guide to Webcasting*. Wiley.

Novak, J. and Markiewicz, P. (1998). *Web Developer.Com Guide to Producing Live Webcasts*. New York: Wiley.

Patterson, J. and Melcher, R. (1998). *Audio on the Web: The Official IUMA Guide*. Berkeley, CA: Peachpit Press.

Reese, D. E. and Gross, L. S. (2001). *Radio Production Worktext: Studio and Equipment* (4th edn). Focal Press.

This book's website at http://www.web-radio-book.com.

5 Established radio broadcasters on the Web

How have established terrestrial radio broadcasters responded to the arrival of the Web as an additional means of distribution? A very large number of them have decided that they should give it a try in one form or another. We may see this as partly professional curiosity: Does this medium have anything new to offer the broadcaster? But there is also the sense in which stations fear they cannot afford *not* to register their presence there, at least once they see a competitor station has decided to experiment. So radio stations the world over have begun to incorporate the Web into their strategies, before perhaps being sure precisely what they hope to achieve by doing so. The deciding factor is that it costs very little to get going on the Web (in professional broadcasters' terms): no additional licensing is necessary (though see Chapter 8 on copyright), the programme output is already paid for, so what is there to lose when it may be possible to add audience in this way?

We can categorize five levels of involvement in web radio by broadcasters:

1 The station website.
2 The simulcast stream of the terrestrial output.
3 Archive streams of parts of the terrestrial output.
4 Investment in creating additional 'side channels' of new programming which target niches within and to the side of the broadcast audience.
5 Using broadcast expertise to create content for third party streaming sites.

Most radio stations now have their own website. A proportion now also simulcast and of those much smaller numbers have yet been persuaded to add archive streams or new side channels. Naturally, the availability of funds is something of a determining factor, although the size of the parent broadcaster is not necessarily an indicator: stations making imaginative use of the Web range from the very large to the very small. The MIT directory of the world's radio stations (http://www.radio-locator.com/) gives the most up to date and comprehensive impression of the ratio between the stations just with websites and the webcasters. It traces radio stations through their websites and then indicates which of them also offer streams. Of course, what this doesn't reveal is those stations without websites, nor does it tell us whether the streams are simulcast, on demand or side channels, until we investigate.

This chapter, then, aims to illustrate how established stations are using web radio through looking at three case studies in some detail. For insights into the best ways simply to add a text and graphics website to an existing broadcast presence (if there are any stations yet to do that), the best advice is to consult one of the texts or websites I have listed at the end of Chapter 7. The purpose of the case studies below is partly to show how web radio fits into the overall strategies of stations who already serve their broadcast audiences very effectively and partly, as a complement to the preceding chapter, to show which of the technical options they are choosing to do so.

Each one of these examples, and those in the following chapter, raise a number of different themes for web radio practitioners to consider, to which we will return throughout the remainder of the book.

My criteria for selecting these three examples from the thousands of radio broadcasters who have added streams to their websites have been simply to look for stations from around the world within each of the three main sectors of the industry I outlined in Chapter 1: commercially funded stations, centrally funded public service stations and voluntarily supported alternative or third sector stations. Beyond that, my selection has been fairly arbitrary, although these are three very positive examples of stations making imaginative use of distinctive strengths that web radio adds over and above their experience of conventional radio broadcasting.

Interactivity on the station website

Each of the examples below have very effective websites in their own very different styles. They are effective because they allow the visitor to navigate their way around the site very quickly and directly, while keeping each page small, both in terms of kilobytes and scrolling length, so that it opens with minimal delay (see Chapter 7). Before we've clicked to listen (near the top of the first or second page) we have a clear impression of the type of station we've come across, if we don't know already. The design of the site complements the sound of the station.

Interestingly – and coincidentally, as I didn't pick them for this reason – none of them make much of the chat room, discussion page or bulletin board. They encourage email comments addressed to the station and indeed often build the immediacy of the quick email into the live broadcast/stream. But they don't provide a space on the site for active online discussion between listeners. This illustrates an important point for prospective webcasters to consider: chat rooms and the like, if they are to be dynamic, up to date but not outside the station's control, really demand the full time attention of a moderator. A moderator is the person who casts their eye over every email submission before it's posted publicly on the site in order to maintain some minimum level of discussion and to filter out the inevitable deliberately offensive comments or those which might damage the station's reputation (or bank balance in the case of libel; see Chapter 9). Clearly, the cost of that staff time is a luxury this sample of stations have decided is not worth the investment. Radio Netherlands comes closest with its 'guest book' on its home page, though its contents show it to be on a fairly long-term rotation and not demanding to manage.

Contrast these examples with the BBC's widespread use of moderated discussion forums across its radio sites or with US talk radio format stations, which thrive on the aura of controversy and additional attention to support their shows on air. This level of active public engagement may be an appealing new strategy for an established station, but – if successful in attracting emails – it is bound to be time consuming.

But, until you stop to think about it, the absence of that kind of online discussion doesn't have to make a radio station's website feel less interactive. Our first two examples here offer those who are interested and have the time several options for interacting in visual, search mode – which stem directly from and add to the on-air content. In Radio Netherlands' case, we can describe this in terms of offering several layers of engagement, through which listeners can 'mine' for information they find interesting. In other words, they can dig as deeply as they wish. Thus, an on-air prompt or a browse around the (newspaper like) site may lead them to an archived radio feature, which may in turn lead them to a link to another relevant site for further detail . . .and so on. Virgin Radio's site, on the other hand, draws listeners into it – again with frequent on-air prompting – by offering side channels of things to listen to, like a star interview or an on-demand play of a new release, plus visually based entertaining things to do, plus carefully targeted visual adverts which typically provide the 'call to action' for on-air campaigns and invite the viewer to click through to find out more.

Virginradio.co.uk case study

Since Virgin Radio won their commercial licence to transmit on AM back in 1993, they have looked for other platforms to give their rock music listeners across the UK clearer reception and better sound quality. (Virgin did manage to gain an additional FM frequency within London in 1995.) So the station were quick to begin experimenting with streaming using RealAudio soon after it became available on the Web in 1996. They were also first among their competitors onto analogue satellite through a deal with BSkyB and more recently have gone on to add slots on Sky Digital satellite and the Digital One DAB multiplex.

Although the early sound quality on RealAudio was not great and the servers crashed fairly regularly, over 5 years the virginradio online experiment has been rewarded with sound quality that is now significantly better than AM and signals that are comparatively very reliable. Interruptions are usually down to local Internet congestion rather than server failures. Their policy in developing their online presence has been to take full advantage of the technology's scalability and grow steadily in response to audience interest, making sure they always build in 'redundant' overcapacity to their steadily increasing bandwidth requirements. A close, dynamic integration between the IT department's development of the website's content and design with the online streaming has been vital to the success of both.

Figure 5.1 The home page at http://www.virginradio.co.uk/ with the pop-up player for the live stream (in this case it's playing through Windows Media Player, though this is disguised by the 'skin' the design team have created for it in-house). Images supplied by Virgin Radio.

Virgin Radio's target audience is 18–24 and predominantly male, which coincides with the profile of early adopters of web radio. As one of the very first stations to appear preloaded on the RealPlayer tuner, use of the virginradio live stream has reflected the spread of web radio. So the station has maintained a strong presence in the US, with no offline promotion, but helped by the high recognition of the Virgin brand from the transatlantic record label and airline. MeasureCast recently rated virginradio the third most listened to web station in the US, with 25 613 unique listeners in March 2001. Global demand for streams fits closely with the weekday office routine, beginning at 9 a.m. GMT in the UK and followed 5 hours later by the American East coast and the West coast 3 hours after that. Forty to fifty per cent of their web radio listeners are in the US, with very slightly less in the UK. The remaining 10–20 per cent are scattered worldwide. However, web listening represents only about 1 per cent of their total audience across all platforms, which explains why the owners have never been tempted to go overboard on investment in the hardware. The consistent demand pattern indicates that most listeners stay tuned in throughout the working day.

In line with their policy of being a radio station for all platforms, virginradio now stream on Real, Windows Media Player and QuickTime. The demand from RealPlayer listeners still represents about 60 per cent of the total, with WMP catching up fast over the last 2 years to around 40 per cent and QT on 1 or 2 per cent. The online team manage all the encoding for all three formats in-house. Thereafter, the QT server operation is handled by the specialist edge of net service, Akami, and Real and WMP outputs are forwarded on dedicated lines to four servers Virgin rent in the central London 'co-location centre' of their current ISP, Level 3 Communications. Being a major online player, the company have been able to shop around over the years to find the best current deal guaranteeing them high standards of connection to the Web. Using the two servers per format is essential as a back-up in case one crashes, but also allows peak loads to be spread. The two Real servers run on a Linux OS and are much the more stable. The WMP servers compensate for less stability by allowing each request for a stream automatically to default to the second server if it fails to find the first. Neither the Real nor WMP have needed any additional relay server arrangements to support their international service.

At the moment, Virgin Radio's online policy is to offer the best quality streams they can at lower encoding rates of 22–30 kbps. They intend to wait until there's been a substantial take up of higher bandwidth connections before increasing the upper end of that range. The live output from the Virgin Radio studio desk splits into analogue and digital paths for their different transmission platforms and passes through standard broadcast compression. The online feed takes mono signals from the digitized path before processing them separately through the three encoders. Through experiment they have found out a lot about maintaining a good dynamic range for rock music by adjustments before and within the encoding settings. Very useful in this learning process has been spontaneous email feedback from listeners noticing the changes and commenting on how they sounded to them.

Virgin Radio regard their online simulcast service as a success within the capabilities of the existing technology, and their strategy is now to add a number of more targeted web-only services to appeal to different niches within and beyond their established audience. In November 2000, they launched the online Virgin Classic stream and in April 2001 Wheels of Steel. Virgin Modern and Virgin Lite are planned to follow by the end of 2001. These side channels are fully automated and so cheap to run within the established online set-up. But again, the policy is to test the water and think about investing in additional DJ presentation as and when audiences for these services increase significantly. The website also offers archive streams from time to time, for example carrying edited highlights of the breakfast show, special interviews or music events. These need promoting independently of the live stream and attract far fewer users. For example, a joint promotion with Amazon.co.uk, to coincide with the release of the latest Oasis album, had a well-trailed live interview with members of the band only available on the website. This was then archived there over several months to gain maximum audience for it.

The initial investment in staff time for the streaming operation was mainly (a) in researching and arranging the server requirements, (b) the additional engineering for routing the appropriate cables and connections from desk to encoder, and (c) roughly an intensive day for the small online team to set up each new channel. From then on, staff time tied up in maintaining the streaming operation is low because few day to day problems arise. In fact, most time consuming for the team is the analysis of the detailed metrics data returned daily from the servers.

As a commercial operator, these data are vital for virginradio.co.uk. Advertisers like the fact that they can get next day feedback on the effectiveness of a given promotion or campaign, while it is in progress instead of waiting for the usual post-campaign analysis. Virgin Radio's total advertising operation combines the ad insertions to the radio output from the various different platforms (AM national, FM London, DAB, satellite and online) with the visuals on the website. They use conventional technology for firing different ad sequences onto each platform during breaks. Having researched automated radio ad insertion software, the team have found it too inflexible as yet for their live operation. Many of the on-air (offline) promotions (competitions, quizzes, more info, online magazine, etc.) are directed to encouraging listeners onto the website, where advertising can be further differentiated towards niche audiences, nationally or internationally. Web listeners already online are much easier to target in this respect because they are only a click away from the advertiser's own site if they're interested. And for many online advertisers, Virgin's target audience represents the kind of technologically literate, upmarket niche they would like visiting their own sites. The next aim is to synchronize the appearance of banner ads on the website with on-air advertising to make the 'click through' even shorter and more effective. Another advantage of the combined web radio and website is that the marketing team can target each different section of interests among the total audience much more specifically, a week at a time.

Sources: Steve Taylor, Group Enterprises Director at Virgin Radio; David Jones, the Head of IT at Virgin Radio. Virgin Radio is part of the Scottish Media Group.

The simulcast stream of the terrestrial output

As demonstrated in these examples and thousands more, this is technically very straightforward to get up and running. The questions about new audiences that follow may take more time to figure out. The answers usually involve additional resources.

In Virgin Radio's case, the biggest question has been what to do about on-air advertising. Ads that talk to a London audience are obviously wasted on a listener in New York, so they have to manage the insertion of different ad breaks for each of their simulcast platforms. The advantage of being online here, which justifies the additional effort, is that much more of their on-air advertising and promotion can direct listeners to follow through on the website. The addition of this visual, non-real-time and interactive tie-in overcomes some of the limitations of the sound-only campaign.

Radio Netherlands has a very different challenge: how to replicate its global terrestrial transmission network online.

Radio Netherlands case study (Radio Nederland Wereldomroep)

Radio Netherlands has been Holland's external broadcast service since 1947. It is based in Hilversum, a public service broadcasting centre rich in historical resonance for anyone familiar with the names on the old style European medium wave tuning band. Its terrestrial output is carried on transmitters around the globe, from Bonaire in the Caribbean to Madagascar and Singapore in the South, to Germany and Russia in the North. In addition, Radio Netherlands has direct satellite broadcasts on IntelSat, AsiaSat and Astra, plus 5500 partner stations who relay parts of its schedule locally around the world. Programmes are broadcast selectively in Dutch, English, Spanish, Bahasa (Indonesia), Portugese and Papiamento (Caribbean). The cumulative audience is estimated at roughly 50 million worldwide. On 1 July 2001, Radio Hilversum announced it was stepping into the North American short wave frequencies as they were relinquished by the BBC World Service, with the intention of switching them to DRM transmission in the next few years.

Figure 5.2 The Radio Netherlands radio home page in English (at http://www.rnw.nl/en/index.html). Screen shot reproduced by permission of Radio Netherlands.

Radio Netherlands' approach to developing their online presence has been evolutionary. Their first website appeared on the Net in 1994 and they followed that with early experiments in streaming from 1996 to 1997 through an arrangement with World Radio Network (WRN). But they began running their own Real server in-house in 1998. Demand for streams has roughly quadrupled each year since then, to a current weekly reach of around 25 000 listeners per week, mainly from outside Holland.

Programmes are mainly speech based, but cover a very wide range of content from internationally oriented news through to highly creative entertainment shows. Online, these are made available either on a single live stream or through a system of rolling archives. The live stream takes feeds from different live language broadcasts in turn, calculated on the basis of approximate peak listening across time zones. So Spanish, Dutch, English and Bahasa language programmes are arranged in regular 1- to 4-hour blocks across a 24-hour cycle. This is obviously designed less for continuous listening in any one language and more for 'appointment' listening to particular regular slots – and consequently the live stream only receives about 25 per cent of Radio Netherlands' total web audience, as against 75 per cent for its archive streams.

The archive streams are mainly extracted from this live stream's daily schedule and grouped by language and on a 24-hour cycle. So visitors who selected the Spanish or English languages on their way to the radio section of the website are currently each offered around 11 hours of the preceding day's programming, usually split into 1-hour blocks; Bahasa Indonesian visitors have 4 hours of programmes; Papiamento and Portuguese speakers around 1 hour's worth each. All these files are offered both as on-demand streams and as downloads (which are especially useful for rebroadcast by partner stations). The choice of Dutch language programmes and bulletins is naturally more extensive. This complex archiving operation is managed by an automated script within the streaming server software. However, Jonathan Marks, the Director of Programmes at Radio Netherlands, is aware of the drawbacks of this time-based archiving and aims to replace it with a programme-based system as soon as they can get hold of new software to link their station programme management system (Dalet) into the web server. In addition to programmes arising from the live stream, the site also keeps a 'sound library' of pre-recorded features which they judge to be of longer term interest. These are on demand only and typically edited versions of features or interviews broadcast in the preceding few months, framed on the site within their own text page of background information and relevant links.

Currently, the radio streaming server at Radio Netherlands' operations centre in Hilversum is running RealServer software on a Windows NT platform. There are plans to add a WMP server as well. The server supports up to 3000 simultaneous streams at a bandwidth of either 16 or 20 kbps (SureStream). They have experimented with specialist EQ products between the output from their Studer studio mixing desks and encoding computer, but have not found them to significantly improve the sound of speech over and above the quality RealProducer achieves at their low bit rates. As the programmes are mainly speech, this lower range of connection speeds is perfectly adequate. Most important, it takes into consideration the lower bandwidth that is usually available in the chain from Europe to listeners in Indonesia and South America. The streaming is all in unicast mode and, as yet, does not involve any overseas relay servers. Because of the bias towards on-demand listening, this arrangement has mainly proved sufficient for now, since simultaneous demand is well spread out across the day. However, Radio Netherlands has a major role as an international news service and capacity problems do sometimes arise when particular events, such as major sporting or royal occasions, create surges in the demand for live streams. For example, as news began to emerge of a massive explosion in the Dutch town of Enschede on 13 May 2000, the clamour for more detail quickly exceeded the station's server capacity and forced the closure of the online site until demand had abated. Director General Lodewijk Bouwens comments from the Radio Netherlands experience that 'Webcasting . . .is simply not ready for prime time'.

As an average, the small online department at Hilversum reckon it takes only around 2 hours in a day to maintain the streaming server. The web radio streams are very much a part of the overall online presence. Thus, the constant process of updating news and other information on the main website is closely integrated with the 24-hour cycles of the live and archived radio streams. (Radio Netherlands also has a television service in English and Dutch, and makes some on-demand video archive available from there through the home page.) As an external service, Radio Netherlands sees its role as representing a reliable, balanced source of international news and European cultural information and entertainment to the rest of the world through as many platforms as possible. Through emails and other interactions with the website, they are particularly aware of providing a point of contact for listeners from the former Dutch colonies in Indonesia and their scattered diaspora. Conversely, the station also attracts a significant North American audience among European expatriates and others. The online presence is therefore a natural extension of Radio Netherlands' long experience of outward looking, international broadcasting.

They are ready to expand their online service to keep pace with demand, but they are in no rush to make the investment in stepping up towards broadband delivery – as many of their competitors have done – until such time as it becomes significantly more widely adopted among its potential audience.

Sources: Jonathan Marks, Director of Programmes at Radio Netherlands, and Radio Netherlands (2001) press release.

Archive streams of parts of the terrestrial output

Radio Netherlands' approach neatly illustrates how archive streams can be used both to overcome the scheduling difficulties posed by webcasting across time zones and to make efficient use of available bandwidth. This strategy is particularly relevant for speech-oriented stations or programmes, although we'll meet it again in the context of a music station in the next chapter. It also illustrates another important, but subtle, aspect of web radio. Used one way, on-demand streams become separated from the live experience of listening to what comes on the radio and more like an off-air tape library (as in Radio Netherlands' 'sound library'). But used another way, as a temporary time-shifting device, they can retain many of the live qualities of radio – albeit in an illusionary way. This is an important distinction for web radio practitioners to be aware of, so I'll come back and discuss it in more detail in Chapter 11.

For our next example, we move from the very large, vertical broadcast institution to the very small and horizontal. CFUV FM102 has not yet been in a position to consider offering archive streams from its speech-based programmes or scheduling those it offers in different languages to suit different time zones. However, its live stream is certainly gaining an international audience and so these are questions the station may well need to balance with their terrestrial operation in the future.

CFUV FM case study – a small Canadian university and community station

The University of Victoria lies on the southern tip of Vancouver Island, just over the Canadian border from Seattle. Like several Canadian universities, Victoria has its own radio station, which grew initially out of a wave of 'public' (or community) broadcasting initiatives promoted by the Canadian Radio, Television and Telecommunications Commission (CRTC) when it was set up in 1968. Based in the Student Union building, CFUV became a fully functioning FM stereo service to the region in 1984, broadcasting on 101.9 kHz to southern Vancouver Island and across the Straits to the American San Juan Islands and on cable all over the Island, the Sunshine Coast and into the city of Vancouver on the Canadian mainland.

The station depends for its organization and management largely on appointments from among the students studying at the university, and has a total volunteer force of around 250, which extends to include members of the wider community. In order to maintain its independent, public radio status, the station has to raise its own running costs, mainly through donations and fund-raising events. On this basis, they manage to sustain a 24-hour schedule of original programming, 7 days a week throughout the year.

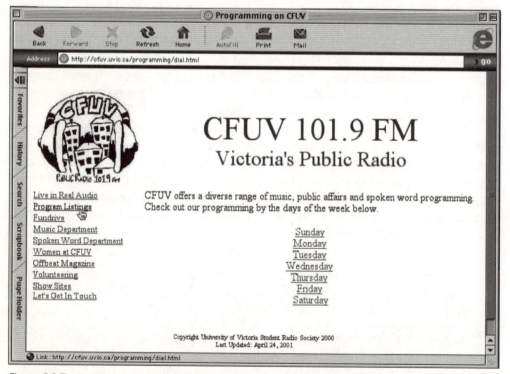

Figure 5.3 The programming page of CFUV, University of Victoria (at http://cfuv.uvic.ca/). Screen shot reproduced by permission of CFUV.

CFUV began simulcasting this output on a live stream in 1998. The output from the broadcast desk is fed in mono to an encoding computer – with no additional processing – and from there via the University's IT network to the server. That is currently still running on the evaluation version of the RealServer software mounted on a Windows 98 machine. Their bandwidth is provided by a 2.8 Mbps ADSL connection, supporting mono streams at 16 kbps only. However, online demand has grown dramatically in 3 years and plans are in place to upgrade to the full RealServer software package in July 2001. This move is hard on the station's extremely tight operating budget, but is now seen as absolutely necessary for their future. Nevertheless, CFUV estimate that maintaining their live stream demands no more than half an hour in any week. The station's modest but highly functional website is hosted on the University of Victoria server.

The radio programming is extremely diverse and aims to provide an alternative to the dominant commercial music format and CBC broadcasting in the CFUV transmission area, an alternative which reflects the minority cultural origins and musical interests of the diverse population the station serves. A summary of the current Saturday schedule illustrates some of the range on offer:

'8 a.m. PORTUGUESE: *Postal Portuguës/Portuguese Postcard*. The only FM Portuguese language radio program in British Columbia! This eclectic program features music and news from the Portuguese speaking world. Tune in for a weekly tour of Portuguese sounds from North and South America, Africa, and Europe.

9.30 a.m. FINNISH: *Soitellaan*. A Finnish program featuring Finnish music ranging from popular modern music to folk and classical. News, interviews and poems in Finnish.

11 a.m. EAST INDIAN: *Rhythms of India*. East Indian music and news.

Noon. IRISH: *Celtic Experience*. Traditional Irish Folk music from Ireland and elsewhere.

1 p.m. GREEK: *The Greek Hour*. Hosted by the UVic Hellenic Students Association.

2 p.m. CELTIC: *Sounds of Scotland*. From the traditional to the contemporary, a wee taste of pipes and drums, country dance and fiddle music, folk, comedy and celtic songs.

3 p.m. SKA: *Skankster's Paradise*. Acoustic healing, battles with cheese, homegrown nutmeg trips and good old Jamacian Ska!

4 p.m. COUNTRY: *Hillbilly Heaven*. Old-timey Country Music.

5 p.m. FRENCH: French music.

6 p.m. REGGAE: *Alive and Dread*. Roots rocking sounds of Reggae and African music.

9 p.m. DANCE: *Boom Shak Attack*. Downbeat dub and electronic explosions.

10 p.m. RAP: *SubZero*.

12 a.m. GARAGE: *Garage Grooves*. One entire hour of swingin' way out, real-gone, outta sight, Farfisa-drenched, Vox-powered, Boss garage 60s punk!

1 a.m. LATE NIGHT: *Longhair's Jukebox*. Curl up to your radio for a weekly dose of pure psychedelic radio.

3 a.m. GUMBO: *TBA*.'

Elsewhere in the schedules are regular classical music slots and spoken word programmes and segments in eight different languages, from arts and poetry to local and international current affairs (http://cfuv.uvic.ca/program-ming/dial.html).

The station management's plan to make CUFV more available online comes from two separate motivations. First, the CRCT have made it clear that they will not license any increase in power to the station's FM transmitter in order to reach any wider terrestrial audience. And secondly, although their present server arrangement does not give them access to detailed metrics data on requests for their steam, it's clear from their email correspondence that an international audience is actively responding to the CFUV mix of programming. The station receives emails from Australia, New Guinea, Bolivia, Argentina, Mexico, El Salvador, California, Texas and many other US states, France, Britain, Sweden, Norway, Finland, Italy, Poland, Portugal, Japan, Hong Kong and a number of African nations. And significantly for the station's future outlook, it is receiving money donations from around the world in response to its on-air 'Fundrive' campaigns.

This is an intriguing development for third sector radio stations which have successfully built voluntary donations from small geographical areas into their survival strategies over many years. Their programming may have been targeted with a local audience in mind, but now the fact that new listeners are tuning in from far-away places provides an illustration of how web radio can redraw the definitions of a community of listeners to include far-flung communities of interest.

Sources: Dean Schwind, Station Manager at CFUV; the CFUV website (above).

The addition of 'side channels'

CFUV creates its diversity of content through the hundred or so different programmes in its live schedule in any one week. Virginradio need to retain their tightly defined music format on their simulcast stream, so to try to increase the breadth of their appeal they are using web radio to add new side channels. Side channels generally take one of two distinct forms. One is the occasional special: an archived interview, which typically begins as a live webcast-only event, well promoted and trailed on and off air, and then subsequently remaining available on the site for weeks or months (depending on popularity) to give anyone who may be interested the chance to hear about it. The other is to add a second or third live stream which offers a different selection of music to the simulcast.

It hasn't happened yet, but it may be that for some broadcasters the side channel becomes their total radio output on the Web. Although this obviously calls for additional resources which must be justified by attracting an audience, this is an option frequently discussed on the web pages of *RAIN* and *Radio Ink* for US commercial radio stations (see, for example, Condra, 2000; Arbitron/ Edison Media Research, 2001, pp. 24–7). The reason is that the side channel does solve several problems for the simulcaster: problems which we'll encounter in Chapter 8 associated with the terms of music copyright and surrounding the question of what to do when your on-air advertising doesn't take notice of your audience online. It may be easier, and perhaps cheaper and more profitable in the long run, for some stations to use their experience and knowledge of radio to create completely new web versions of themselves.

So the decision – to side channel or not to side channel? – returns us to the question I posed at the start of the chapter: what does going online with web radio add to an established broadcaster's existing terrestrial output? In the three examples we have looked at in this chapter, the answer looks clear: they are each in their own ways adding something different to the radio landscape. They are filling in some of the hollows in between the service we receive from the broadcasters and they are doing that either within their immediate broadcast audience or beyond it.

This, I think, is the function of web radio for today: to fill in the gaps broadcasters cannot reach in the present. The examples in the next chapter give further emphasis to this view. Of course, the relationship between the broadcasters and narrow-casters is a dynamic one which will change with time. For this reason, it is important to take advantage of the scalability web radio has to offer and evolve your operation in response to the listeners you hope to serve.

Summary

In this chapter then, we have seen that the addition of live simulcast or archive streams is not technically demanding for experienced broadcasters – of whatever size. Fully fledged side channels take more organizing, but the hurdles here are time and experience more than technical. The test, as ever, lies in the content. How is broadcast content affected by the presence of web radio?

- *Global audience reach.* This is fundamental, though its effect may be paradoxical. CFUV, for example, demonstrates that its existing broadcast programming can attract enthusiastic listeners from overseas simply because it is different from what they can hear on their home radio. The more a broadcast station sounds like other stations around the world, the less interesting it is to a global audience.
- *Workplace listening.* The Virgin Radio study illustrates how central the workplace can be for web radio, whether for a listener just down the road from the studio or on the other side of the Atlantic. The cost of connection is still part of the story, but so is the fact that habitual listening in particular matches well with work in front of a computer – especially when reception from the computer is as good or better than on an analogue radio next to it. Listening on headphones in an office environment may be an additional factor in this equation.
- *Integration.* Radio Netherlands, by contrast, shows how a broadcast speech station might go about taking advantage of Web technology to adapt the way it makes its programmes available. This might well be as useful to its existing terrestrial listeners as those outside its transmission area. The Web operation is integrated within the broadcast function.
- *Advertising and promotion.* On-air advertising clearly poses a problem the more a station extends its audience. If the station continues to target the same local audience on the Web as on analogue it makes no difference. But if the ambition is to extend audience reach the advertising needs to reflect that. Given that the Web audience will certainly be much smaller than the broadcast audience to begin with, the main decision is whether to start

inserting different ad breaks on each. On the other hand, the versatility of the single click from station website to retail site is clearly attractive to the right advertisers.

- *News coverage.* The same holds to some extent for news bulletins, although inserting alternative bulletins is unlikely to be an option for most stations. One option is to shift the station's news criteria to be less specifically local – which will almost certainly reduce its value as news if it was working for the broadcast audience in the first place. Another is to hope the online visitor is interested in your local news. A third is to drop the bulletin out of the online stream altogether (as with Virgin Radio's side channels) and replace it with another ad break or something else.

These latter points may seem like desperate measures for a well-established broadcaster. For some, they should certainly raise some key questions: Why simulcast at all? Who are we hoping to reach? For the Internet-only station of course, there are no existing audiences to lose. Similar issues still apply but, as we'll see in the next chapter, the station is free to make up their own rules in response (see also Chapter 10).

6 Internet-only stations and other adventures in web radio

The examples in the previous chapter clearly have the advantages that (a) they have already established substantial audiences through their broadcast licences and (b) they have plenty of accumulated experience of how to make radio programmes that communicate well with those audiences. Their disadvantage is that, as *broad*casters, they have to play to the middle of a broad range of listeners to hold on to the audience numbers that justify the station's existence. Now we move on to take a look at stations which are using the Web to start from scratch. (Although many of the personnel involved do bring their own experience of terrestrial radio with them to their web projects.) These are the freestyle climbers of web radio who have no ropes to support them. They are exploring a different face of web radio than are the established broadcasters. They are finding out about the spaces that lie in between the vertices of the existing broadcasting world, where restrictions on the access to the electromagnetic spectrum and licences to transmit no longer limit the number of stations that can be on air at one time.

Their challenge is to find those niche audiences and build upwards from zero and so by definition they represent an alternative to mainstream broadcasting. That said, in their very different ways these experimental stations are also exploring the very different financial conditions on the Web as well for clues as to how they can cover their costs in the long term. But principally they all begin with the idea that their programmes *should* be on the air because they have something different to offer.

This is a very diverse set of case studies, in their ambitions, the content of their programmes, geographically and their methods. One characteristic they all share in common, though, is that they take advantage of the simultaneously global and local nature of the Internet in one way or another: they are using radio to communicate within the new context created by the Web. Again, my selection has been somewhat random and without the obvious logic of sectors within an established industry. There were potentially thousands to choose from, but that figure dramatically reduced to hundreds when I narrowed my criteria to exclude stations I have defined elsewhere as collections of music channels or lacking the essential live elements of radio communication.

The first two studies are indeed music stations, which demonstrate two different approaches to getting started online. But they are live radio stations and not automated channels. The music RadioValve and Pulse Radio play is somewhat alike (to the uninitiated) and, although this was not the reason for choosing them, it is a fair reflection of the time-honoured role of 'underground' or 'alternative' music radio. Variations or sub-genres of today's dance music have substantial, young, international (and computer literate) followings but, almost by definition, the music defies playlisting in anything other than a filtered, popularized form. This music has little to do with the 3-minute pop song made for format radio and everything to do with the continuous live event. So web radio is a natural home for its enthusiasts. The second two case studies are experiments in speech radio, one very large and one very small. In terms of content, the contrast with the music stations could hardly be greater, but in the methods they use and their approach to localism and globalism, we see a surprising amount in common, which again gives important clues to the potential of web radio *within*, or as part of, the mosaic of different distribution platforms digitalization has now made possible.

Interactivity and the website

These two music stations for web radio both have to use their websites as their means of forging a community of listeners and building their audience from zero. So, unlike the examples in the previous chapter, they really have to offer on the website a place for listeners to make their presence felt not only to the station, but to each other. It is also somewhat in the nature of the music that the DJ doesn't have much space to talk to the listener during the live show. So again, information about who's on air and a sense of dialogue with the station is best achieved – for those who want it – through text. In these examples, the email forums are moderated and it is made obvious to the listener that this is the case. In the first example, RadioValve have gone for a simple, stripped down but highly efficient website which feels like it exists more as an adjunct to the music and archive streams. On the Pulse Radio site, the emphasis is the other way around: it's the website, the information it supplies about the current dance scene, the chat opportunities, the invitation to join a membership, these are the ingredients that define the station – visual, magazine-like activities to be doing while you listen.

RadioValve case study

RadioValve is a fine example of a well-established, small-scale, independent Internet-only web radio station. It bills itself as a 24-hour Techno music station, and has been devoted to playing the cutting edge and the experimental on the electronic music scene since February 1998. Based in a local music scene in Boulder, Colorado, in the Rocky Mountain west central region of the USA, the station also looks outwards to a global audience, who are young, technologically literate and active seekers after music that is not widely available through mainstream radio.

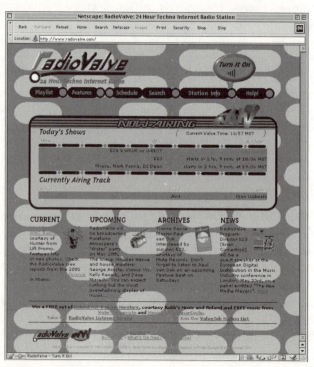

Figure 6.1 The RadioValve home page (at http://www.radiovalve.com/). Image supplied by RadioValve.

The idea for RadioValve came to two DJs/electronic music makers, David Fodel and Brian Comerford, while they were presenting a weekly Techno music show called Electronic Air on their local Boulder community station, KGNU (which in itself is an interesting example of a varied speech and music alternative to the mainstream broadcasters in the area: http://www.kgnu.org/). When KGNU bought an early version of RealServer in 1996 – with the help of public radio grants – the 'Electronic Air crew' began experimenting with the interactive possibilities during their live shows (streaming plus photo images and visits to chat rooms). As these innovations started attracting active interest from listeners and potential advertisers, the possibility of creating a fully independent web radio station began to crystallize.

So when Fodel and Comerford left KGNU the RadioValve concept was fully formed: the station was to focus on giving the widest possible exposure to new electronic music at the best quality attainable using streaming. Wide exposure meant, and still means, optimizing their output for 56 kbps modem users, because they form the overwhelming majority of the streaming audience. At this bit rate, achieving the highest quality meant putting all their acquired knowledge of the technology into developing the best single live stream they could from their one server, rather than trying to maximize output with the commonly used multiple stream, 'micro-niche' model, which would involve them compromising on audio quality. It also meant no bandwidth hungry visual frills like video streaming. They started straight in with the structure the station still uses today, an 8-hour rotation of unique live programming running 7 days a week – carefully scheduled for variety and to balance established artists with new material – alongside an archive of fully produced radio programmes. The 8-hour rotation begins at midnight Mountain Standard Time, so the first repeat coincides roughly with an average US working day, the second with the Japanese working day and the start of the next day's schedule with the Central European working day.

The RadioValve team has since doubled to four with the addition of Brian Kane and Tony Middleton. The station covers its running costs through accepting selective advertising and partnership arrangements. But crucially, the four have day jobs and run the station for the love of it. This has the flavour of a station run by passionate enthusiasts – who also have a highly professional knowledge of what they're doing, both technically and as makers of music radio.

The live output is built around regularly scheduled programming, though it's not fixed and may be interspersed on the spur of the moment with special events, interviews and mini-features on artists, musical styles or geographical scenes. Regular programming originates either in-house from the RadioValve studio or is mailed in from around the world via specialist labels or direct from artists. So 'live' here either means truly live – a set by one of the RadioValve crew or one of a handful of local DJs each week – or recorded live and sent in. In total, around six or ten outside DJs are featured in an average week. Styles vary: some are sets of continuous DJ mixes, others incorporate various forms of DJ presentation or speech. It's the selection and scheduling of DJs that creates the unique sound of the station.

Special events are anything from an internationally renowned DJ dropping in for a live set in the studio to a live dance music event. These outside events are usually again recorded live (to DAT uncompressed) for streaming at a later date. Experience has taught the crew (a) that it's rare to find a live venue which has ready access to a problem-free DSL to link to the streaming server at good enough quality, and (b) that the majority of RadioValve listeners are themselves out and about during the weekend evenings when these events are on. So they are now selective in who they record and they generally package the best of the event with relevant interviews before encoding the programme, either for the live stream and/or for longer term access on the archive stream. The station also keeps a selection of its best archive material ready to hand for back-up purposes, in case of system failures.

RadioValve encodes and serves its streams using standard RealNetworks G2 software with SureStream variable bit rate. But they are continually experimenting with processing the analogue signal between the mixer output and the encoding PC to wring the best stereo sound quality they can from limited bandwidth for their range of music styles. Currently, they are very pleased with 'eStream', which is a programmable DSP product from Broadcast Electronics (http://www.audiovault.com/Product-eSTREAM/eSTREAM.html). This has allowed them to find the clearest, loudest signal across a wide dynamic range. As with the earlier Virgin Radio case study, they gauge the success or otherwise of their signal processor settings from listener feedback.

Since its launch in 1998, RadioValve audiences have doubled about every 12 months. They are comfortably delivering at least 300 simultaneous streams on what is now their second generation server set-up: one dual processor server running Linux Red Hat 6 and plenty of memory, connected via a 100 base-T Ethernet link into two T3 lines to their reliable ISP. Peak simultaneous demand for streams is currently (May 2001) during working weekdays (US MST). However, baseline demand through the MST night remains consistent at roughly 25 per cent of the peak (see Figure 6.2).

This pattern reflects the geographical distribution of the RadioValve audience and, once again, shows the importance of workplace listening,

File Requests by Half-hour Throughout the Week

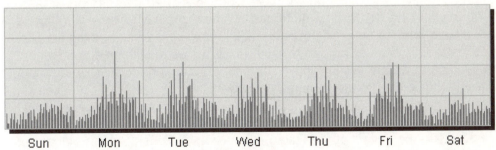

Sun   Mon   Tue   Wed   Thu   Fri   Sat

Figure 6.2 The pattern of file requests from the RadioValve server by half-hour throughout one week in May 2001. Mountain Standard Time. Image supplied by RadioValve.

especially for a live, well-scheduled music station. Their server metrics reveal that 70 per cent of their audience is within the US (with roughly half listening from a home computer and half either from a workplace or educational institution) and 16 per cent from overseas (including 2 per cent each in France and Canada, 1 per cent each in Australia, Japan, Netherlands and the UK). As is commonly the case, around 14 per cent of the data collected is from unsolved or unknown locations. The station's international reputation has led to invites to represent independent web radio at Internet music conferences in London, LA and Hong Kong.

The station takes very careful note of the feedback it receives from listeners, both via the server metrics data and from direct comment on their website's bulletin board. They know their unique identity lies in the variety and surprise in their programming, in their ability to intrigue their audience with new electronic music, while playing enough established material to avoid alienating them. So, although they get plenty of requests to do things differently, they take care not to be swayed into responding with changes in the schedule (or the website) unless they sense a sustained demand from a range of listeners. If listeners want their Techno or House music on demand there are plenty of web music channels and jukeboxes to choose from.

As for the future, the RadioValve crew make no predictions; they are just happy to have survived this far. To quote David Fodel in a recent email to me:

'RadioValve has managed to survive crashing stock markets, Vulture Capitalists, potentially debilitating lawsuits and our own egos for over 3 years, in a fresh new medium where no one has a rule book and there are no easy answers. All along we have been reassured by both music fans, artists and by CEOs of well-funded "competitors" (who have later gone belly-up) that we were on the right track . . .that we had something special, that RadioValve was a good "model" (for what we're still not sure). Bottom line is that we are still around . . .and as a good friend told us on a recent junket to Tokyo, "to continue is to succeed" . . .'

(22 May 2001)

Sources: 'the guys that run RadioValve' – David Fodel (Station Manager), Brian Comerford (Program Director), Brian Kane (Creative and Technical Director) and Tony Middleton (Systems Administrator).

Using a host to handle radio streaming

The small team behind RadioValve have successfully developed their own in-house streaming operation in their office in Boulder. Their strategy, or pattern of development, has been to build steadily outwards from their local reputation on the ground. But, as suggested in Chapter 4, there are other ways of handling the technical side. Pulse Radio is a more diffuse operation, with programmes originating from several cities around the world. Their strategy has been to start on the global level and work towards building connections to local pockets of interest. They have surveyed the options and decided to hire the expertise of an experienced host service to manage the server end of their live stream. There's quite an overlap between the music RadioValve and Pulse Radio play and in the fact that they are based on improvised sets from a variety of DJs. But, in technical terms and their approach to the Internet as a global phenomenon, they provide an interesting contrast.

Pulse Radio case study – Global Dance Radio

Pulse Radio started in Sydney, Australia, but it now streams live music sets from changing locations all around the world to dance fans all around the world. In this sense, it is fully absorbing the characteristics of the Internet and doing with it something its terrestrial radio competitors could not. The combined website and web radio station has grown out of the international dance music scene and sees itself as targeting the middle ground of tastes within that niche. Its home page lists the sub-genres it embraces, with names familiar from the format categories of automated music channels: jungle, techno, house, hip-hop, urban, drum 'n' bass, trance, dance, rave. The difference here is that the shows on Pulse Radio are not automated: each one is a continuous live session from a DJ who combines and blends tracks or part tracks, many of them instrumental, within or across these categories, shifting pace and mood in the improvised moment. Most of the sessions come from studios in 2-hour slots, but some are from live dance events. The target listeners tune in to the performance of the DJ as much as the feel of the individual tracks s/he mixes on the decks. The website gives out information about where next to catch the DJs playing live, so the station acts – in the true music radio tradition – as a kind of proving ground, as well as a place to listen to music played in ways most conventional radio stations find hard to emulate, in spite of its popularity. The ad break or news bulletin has no place on a station like this.

Figure 6.3 The Pulse Radio home page (at http://www.pulseradio.net/). Screen shot reproduced by permission of Pulse Radio.

Pulse Radio started streaming live in 1999, at first as a radio outlet only for local dance DJs in Sydney but, when Colin Kleyweg arrived as managing director soon after, they broadened their ambitions and began hooking up with DJs in Europe and America. As a start-up company, they needed a cost-effective way of connecting DJs in Adelaide and Brisbane and then London, Atlanta and Amsterdam into a reliable server network. They chose one of the no frills professional service packages from Live365.com. Unlike the free hosting Live365 offer to 'personal broadcasters' in return for inclusion of radio advertising, this 'Broadcast365' professional hosting is charged, usually on a monthly basis, for a negotiable number of guaranteed simultaneous streams, with no ad insertion except for the brief ident as the stream is first buffered onto the player (http://www.live365.com/plr/index.html).

The role of the Pulse Radio team is to find the DJs around the world and negotiate 2-hour time slots with them to fit into the schedule. This timing of the slots on the 24-hour clock tends to follow the setting sun, so that Australian DJs are live through the Asia Pacific evening followed by sets from Europe and then on to the US. When DJs are contracted they receive the Live365 encoding software, which they install on their desktop or laptop computer, which they plug into the Internet, ideally via ISDN, though a 56 bps modem will do. The output from their mixer then simply plugs into the computer's sound card. All Live365 streams are encoded in MP3 format and are currently served at low bit rates – Pulse Radio is at 16 kbps stereo. Come their time slot, the next DJ on the schedule goes online, and the software directs their output to the nearest server in Live365's worldwide network of relay servers. As part of the service, Pulse Radio is listed on the extensive Live365 tuner, but the majority of requests for streams reach the network from the Pulse Radio site, or else the visually customized version of the free proprietary Live365 player, which regular listeners can keep on their computer desktop.

Pulse Radio do keep a back-up server in Sydney loaded with music on the hard disk, which they can play in on random selection should DJs miss their start time or lose their connection to a Live365 server.

The Broadcast365 service provides Pulse Radio with some basic listener data, but they get most of their sense of who's listening through their own website server (clicks to listen and email feedback). Having started out with listeners mainly within Australia, their current estimates show that this is now only about 50 per cent of their growing international audience. US listeners make up about 20 per cent, the UK 10 per cent, the rest of Europe another 10 per cent with the remaining 10 per cent scattered around the world. The dance scene generally operates strongly on word of mouth reputation and Pulse Radio are finding that works equally for them: DJs new to the station bring in new listeners from their local scene. As part of the culture of the dance DJ includes a kind of competitive rivalry, the aim is to build some of that edge into the station's evolution to strengthen the online following.

The website is obviously an integral part of that strategy. It has three separate ways of drawing in email contributions to create the sense of the listening audience 'out there': there's a guest book, where comments and 'signatures' are held long term, a bulletin board for medium-term exchanges of feedback and information, and a live email chat room, which encourages real-time dialogue between listeners, DJs and members of the Pulse Radio team. There's also a news section, feature articles and the space to post any information the international dance music fan could want. The aim is for the site to become an international meeting point which links between other dance music websites (such as, currently, Worldwide Dance Web in the UK and Jive Magazine in the US). In this sense, the website and its web station are each integral to the other in the company's aim to keep growing their audience to the point where they have a financially sustainable operation.

The next technical step will be to find a peripheral or edge Internet service which can add higher connection speeds as more listeners come to expect broadband quality. The company is waiting for the price of those higher grade streaming services to fall within their means.

At present, Pulse Radio has a small, full-time staff team, who act as the co-ordinators of a much larger loose group of around 100 volunteers, including writers, DJs, dance music entrepreneurs and web designers. The expectation is that, as with a great deal of Internet activity, the station will be driven by the passions and enthusiasms of the people who want to get involved.

Sources: Colin Kleyweg, Managing Director of Pulse Radio Pty Ltd, and the Pulse Radio website.

Exploring speech radio alternatives

Pulse Radio's global to local strategy has something in common, from a technical point of view, with the next case study. Both use the World Wide Web as a means of linking disparate geographical communities in an attempt to create a 'many to many' type of radio communication as opposed to the 'one to many' broadcast model we are used to. Of course, impressive international hook ups through various intricate combinations of ICT pathways are nothing new to the established vertical broadcast institutions, but something very different is happening when it is organized at a grass roots level with the aim of making those connections horizontal in the way the Internet now makes increasingly possible.

The Radio Voix Sans Frontière project provides an important illustration of the way web radio can fit into the mosaic of delivery by conventional terrestrial transmission routes, and now by digital satellite direct broadcasting as well. In doing so, the one-off event perhaps most closely echoes the aspirations of the early radio broadcasters, discussed in Chapter 1, to create the means for a kind of global conversation between peoples. This is a study of an experiment in global speech radio. Clearly, the transmission took a lot of arranging. However, the technical detail is in fact relatively straightforward and applicable in many less ambitious situations.

Radio Voix Sans Frontières (Voices Without Frontiers) case study

All around the world, the massacre of peaceful protesters which took place in Sharpville, South Africa, on 21 March 1960 has come to symbolize the wider struggle against racist oppression and discrimination. Every year now, the hundreds of member stations which make up AMARC (the World Association of Community Radio Broadcasters) organize a radio event to mark what has become the International Day Against Racism. The Radio Voix Sans Frontières (VSF) event of 2001 was their most ambitious yet.

VSF is an international co-production of radio programmes on the broad theme of anti-racism, created from their own perspectives by community radio stations scattered around the globe. The programmes were transmitted through an intricate international network on the day of the 21 March 2001 to over 600 stations who were willing to rebroadcast some or all of them within their own schedules on their local analogue transmitters. The 24-hour schedule was also made available directly to as many individuals as had access to digital satellite receivers or web radio connections. In total, it was a mammoth undertaking; the object here is to focus on the various roles the Internet was recruited to fulfil within it.

The VSF team set up three centres to co-ordinate the operation and act as the physical hubs which would receive and redistribute programme material in the build-up and during the 24-hour broadcast. These were the Centre for Democratic Communications in Johannesburg, and the radio

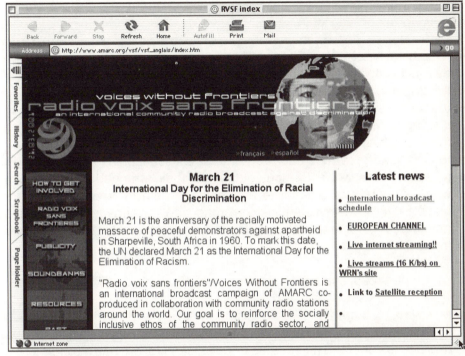

Figure 6.4 The VSF project's website (at http://www.amarc.org/vsf/). Screen shot reproduced by permission of AMARC.

stations Orange 94.0 in Vienna and Radio-Centreville in Montreal. The functions of each hub were many and varied, but the main ones can be summarized as follows.

(a) In advance of the broadcast:

- to receive pre-recorded programmes from contributing stations, either through the post or by file transfer on the Internet;
- to make those programmes available for any participating station to download as MP3 files so they could include whichever they chose in their own independent schedules for the day;
- in consultation to draw up three separate schedules, interlinking at various points, for three separate live transmissions: an International broadcast from the main hosts in Johannesburg, a European broadcast from Vienna and a North American broadcast from Montreal.

(b) During the broadcast:

- to host the live output from their studio through their allotted period of the day, including live link-ups between the three hubs at the start and end of the transmission (at 00.00–01.00 and 23.30–24.00 UTC);
- to receive live feeds at the arranged times from contributing stations in streaming MP3 or Real format on ISDN lines or faster and retransmit them into their schedule;
- to incorporate pre-recorded programmes as scheduled;
- to transmit the whole 24-hour output via their arranged routes, which were permutations of satellite, higher bandwidth Internet streams (for participating terrestrial stations to rebroadcast), lower bandwidth streams (for direct web radio reception by the public) and their own local analogue transmission.

(c) After the broadcast:

- to collate captured highlights from the live feeds and pre-recorded programmes onto each hub's streaming server, there to be made available as on-demand streams or downloads for anyone's own interest or indeed later rebroadcast. These archives can be found via the VSF Europe website (see below).

The aim here was to maximize global access to the programme material – although the organizers at AMARC know very well how far they have yet to go in filling the gaps. The programmes were deliberately multilingual, in the international spirit of the event. The overlapping schedules will be more easily understood by visiting http://www.amarc.org/vsf/vsf_anglais/21mars/horaire.htm, where they are expected to remain until the build-up to next year's event. To take one high-profile example, this meant that from around 15.00 to 16.00 UTC, anyone online could have tuned into a discussion between young people gathered in the UN headquarters in New York about 'empowering youth to fight racism', which included the live participation of Mary Robinson, the UN High Commissioner for Human Rights. Or among the 4 hours hosted from Johannesburg were programmes made by new participants in radio from around the Southern African nations, who had attended skills workshops held during the previous week on 'using digital sound' and organized by AMARC, the UK government's Department for International Development and the British Council. Elsewhere in the schedules were contributions from communities in all quarters of the western hemisphere, from Brazil to Northern Canada, from Finland to South Africa. A major target for the project next year is to increase participation eastwards from the Middle East through Asia to the Asian Pacific.

The total streaming operation was divided between those streams at higher bandwidth intended for live rebroadcast by whatever route (i.e. through other stations' studio desks, which allowed local input and context to be added en route to local transmission) and those at lower bandwidth for public consumption globally. Thus, an online listener in search of the live International broadcast stream was directed via hyperlinks to the World Radio News (WRN) website, which ran a 24-hour service in Real format (as well as carrying the same transmission on its global satellite service). Alternatively, the European broadcast live stream was routed from the servers at freirad.at in Innsbruck, either directly or via relays organized through the globally positioned servers of Live365.com (see also the earlier Pulse Radio case study). This European service was only available online as an MP3 stream, which of course means it could be received by any of the major streaming media players. In other words, it was important to keep unpredictable direct demand from the public away from the streams intended for rebroadcast by radio stations. (The 24-hour North American broadcast was delivered directly only through the well-established AIROS satellite network and so falls outside the immediate subject of this case study.)

To pursue the detail at the European hub in Vienna a little further, a server (running a Linux system) in the studio at Orange 94.0 (http://www.orange.or.au/) received all the incoming live feeds and stored the pre-recorded programmes as MP3 files. The output from this main server was fed to the studio desk, where it was remixed and tied into the live continuity presentation. (The live stream went direct and the stored programmes were 'called up' on a separate Windows computer.) Live hand-overs between locations were tricky because of the time delay in buffering the stream (5–10 seconds), so at the junction the two studios had to cover the gap using a live phone link as well.

The mono output from the studio desk was split three ways to feed an RA encoder (RealProducer on Windows), an MP3 encoder (Liveice on Linux) and an ISDN line. The RA and MP3 streams were encoded at 48 kbps and directed on a fast network connection to the local Silver ISP (http://www.sil.at/) for the rebroadcast side. The main streaming server at Silver ran Real server software and Icecast software for MP3 on two separate ports (addresses). It was crucial to ensure they always maintained surplus bandwidth to the rebroadcasting stations. This they achieved by negotiating for a single relay server in Holland to multiply the RA streams and four relays around the world for the MP3 stream.

The ISDN link carried the output to another server housed at Freirad (http://www.freirad.at/), which encoded it on Live365 software to feed into their global network of relay servers for public online listening.

The outcome of this feat of radio integration was something of a triumph for the technology in supporting a truly global event. The team are still in a lengthy process of evaluation of the project as I write, but there were hardly any lost connections between the hubs and output servers. The main casualty appears to be that some of the automated archiving of the live output didn't work as planned. For the pre-recorded items on the schedules this is obviously no loss, but it means that parts of the live feeds could not be included in the public archive of the event, the 'sound bank' at http://www.amarc.org/vsf-europe/.

Sources: Sruti Bala at AMARC; Hermann Schwaersler and Roland Jankowski at Orange 94.0.

Web radio across the digital divide

A significant pattern has been emerging from the case studies I've included in these two chapters: web radio tends to be complementary to and not necessarily in competition with its parent, analogue radio. It seems pretty clear at the moment that a commercial model for web distribution is not about to sweep away terrestrial radio broadcasting as we know it – nor TV or the newspapers for that matter. On the infrastructure of the Internet as it exists at the moment, the strength of web radio is in doing things traditional radio broadcasting cannot do, or do well.

This next study takes the reverse perspective from VSF, looking at the Web from the receiving end. It emphasizes two crucial points about the combination of radio listening and Internet distribution. The first is just how indispensable a part of everyday life access to a radio is in many, many parts of the world – as it was in the industrialized world between about 1930 and 1950. The second is the technological chasm that separates Internet users in today's affluent, wired world and people living in the developing nations, who have access to minimal ICT infrastructure. This project creates a small bridge across the 'digital divide' by harnessing the timeless qualities of radio listening together with the Internet's power to inform. It certainly takes us across definitional boundaries beyond the kind of web radio we have been considering up to now. We can easily picture though how one day, with the right resources, it could become part of that web radio network. But more important for now is the different light it sheds on the alliance between radio and the Web for the end-user. It reminds us in the West of the many millions of people who could increase the global audience for web radio and contribute to its potential for diversity.

Kothmale Community Radio Internet Project (KCRIP) case study

The telecommunications infrastructure in rural Sri Lanka is sparse. For those who do have access to a telephone line, connection to the Internet is prohibitively expensive because the nearest ISPs are in major towns or cities to which connections are likely to be on a long distance tariff. Personal computers are well beyond the means of most private residents. Literacy rates are increasing, but nevertheless low by western standards. Consequently, awareness of the Internet and the education and information resources it has to offer is low. Against this background, the Kothmale

Figure 6.5 The home page of Kothmale Community Radio (http://www.kothmale.net/), which links to further information and fruits of the Internet Project. Screen shot reproduced by permission of Kothmale Community Radio.

Community Radio Internet Project has experimented with using analogue radio to bring the Internet into the lives of its local listeners.

Kothmale Community Radio was set up in 1989 under the auspices of the Sri Lanka Broadcasting Corporation to serve a rural population in the centre of the country, 4 hours drive from the capital, Colombo. Kothmale is on a hill surrounded by tea plantations and paddy fields, and its transmitter covers roughly 230 000 inhabitants of villages and small towns within a 20–25 kilometre radius. For most of those people, the radio station is the main source of news and information that directly affect their daily lives. The station has a paid manager, but is operated and presented by local volunteers. The Community Radio Internet was initiated by UNESCO, who provided computer equipment (three PCs and one server) and initial training, with the support of the Sri Lankan Ministry of Post, Tele-communications and the Media, who provided Internet connectivity to the radio station on a 64 kbps line. The project went into action in 1999. Support and evaluation during the experiment is also given by the University of Colombo.

The crucial Web/radio interface is provided in a daily 1-hour programme called 'Radio Browse the Internet'. Its aim is both to raise listeners' awareness of what the Internet can do for them and then take their requests for information, which trained local volunteers research and translate into the local languages of Sinhala or Tamil. The real importance of the radio side of the equation though is that the information is discussed on air by local people and given a local context. Yes, this is a horizontal, two-way communication but the net direction here is from the global to the local. The kinds of information include, to mention a few examples: improving farming practices; new, low cost engineering solutions; discussion of global warming and its consequences; facilitating reforestation projects; family health care. Research from each request is filed on a database and held by the station as a permanent resource. Radio browsing in this way is the start of a process of encouraging people to visit the radio station regularly to learn how to use the Internet themselves. There are two further terminals in local libraries which connect to the Internet via the Kothmale server.

Since KCR has had access to the resources of the Web and email, these have greatly influenced other programmes across the weekly schedule. News programmes especially have been transformed so that they can report a far greater range of stories and background as they are relevant to the community and its development.

Local support for the project is enthusiastic. So much so that access to the terminals has to be rationed at popular times. The potential for expansion is self-evident, but first the project needs to become self-sustaining financially by covering the cost of maintaining the leased line, which has been agreed at US $1000 per year. The station is allowed some commercial activity but it is limited under the terms of its licence from SLBC, so much of this money is being raised in true third sector tradition through fund-raising and voluntary donation within, and perhaps eventually beyond, the local area.

The KCR website (see above) is beginning to collect music and song from the region as on-demand RealAudio streams – recorded by members of the community in the radio studio or on other local recordings. It is not yet at the stage of putting its programmes on the Internet; however, other similar centres are now planned across Sri Lanka and it would then be possible to envisage some exchange of programme material becoming useful between communities whose experiences are similar. A similar online exchange of programming is being successfully tried at another radio Internet project in West Africa (UNESCO, 2001, p. 10).

The KCRIP initiative and a handful of similar projects around the world represent a very successful, though small, first step across the digital divide. UNESCO is developing a global programme to promote similar Community Multimedia Centres in other economically and technologically marginalized regions, such as Sub-Saharan Africa and rural SE Asia. To quote from a recent UNESCO pamphlet, 'Including the Excluded', which summarizes the project:

> 'Being a participatory radio programme, Radio Browsing of the Internet has taken into account the desires of rural communities to assimilate knowledge collectively, in contrast to the prevailing mode of individual access to the Internet. More importantly, the project enables the community to produce knowledge collectively and to package and disseminate it in the appropriate manner to meet immediate community needs and priorities.'

A very useful report summarizing Kothmale and other related projects is published at http://www.unesco.org/webworld/public_domain/kothmale.shtml.

Sources: Wijayananda Jayaweera, Regional Communication Advisor, UNESCO, Kuala Lumpur; Tanya Notley, Australian volunteer worker at KCRIP; Sunil Wijesinghe, KCR station manager.

Summary – web radio is an experiment

What I hope to have indicated in this chapter is something of the range of expectation and possibility that comes with the arrival of a novel way of making and transmitting radio. There will surely be a whole lot more experiment and innovation before web radio becomes a settled, mature medium. That again is down to the vision and imagination of those who use it.

The one thing these disparate examples share in common is that they are all exploiting the additional horizontal characteristics of the Internet as a method of distribution. The Kothmale experiment is still partially within the framework of conventional radio broadcasting, but the ways in which it is useful to its particular community of listeners add a radical new dimension. The analogue stations at the end of the chain in the VSF event are, most of them, similarly operating under licences and so fitted what was on offer into their own schedules. But the online stream from VSF, though it worked to its own highly organized schedule, was a much more free-flowing event in its own right. It had no externally fixed points to accommodate, like bulletins on the hour or ad breaks. What it did have on its side to replace those reassuringly familiar patterns of broadcasting was a sense of unpredictability, surprise and adventure generated entirely through peoples' conversations, experiences and opinions. The other two case studies, in their own ways, make use of similar qualities in a musical context: they can remake the structure of presentation in whichever ways they feel suits the content rather than the other way around. They revisit the 'old-fashioned' notion of the DJ improvising and 'throwing together' their unique choices from different types of popular music in ways that deliberately do not fit the formats of commercial terrestrial radio.

This free form approach to radio is, of course, not the end of the story. In the coming chapters, we'll look in more detail at the essential qualities of radio listening that are likely to keep us tuned in and coming back for more. The real point of departure from what the radio broadcasters have learned is that their training has been to appeal across a wide range of types of listeners and to try not to lose too many to rival broadcasters on the margins of that range. Web radio is about finding a core of listeners for programmes you are passionate about and building outwards in direct response to what they enjoy about your output. This is certainly a case of starting in at the bottom, but it is also an experiment in seeing if we can reinvent or reinvigorate the style and form of radio in order to keep it flourishing in a multichannel twenty-first century.

7 One voice in a very large crowd: getting heard

The Web redraws the map in the competition to find and keep the eyes and ears of an audience, as many so-called 'dotcom' companies have discovered to their cost from late 2000, once the first rush of excitement over the e-commerce revolution had begun to wear off. While large personal fortunes continue to be made on *speculation* that online businesses should be as profitable as parallel offline businesses – only with faster returns – there is little evidence yet that anyone has worked out how to achieve sustainable *operational* profits from an Internet-only company. This is certainly as true – or maybe more true – for web radio stations as any other online venture: there has been as high a casualty rate among commercial web radio operators as any other dotcom sector, in the recent shakeout after the loans dried up. The swift descent into receivership of the webcasting portal company BroadcastAmerica in early 2001 is perhaps the most notable to date. So this book makes no claims to offer a route map for financial success in web radio. When someone does manage to draw such a map, we will hear about it soon enough. But, once again, these are early days in what is undoubtedly a unique new form of distribution and, just as analogue radio did in the 1920s and 1930s, before it really knew precisely how it might earn its keep, the first thing to concentrate on is establishing an audience. And that will be done by offering interesting web radio programming, not simply by throwing sites at the Web and seeing what sticks.

As we have seen, web radio stations are divided between those operated by existing terrestrial or satellite broadcasters (broadly speaking those discussed in Chapter 5) and those smaller stations who are heard mainly or only on the Web (as in Chapter 6). Established broadcasters have an obvious advantage in their own territories that they already have the ears of a radio audience, so they can promote their side channel or their archive streams to them. It's less likely that they need actively to promote an online simulcast to those same listeners, though they will incidentally have been made aware of the station's web presence and so will realize that they can tune into a live stream if needs be – for example if they are travelling outside the terrestrial transmission area or if it's more convenient to listen online at work.

So this chapter is primarily concerned with using the Web to find an audience. We can divide the task of getting any kind of radio station noticed in two:

1 What you do off air to tell potential listeners you exist and let them know where to find you.
2 What you do on air to build a relationship that brings first time listeners back for more and gets them spreading your reputation by word of mouth – and the Internet's powerful equivalent, email.

The available means of doing both are very different for web radio than for a terrestrial station. Those differences are produced partly by the global scale of the thing and partly by the new, unfamiliar, horizontal nature of the relationship that exists between producer and audience (or potential audience) on the Web. So that's where the chapter begins. It then goes on to consider new strategies for the old problems of getting known and building audience.

Some audience principles – push and pull

The Internet is a two-way technology: broadcasting is one-way. The differences in terms of promotion may at first seem subtle, unimportant even. After all, big or small, a receiving audience is a receiving audience, isn't it? Either they tune in to you or they choose some other station. But the closer you look, the more radical the difference becomes. And anyone getting involved in this new audience relationship needs to recognize there's a lot we have yet to learn about it. Both sides of the producer/audience relationship are in a process of evolution.

Levinson (1999), among many other media observers, notes that, from the producer's point of view, this two-way technology combines 'push' with 'pull' functions in a much more powerful sense than conventional broadcast technologies. He defines push technologies as a form of 'special delivery':

> 'i.e., programs that, once set, automatically bring selections to customers, in contrast to "pull" technologies which require the user to search the . . .Web anew for each desired selection.'
>
> (p. 129)

So broadcasting is predominantly a 'push' technology in the sense that the producer determines the content which fits the schedules that are offered to – pushed towards – the listener in real time. Beyond a general under-standing of what their target audience likes, periodically supported by some specific audience research here and some received feedback there, station managers, schedulers and producers do not need to know much about the precise individual preferences of their audience. Only after the event do they assess how many they have succeeded in appealing to by examining their ratings. The Internet started out entirely as a 'pull' technology in the sense that content was put onto the system to be pulled off as and when the receiver needed it. The power of the search engine enabled the receiver to be the more active decision maker in arranging what to receive and when to receive it.

We find a vivid example of this shift from push to pull in the supply of news. In broadcast news, the senior editors determine the selection and sequence of stories. On the Web, where I can personalize 'my news' on my home page, I choose the categories and sequence of stories I want presented to me according to my own interests. The process is automated to my specifications. The stories themselves though are, by and large, originated and put together by the same news agencies and journalists as supply the conventional mass media. The Web today has become a hybrid between push and pull, and a web radio station needs to incorporate both into its strategies.

The push dimension means working to keep listeners returning because they can rely on your station to provide the particular kind of radio content they like. The pull dimension means tailoring the way you make that content available more to individual listeners rather than taking an 'across the board' broadcaster's view of their audience. We have seen examples of both in action earlier. NetRadio.com (see Box 2.1) markets itself as the single station which anyone can rely on at any time to cater to all their musical tastes: 'Listen to the music' (push). But at the same time the site is in fact a container for a range of musical niches: 'The choice is yours' (pull). Hilversum (see Box 5.2) offers some of its usual broadcast output as a live stream – a global extension of its push strategy. On the other hand, its website offers a whole array of stored items in the expectation that visitors will pick and choose (pull).

So you can expect the potential listener to web radio to be a much more *active* participant in the process of choosing the station or programme to tune in to. This is partly a function of apparently endless choice (though we could argue about what that means in fact – see Chapter 10) and partly a function of the amount of the user's attention the computer demands. This means two things so far as getting noticed is concerned:

1 On the one hand, the web radio audience are likely to be more deliberate seekers after something new, something not already to hand on analogue radio, and so there's more chance of them coming across your station in their search. Niche audiences will work that bit harder to find niche content, because they are dissatisfied with the mainstream, so – until they find their niche station(s) – they are mentally in 'search mode'.

2 On the other hand, this same restlessness may equally work against you. The scale of the choice on offer is just as likely to tempt them to move on to try the next on screen. The computer – if that's where they're listening – is more demanding of the innocent listener's attention than today's handy radio. It's harder to use for one thing, then there's the waiting and watching while your player application opens and buffers the stream; and, while that's going on, the listener's eye is already likely to be roving down the list of competing offerings they also have on screen in front of them.

Just as with the initial popularizing of analogue radio, both the listener and the webcaster are excited by the novelty and the new choices open to them. We can regard this as a temporary phase on the way to a state of equilibrium once the technology has matured – or relative equilibrium at least. That is bound to take time though. Even when web radio approaches maturity in a lead country like the US, it will still be a novelty elsewhere in the world. For the purposes of the present chapter then, we should think of web radio listening as highly volatile in the medium term.

The hyperlink is the key

The URL is the web radio station's equivalent of the analogue radio frequency. The hyperlink is the simplest, most versatile way of publicizing its existence online. The question for the station manager is deciding where best to try to place those hyperlinks so they'll be effective. As with all good promotional strategies, a certain amount of lateral thought is involved here.

Hyperlinks fall, roughly speaking, into four categories:

1 Commercial advertising links.
2 Links 'in kind'.
3 Submitted links.
4 Reciprocal or associative links.

The strictly *commercial* hyperlink typically appears as a prominent button icon, often part or whole of a banner ad, which says something like 'Click here for . . .'. (Hence this is also known as 'click-through' advertising.) This kind of link you pay for and, as with any other visual form of advertising, is charged according to an assessment of the number of people who will see it. We can identify two strategies for placing a click-through link: a scatter gun approach or something more targeted. The scatter gun promotion buys space on a web page just because it has a known high 'hit rate', more or less irrespective of whether it has anything to do with your business, in this case web radio; the targeted promotion finds 'like' sites where the space costs less because the traffic is less. (These are not necessarily other web radio sites, but especially sites where people are likely to go in search of related information.)

A variation of the commercial link is negotiated '*in kind*'. In other words, no money changes hands, but a formal, cross-promotional agreement is made between companies in related or mutually supporting sectors. In traditional radio terms this is akin to sponsorship in kind, where discounts on goods or services are given in return for a favourably placed hyperlink on your site. If you are a well-visited station, those suppliers may also want to associate themselves with you by carrying a link to your station on their site.

But the non-commercial ethos is also strong among Internet users. It was constructed in the first place as an information exchange network and therefore links placed purely on the basis of facilitating the search for specifically related content remain fundamental to its operation.

Search engines, directories and portal sites depend on *submitted* URLs, to which they then provide hyperlinks. In principle, they provide a free service. However, the popularity of the Web, the ever increasing number of its pages, and the mixed economy of information and commerce it now serves do place great strains on these search facilities. So although submitting your URL is free, it is becoming more usual to pay for a better position on the listings returned in response to the key search terms you select. Web radio stations form a large community in themselves, quite distinct from the rest of the Web's content, so it makes sense to take advantage of this and concentrate on submitting links to specific web radio directories. Because these are small enough to work on the principle of browsing within categories or geographical regions, there's not the same incentive for them to charge: they gain their value from being inclusive. Also, think laterally and consider the value of positioning your URL on appropriate specialist 'lifestyle'-related portal sites that might appeal to your target audience.

The *reciprocal* or *associative* link is also defined by content. It may be negotiated on a non-profit basis – typically through an exchange of emails – and usually appears simply as coloured, underlined text, inviting the viewer to follow a trail in that direction if they are interested in finding out more. Alternatively, many sites now – including radio sites – give a simple invite for you, the visitor, to copy a link to their site from your own, if you like it. (A text version of spreading the word.) A reciprocal link is, as it says, a mutual arrangement between two sites. An associative link is mutually agreed but one-sided and may well be temporary, for example a link from an online newspaper article to a web station that's carrying a relevant or related programme or interview. Especially among 'third sector' web radio stations, this kind of linking creates communities of like-minded stations, mutually connected and not in competition with each other.

So, whether it is paid for or by mutual agreement, the hyperlink is *the* currency of web promotion. The so-called 'netiquette' of linking is evolving all the time, but the common sense advice is to ask the webmaster if you're not sure whether there might be some objection to linking to a given site. The next two sections suggest some of the more obvious starting points in developing your strategy for placing them.

Web radio portals or aggregating sites

Streaming hosts

For small stations wanting to get noticed, there's a lot to be said for operating through a specialist web radio host. Sites like Live365.com and StreamAudio-.com act as portals to the huge number of stations that stream through their servers. So people actively looking for new, 'different' stations are likely to search there. They can use the host sites to select a handful of stations that appeal and create their own personalized push button tuners. When they tire of one station or another goes off air, yours may be the next they try.

The price you pay for this kind of arrangement is that you have limited control over your station's independent exterior identity – irrespective of the brilliance of your content. Yours is associated with the hundreds or thousands of other stations with which you are in very direct competition (more so in some of the pre-set categories than others). You may or may not have your own web page on the site itself and you also undertake to appear in conjunction with a small amount of advertising which is organized by the host.

Streaming media players

If, on the other hand, you run your own server, in the process of acquiring the streaming software your URL will normally be automatically registered on the regularly updated lists of stations that appear as part of their player application. (As all the best known webcasters use the major streaming software, you may gain some small additional advantage if your station's name and category puts it alphabetically adjacent to one of theirs.)

Beyond this 'tuner' service, it is always worth remembering that each of the streaming software companies is on the lookout to enhance their own profile, and so they like to associate themselves publicly with stations that reflect well on web radio in general and their own format name in particular. So it's always worth letting them know in advance if you plan any programming that exploits the characteristics of web streaming in interesting or unusual ways. Or perhaps a live webcast of a significant special event. Here, of course, the usual media hook of an exclusive with a high-profile 'personality' will help focus marketing minds. If they like your programme idea the companies will give it plenty of free publicity, maybe in the form of 'site of the week' or else as part of their widely circulated email newsletters.

Other online radio tuners

In Chapter 3, we met the dedicated web radio tuners, Kerbango (as I write now sadly mothballed), iM Radio, Akoo Kima and Penguin Radio. Each of these companies offers their own online web radio tuning service independently of their hardware tuners and are well worth a visit. Again, these are, for the time being, free services. Bearing in mind their line of business, it's not surprising that their main criteria for accepting your station onto their lists are based on the strength and reliability of your streams. And there are many other similar, more or less specialist, tuning services out there (see Box 7.1). You will find that a rating for the strength of reception is becoming an increasingly prevalent feature of these listings. This reflects their wish not to associate themselves with repeatedly failing connections and to try to improve the overall sound quality of 'their' medium as the newer technology allows. So if your stream is weak for some technical reason, obtaining useful listings on some of these sites may involve you in additional costs to upgrade your hardware, even though the listing itself is usually free. (Being listed in this way should bring extra listeners, but if the demand for streams then means you get rated as having an unreliable signal the net effect will be counter-productive.)

Box 7.1   Some useful free radio tuner sites

http://www.akoo.com/
http://www.apple.com/quicktime/qtv/radio/
http://www.comfm.com/live/radio/
http://www.cyberradio.com/
http://www.penguinradio.com/stations.html
http://www.radiofreeworld.com/ (part tuner, part web radio directory)
http://realguide.real.com/tuner/
http://www.shoutcast.com/directory/
http://windowsmedia.com/radiotuner/defaultalt.asp

As a general observation, most of these tuners are organized according to formats that are familiar from terrestrial radio: mainstream music classifications like AOR, R&B, Country, Jazz or Classical, plus minority genres and sub-genres, plus generic Talk or News categories, and often finally a catch-all Alternative category. A high proportion of those music stations are, as we've noted, music-only channels. Some tuner sites aim to cover all or most of the bases, while others specialize. This is not surprising as most of them operate from the US, the home of format radio, which also happens to be where web radio is most established. Clearly, for many stations it is helpful to try to ally themselves to an audience sector in this way, but others coming from outside the format tradition may be uncomfortable with the limitation.

Web radio directories, large and small

Pre-dating the web radio tuner and somewhat more open in their organization are the web radio directories – though as time goes on the distinction is become harder to draw. The classifications in directories are typically geographical first and then alphabetical second. A listener more interested in spoken content rather than musical category is going to find this a more useful basis for searching. In this case, for each station they will be presented with a single line of text which begins with the station's name, followed by a description of its output, a choice of live or archived streams (whichever is on offer) and often a choice of connection speeds. The station's name is usually also a link to its website, while the streaming options link directly to the designated server address.

Boxes 7.2 and 7.3 show examples of two such long-standing directories, which aim to offer fully comprehensive, global and up to date listings. Of course, it is in the nature of web radio that some stations come and go on a regular basis, so the task of keeping up to date with what is actually online is no small undertaking. These directories actively look for new stations coming online, but it is obviously in your station's interests to inform them of your URL. Having decided to take this step though, it is important to maintain consistent and reliable streams: listeners are generally invited to alert the directories to stations they cannot connect to. Their webmasters will then check and will de-list stations that they cannot find (eventually; this may take quite a long time).

Box 7.2

The Massachusetts Institute of Technology (MIT) has a long-running research programme on international broadcasting. Their Radio-Locator at http://www.radio-locator.com/ is a huge database of radio stations around the world whether they are streaming their output or not. Its aim is to be as comprehensive in this as possible. There are various ways you can search the database – for example, Internet-only stations, country by country. Having found a station, Radio-Locator gives terse information and a link to the website. Unsurprisingly, it is particularly good on North American stations.

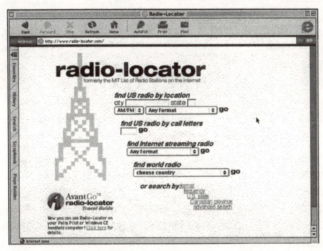

Figure 7.1 The MIT Radio-Locator home page with its range of different search options. Screen shot reproduced by permission of Theodric Young.

Box 7.3

The Live-radio directory home page at http://www.live-radio.net/ specializes in stations which stream on the Web rather than terrestrial stations with websites. The search is by country, in which case you get both simulcast stations and Internet only. There is a separate search if you want Internet only. On the country lists there is space for your own very brief description of the stream. From there, the visitor can either click through to the website or directly to receive a stream. This is a useful resource because it shows at a glance which software and bit rates stations are offering.

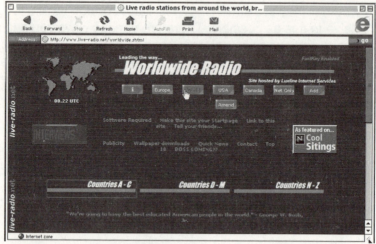

Figure 7.2 The front page of the Live-radio directory. Screen shot reproduced by permission of Brian Buckley.

However, 5000 is a lot of stations to look through when they come in all shapes and sizes. So, at the other end of the spectrum are small directories, specializing in listing particular categories of stations. These might be according to musical tastes or the governing ethos of the stations, as is the case for the Radio4All directory (Box 7.4).

Box 7.4

Radio4All is an American-based website which campaigns for greater freedom to broadcast. It is conspicuously opposed to corporate domination of the radio industry. As well as providing many links to other campaigning sites, it operates a directory of web radio stations which take a similar view at http://www.radio4all.org/. There is a bias towards North American stations, but it also collects together an interesting range of supportive international stations.

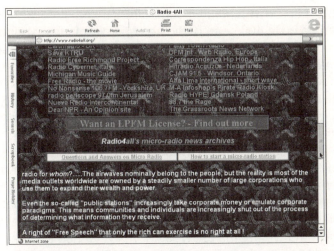

Figure 7.3 Part of the Radio4All.org home page, showing some of its links to 'alternative' web stations and information sites, and a statement of its allegiance. Screen shot reproduced by permission of Radio4All.

These small directories set themselves up as beacons on the Web to attract like-minded audiences. They are typically run by enthusiasts and so often don't have the resources to actively trawl for stations to include. It is up to web stations themselves to seek out suitable specialist directories and request a listing. On this more manageable scale there is then a symbiotic relationship between directory and subscriber, and it is equally important for the directory to have a reciprocal link from each of its listed stations. This model is quite a departure from traditional broadcasting: instead of competing for niche audiences in isolation, the expectation is that listeners will be shared between stations.

Outsourcing promotion

With all these possible hyperlinks to explore and negotiate, the organization of an online promotion strategy can be a time-consuming business for a new web radio station. If it's a commercially run station, it's important to be able to show potential advertisers some healthy audience figures quickly, so a concerted promotion strategy is essential. A number of companies on the Web specialize in developing such strategies and their expertise can save a new station a good deal of money.

For example, http://www.submit-it.com/ offers a straightforward service to get your site listed on up to 400 search engines and directories, and to keep it listed by running monthly checks for $59 a year (February 2001 prices). They also offer additional promotional tools, like targeted emails, for a separate small monthly fee. Or companies like http://www.virtualdomain.net/ offer a more comprehensive service to develop a promotional strategy for which they charge considerably more. Try putting 'net promotions' or 'web promotions' into a search engine. Alternatively, you might decide to do your own research and register with a service like http://www.searchenginewatch.com/, which specializes in providing up to date news and tips for getting the most from your search engine placements.

A disadvantage of this rapid launch strategy is that you cannot be sure how large an audience to plan for in the first weeks or months. This in turn poses the question of how many streams to invest in. For a launch to make its mark, it is essential not to have too few streams to cope with peak demand. On the other hand, overspending on bandwidth can be a costly mistake, which may be difficult to recoup.

For small, third sector stations though, what is a dilemma for the major broadcaster turns out to be a great advantage of web radio: for them it may well be better to build slowly and from a very low base in broadcasting terms. So the building of promotional links can take place over time, making outsourcing unnecessary. The promotion garners audience at a steady pace, which allows the spending on bandwidth to grow in step.

Registering your own domain name

So, if you are not using a host to get your web station online and you are not outsourcing the development of your presence on the Web, you may need to think about registering a domain name for your new website. Finding the right domain name is a potent way of getting your station noticed. Three things to note about choosing a domain name follow:

1 It should be as obvious and easy to remember as possible.
2 It should provide a recognizable 'hook' that conveys something about your station to potential listeners.
3 Competition to be the first to register names and permutations of names is intense.

The international body in charge of controlling the form and method of assignment of domain names (albeit loosely) and therefore for opening up new designations is the International Corporation for the Assignment of Names and

Numbers (ICANN), and their website (http://www.icann.org/) is a good source of information on the current rules for domain naming. One significant parameter to be aware of is the name (the bit which follows, usually, www. and before the first /) can now be up to 67 characters long. That includes the final suffix, .com, .co.uk, .net, etc., with each 'dot' counting as one character. So with some lateral thought you can make your name quite descriptive, and the more relevant key words it includes the higher it is likely to show up on a search engine's results. ICANN is also responsible for accrediting the hundreds of e-businesses that offer various kinds of registration deals under its guidelines which ensure that you and only you are the legal owner of that name for the duration of the contract (typically 1–10 years), assuming of course someone has not already registered it before you. These agents make registration easy and cheap, and the service includes the laborious task of checking whether the name you choose and its permutations (same name but with a different suffix) have already been claimed. They are easy to find by entering searches for 'domain names'.

The front end – web page design

Perhaps contrary to the common image, it is perfectly possible to be a regular listener to a web station without ever having visited its website. If I click on a 'listen now', 'hear it' or similar link from a directory or online tuner, my computer opens the appropriate player and connects directly to that server stream. The web page never appears on my screen, only the information carried on the player. And if I like the station its metafile remains on my computer's desktop until I move or delete it. The same principle applies if I use a dedicated web radio tuner like Penguin Radio.

So, in planning your station you can either think of the website as more or less important to the listener; as more a part of the station or less. That said, unless you are with a host service, you need to have one. The website is at the least:

- the public face of the station – probably the first point of contact for the audience and certainly a major source of crucial information like schedules;
- the only means of contact from a search engine, because they rely on indexing key words in text form;
- the point of interaction for your listeners to choose archive or live streams and to write in via email.

At the other end of the scale, the website can become as integral a part of your station's identity and the listening experience as you want it to be. Many established broadcasters have taken the visual power of the website very much to heart to bring their listeners 'into' the station by creating their own online equivalent of the fan magazine, as demonstrated by the websites of stations like Virgin Radio (http://www.virginradio.co.uk/) or the BBC's Radio 1 FM (http://www.bbc.co.uk/radio1/). To take a few examples of the kind of things the listener may be offered:

- photos and biographies of presenters and featured personalities;
- perhaps a studio webcam;
- a chat room where they can hold email discussions with other listeners, presenters and special guests;
- online competitions;
- instantaneous feedback of opinion or online votes;
- background information or links to other sites where they can find it.

All of these interactive functions of course require designing, staffing and keeping up to date. In this sense, there is the possibility for some of them to have a counter-productive effect if they do not live up to expectations. The user of the website must get the sense that there is someone at the other end of the line, that it is a live visual space in the same way as radio is a live aural space. And a popular station is likely to attract a lot of online visitors and reaction. Firing emails into a void and not knowing whether anyone has read them can be a discouraging experience. This is soon reinforced when the visitor notices nothing on the website has changed for a fortnight except the date and the hit counter.

As a rule of thumb, it is absolutely vital for a new, little known station, which is hoping to attract 'passing trade', to have a site which gets the visitor to the 'listen' button with least delay, even over a 14.4 kbps link. Anyone who's used the Internet knows the frustration of so-called 'blue bar blues' – staring at your browser's motionless progress indicator and a half complete web page. A survey by Jupiter Research in September 2000 found that 84 per cent of US Internet users left websites because of slow or broken links and 68 per cent because they couldn't find what they were looking for (Lake, 2001). Sites of established stations – and especially of a terrestrial broadcaster – can afford more complex pages which take a bit longer to open (within reason) on the assumption that the visitor has gone to it for a purpose and are prepared to wait (or queue up) for a short while to be 'let in'. On the whole though, a slow website is nothing but an obstacle to listening.

So, many hidden traps lie in wait among the many attractions of designing your own website, and perhaps especially for the unsuspecting radio person. There are plenty of examples out there of web stations whose web pages are as likely to put potential listeners off as attract them. In this respect, an experienced web designer is an invaluable asset, if not as part of the station's permanent team then contracted on a regular basis. Failing that, there are many excellent books and websites on the essentials of web design (some are suggested at the end of the chapter). For a web radio station there are a few golden rules, which are all variations on the same theme: keep it simple. The writers of software will continue to give us more powerful, more elaborate tools to play with, but remember that they are using very different hardware from most of your potential listeners. We've seen how we can select against whole sections of potential audience by the connection speed we choose to stream at (Chapter 4). It's just as easy to do the same by offering them a website they cannot open or which demands they spend 20 minutes finding and downloading the latest plug-in software before it'll let them anywhere near your audio stream.

Crucial points of web design to remember are:

- The first page (either the home page or whichever is linked from directories and search engines) must open fast, even over lower connection speeds. Either an arresting image or your station logo should come up within 5 seconds and the rest should follow very soon after. (The same rule you'd apply to holding the listener's attention at the start of a radio programme.) So you must test it through a typical user's modem.
- Think very carefully what you are trying to achieve before you design in moving images like a Flash movie. These may be great for some sites that want to make a big first impression and hold attention among users with more expensive hardware, but is that you? A movie holds the listener up on their way to your radio content – and for too long over a slow connection. I know I have very little patience with movies that take time to load – and they'd better be *really* good once I've waited or else it's on to the next site.
- If you do decide to use larger embedded files like Flash or Frames, always offer an alternative text-only version alongside (and, by way of strategic research, monitor how many hits you get through each route).
- Don't try to be at the cutting edge in using the latest software versions of anything on your website, which require the latest plug-ins or updates. Allow plenty of lead time for other non-radio websites to have persuaded your audience to download them first. A potential listener looking for radio may accept the occasional demand to upgrade their player software, but is perhaps the least likely person to be tolerant of a diversion to hunt for visual effects.
- Work with as basic a colour palette as you can; 256 colours should be plenty and you certainly don't need thousands or millions. They just add time to the loading.
- The visitor to your site should never be more than three clicks away from hearing your audio and preferably less. Show them you're making it easy for them to enjoy your programmes. By the same token, don't hide the 'listen'

button low down on a scrolling page. If you need more pages on your site that's OK, but make sure they appear as secondary to your audio streams, otherwise you'll look more like a website with a bit of audio rather than a web radio station with a website.

- Where possible, keep at least the front pages short, so they just fill a single screen without scrolling. The information that's out of sight again holds up the page opening.

The best way to begin planning the design of your website is to study other people's – over a modem with the kind of connection speed you'd expect your listeners to be using. The case studies in the preceding chapters would make a good starting point.

Reputation

It's one thing to go through the technical stages of getting a station safely online, but quite another to establish a reputation that is going to spread the word that it's worth listening to. Reputation is a complex of factors, which for web radio crucially includes:

- technical reliability of streams and ease of access to the station;
- clear identification with a specific audience – much more specific than in broadcasting;
- reliability and variety of content plus the ability to surprise;
- a well-integrated balance of interactive resources to involve the audience, which don't exclude or marginalize those who just want to listen by, for example, talking too much about visual content on the screen;
- but enough opportunity for dialogue with those who want to really involve themselves in the station – through email, bulletin boards or chat rooms, phone-ins or other audio contributions, regular news and updates from behind the scenes;
- well-signposted policies on the limits of those interactions – i.e. whether or not they are moderated by the station and, if they are, according to what criteria (see Chapter 9);
- for smaller stations, independence from or conversely association with other online or offline stations or web radio streams may well be significant.

These factors really need to be in place before any promotional strategy is worked out: marketing budgets are likely to be wasted if they are not. And the more securely they are in place the easier the job of getting noticed becomes.

I have emphasized already the importance of getting the transmission side right and maintaining the highest reliability of streams. This is not only vital for the individual station, but is also very important for the greater good of the whole project of web radio – just as the use of reliable and rapidly improving transmitter technology was an essential factor in the early growth of terrestrial radio. In later chapters, I will come on to consider different aspects of content in more detail and the points of similarity and difference between web and analogue radio content. Suffice it to say here that a genuine, sustainable foundation on which to build a word of mouth reputation is very much at the heart of getting noticed among the mass of competition that flows daily through the Internet.

So, the last of the above bullet points deserves a few more words in this present context. The web radio station needs to take a strategic decision about its position in relation to competing stations. Is it trying to out-compete others providing very similar content or to strike out to find an unmet demand and offer something significantly different? (There is, of course, nothing new in this question to media economists and marketing experts.) A very high proportion of web stations at the moment are competing in markets that are well established offline and most especially in commercial music formats. It is extremely difficult to promote such a station in isolation amid the dense crowds of international competitors, and the only realistic way to achieve significant ratings has little do with content and a lot to do with market muscle to pull in your audience. Hence, a prevalent strategy is to join a big name aggregating site like Yahoo! Broadcast.

In this multichannel environment, there are no guaranteed formulae for the new starter. The consequence of an excess of choice, of information overload, is a certain level of self-protecting resistance on the part of the audience or potential audience. In a noisy environment, our aural senses impose their own filters to allow us to hear more clearly; in a quiet environment, we can be much more responsive to individual sounds. Joining a busy portal like Yahoo! Broadcast does not provide an automatic introduction to an audience or a right to be heard. The alternative to standing in the middle of the market square is to get on with doing something interesting on a side street and let those who are curious come and find you. Web radio is more suited to this strategy than broadcasting.

Offline promotion

A surprising amount of the news about what's going on online is found through offline sources – especially those primitive media, the newspapers and magazines. So a promotion strategy for a web radio station needs to include this type of conventional outlet.

An established terrestrial station already has its access to offline promotion within its transmission area. For the new station, though, which doesn't have that brand leverage, the question is how to get into the news and, crucially, where in this global marketplace. Unlike the launch of a new terrestrial station, there is little point in thinking in terms of an expensive build-up to a big splash as the station 'goes live'. Web radio starts small. It has to be there, available online and already doing something relevant before the offline press in any part of the world are going to take notice.

Buying newspaper or poster advertising campaigns has been tried and tested for promoting new local radio licences over decades, but it is unlikely to be cost effective for web radio – unless perhaps your station is intended to have a very particular local appeal not already catered for by the terrestrial competition. Once again, this returns us to the question of the station's content, *who* it might connect with, and exactly *where* it is likely to get those people talking about it. The launch of another Chart Hits music channel is news almost nowhere in the world by now, but a new radio station that has something obviously different about it just might be. If your station will appeal, for example, to particular 'expat' communities around the world, who have little other radio contact with their home country, region or city, then you need to research where those potential listeners are concentrated and get press releases out to their local newspapers, magazines or company newsletters. Once you have established those kinds of links with some real listeners, *then* the usual push strategies of media promotion may be relevant: staging well-timed newsworthy events, trailing visits from well-known guests to the station, perhaps online competitions (see, for example, Keith, 1997, Chapter 7).

Building a brand

A brand is a reputation built over time – a name or logo which, in the instant that it's seen or heard, conjures immediate recognition and particular associations. A strong brand is the holy grail of today's marketing strategists. But it is an elusive commodity because it depends on so much more than mere marketing. The strongest radio brands are those built up over the decades on the strength of their relationship to a broad range of individual listeners – the BBC being the oft-cited classic example.

Established terrestrial stations with strong global brands have a huge head start when they go online. Hence, the BBC has been able to further strengthen its brand in a global context by building an excellent website that lives up to people's pre-existing expectations of the brand. (It could equally have damaged the brand in the long term by offering an indifferent website.) Two mutually supporting stanchions that frame the BBC brand are News and Radio, and these also now provide the solid foundation for the website to reach new audiences with the five national networks online plus the multilingual World Service.

An example of a more recently established brand transferring successfully onto the Web is Virgin Radio (see Chapter 5). The web station is owned by the Scottish Media Group and its offline parent in the UK has long ceased to have any financial connection with Richard Branson's shrewdly built global brand. Nevertheless, virginradio.com appears to be benefiting from some association with its former owner on the Web. Branson's brand has gained a solid foothold in the American market, largely through the visibility of the Virgin Atlantic airline, but supplemented by online marketing of other products. The online stream of the Virgin Radio station is given third place in the MeasureCast Top 50 most listened to online stations in the US during March 2001, while its sister station, Virgin Radio Classic, is at number 28. This to the most developed web radio audience anywhere in the world and in competition with many well-known American radio brands in that same Adult Alternative/Classic Rock music market.

It is too early in the development of web radio to talk of substantial Internet-only brands in the same breath as these examples with their offline roots. Indeed, as I write the bursting of the 'dotcom bubble' is vividly demonstrating the folly of trying to create brands without histories. A plausible concept and pure marketing are no substitute for an earned reputation. Having said that, the speed of today's ICT world does certainly accelerate the pace at which reputation can be earned and consolidated. So we do have examples of some formidable brand names emerging in the short life of web radio – but as creators of the infrastructure rather than content – the most prominent example today being the Real brand.

Summary

The challenge for a web radio station then is to develop the kind of content that will distinguish it from the sheer mass of online competition. The lessons sketched in this chapter suggest two alternative strategies. One is to be a very powerful offline brand and use that leverage to vigorously promote your online station, slightly adapting your experience of conventional push-type methods to this new environment. The other strategy, for the vast majority of smaller web radio ventures, is to start small and concentrate on creating reputation, not marketing a brand.

The Web offers many aids in this because promotion online is generally cheap, if not free. It certainly is not an exact science, and the major cost is likely to be the time you invest in visiting other sites and learning from what you see as their strengths and weaknesses. What would connect you as the receiver – as the motor of this pull technology – with any given site?

The answer lies in the way a station uses hyperlinks in conjunction with its content. Remembering what we've said about the two sides to the Web – the sharing and the commercial, which correspond roughly with the pull and the push of the technology discussed at the start of the chapter – the choice here is between forming or joining mutual alliances of links or else placing them as advertising to be bartered, bought and sold. The former tend to make the listener's searching easier because they act as sort of self-sorting sub-networks. The latter stand to attract more visitors in the short term (provided the links are well placed) and are more likely to propel a station nearer to the centre of the marketplace, if that's where they want to stand.

Either, or a combination, of these two strategies can be usefully supplemented with well-researched and creative approaches to the offline media. Again, an organization with a viable offline brand is at an advantage here because, apart from their existing promotional experience, they have their track record of content with proven wide appeal in their transmission area(s). The single advantage the Internet-only station can rely on in the offline world is if they have something different to offer.

In all cases, for all stations that want to create a sustainable presence on the Web, the evidence so far points towards investing any available time and money in the content first. Just as in the early adventures in terrestrial radio, only when you know you have something some people want to hear is it worth spending to let others know about it.

Further reading

Flanders, V. and Willis, M. (1998). *Web Pages That Suck*. San Francisco: Sybex.

Keith, M. C. (1997). Promotion. In *The Radio Station* (4th edn), Chapter 7, pp. 200–218. Focal Press.

Sakai, D. (1999). *The Targeted Audience. Internet & Database Marketing Strategies for Broadcasters*. Washington: National Association of Broadcasters.

SearchEngineWatch website – http://www.searchenginewatch.com/.

Siegel, D. (1997). *Creating Killer Web Sites* (2nd edn). Hayden Books.

Spinelli, M. (1996). Radio lessons for the Internet. In *Postmodern Culture*, Vol. 6, no. 2 (January). Oxford University Press.

Web Developers Journal online – http://www.webdevelopersjournal.com/.

8 Copyright on web radio

There's no getting away from it, the easier digital technology makes it to store, search and distribute creative works at high sound quality, the more fiendishly complicated it makes protecting the intellectual property rights of the creators. This is true for all copyright material that might appear on a web radio site or its streams, but by far the greatest problems are in the arena of popular music. It is invariably the case that legislation follows in the wake of new technologies, where they change the way we do things, and in the ICT ocean the previously serviceable raft of copyright law is having an especially hard time keeping afloat. This uncertain state of affairs should not deter the aspiring webcaster, but it is important to be aware of the potential for finding yourself on the wrong side of some hastily drafted legislation which is attempting to maintain the copyright status quo. Hence this chapter.

The problem is fundamental: the distribution of analogue sound has been easy to police because it had its own natural barriers or points of exchange with the public, whereas in the decentralized world of digital distribution policing copyright becomes extremely difficult – and maybe ultimately impossible. Until quite late in the Broadcast Century, music used to exist in one of three clearly definable forms: as live performance, as sheet music or as sound recorded onto some physical medium – usually as mass produced singles and LPs on vinyl or analogue cassette. It was relatively easy to manage the assignment of the rights to use music in one of these forms because each involved a controllable point of sale, where the price could comprise the various costs of production plus a proportion to pay for those rights. When analogue broadcasting came along, after some early doubts, that too proved eminently controllable because the electromagnetic spectrum on which it took place was a finite resource which, by and large, could be regulated by international agreement and managed under national licensing regimes. Payments for rights to broadcast live performances or from recordings were amenable to negotiation between the limited number of known, licensed broadcasters and the holders of those rights.

Music piracy did, of course, exist in the analogue era and it flourished as a by-product of the global demand created by the recording industry, especially through the sale of unlicensed cassette copies. In most territories, the lines between legality and illegality were clearly drawn, though, and fairly easy to understand for anyone who cared to ask. Pirate radio presented no more than a minor blemish on the orderly surface of the copyright agreements as far as their avoidance of payment for airplay was concerned. But, in the medium to long term, most pirate music stations could reasonably claim to have cleared that debt many times over by creating demand for new records and so boosting revenues for copyright holders. In some cases this effect was huge. For example, the offshore pirate stations in 1960s Britain were promoting new music to 45 per cent of the population during any week in 1966, according to NOP (the National Opinion Poll, cited in Lewis and Booth, 1989, p. 84), at a time when sales of records *not* played by the nation's legal broadcasters was booming. Similar, if smaller, effects could be claimed for the breaking of any number of 'underground' musical forms into the popular mainstream since then.

But the technology of digitization separates the music recording from the medium it is captured on; in other words, from the physical product. OK, the CD is a physical product, but unlike its analogue predecessor the information it contains is highly reproducible. Unlike analogue broadcasting, this can be achieved extremely cheaply and with minimal loss of sound quality. So the whole system for collecting copyright payments has to adapt to this virtual new form of listening. The factors which make collecting payment so difficult can be summarized as:

- Physical – music can be moved from A to B entirely electronically, leaving very little detectable trace.
- Structural – the Internet is designed for sharing data horizontally.
- Economic – once you have access to an online computer, sending and receiving can be extremely cheap relative to the perceived value of the goods.
- Scale – this is truly a global phenomenon, ignoring borders and jurisdictions and involving millions of private individuals.

The two collection points these factors most seriously threaten are:

1 The point of sale of recorded music – where downloads replace the CD or another physical format.
2 The blanket licence fee for the right to broadcast music – through streaming.

Returning to our distinctions in Chapter 2, web radio only involves the second of these, though it has become caught up by association in the fierce battles over the first to reassert the rights of the owners of copyright.

Most books on making radio tend not to go into the details about copyright arrangements – which on the face of it have come to involve nothing more interesting than a streamlined system of paperwork and station accounting (see, for example, Keith, 1997, pp. 96–7). But in this book, once again we find that the Web puts radio into such a different context that it forces us back to first principles to understand the issues and potential pitfalls.

So, most of this chapter looks at copyright from the point of view of streaming music. Much of that discussion, however, is also relevant to other areas of performance copyright, for example published recordings of readings or dramas. Towards the end of the chapter, I make brief mention of some relevant aspects of text information on a station's website. The complexity and current uncertainty surrounding the whole subject of copyright on the Net make it impossible to offer more than a summary of the issues to be aware of here. The chapter is not intended to be a legally watertight guide for prospective stations. For more detailed and legally authoritative information, refer to the 'Further reading' section at the end of the chapter.

Established music copyright arrangements for terrestrial broadcasts

There are two components to the established models of music copyright: the writing of the song or piece of music and its performance. Both are recognized internationally, whether or not the writer of the song also performs it. Different territories have evolved different arrangements in respect of both – and a few territories have no tradition of copyright for either. These components underlie the existing arrangements for the payment of licence fees radio stations pay for the right to broadcast music. Figure 8.1 gives a simplified visual summary of the main copyrights relationships.

The song publisher

Take any (published) record from your collection and you'll find for any given song there is a credit for its writer and a publisher. For example 'Imagine', written by John Lennon and published by Lenono Music. In this case, all rights to perform that song are administered on behalf of Lenono Music by the much larger BMG Music Publishing (part of the international Bertelsmann Corporation). If I want to give a public performance of 'Imagine', live or on record, anytime within the next 50 years or so, I should ask permission through BMG Music Publishing, who may refuse or make a charge or let me do so for free. (Copyright usually expires 70 years after the originator's death in European law.) The songwriter or the publisher may also sell on all their part in the rights to the song to another person or organization, who then becomes the owner of those rights.

Early radio broadcasters negotiated agreements with the music publishers' representatives to pay a very small fee to each publisher every time a station broadcast one of their songs. To make the collection of these performance rights fees (or royalties), manageable broadcasters now pay agreed blanket fees to their national performing rights organization, which exists to trace the publishers and distribute fees in proportion to the number of plays their client stations list. Performing rights organizations collect fees on a national basis and redistribute them internationally. So, for example, the Performing Rights Society (PRS) collects from all local and national UK stations (see http://www.prs.co.uk/), while in the US, with so many more stations, the job is shared by three organizations, ASCAP (http://www.ascap.com/), BMI (http://www.bmi.com/) or SESAC (http://www.sesac.com/), as indicated on records released there. A useful list of other international performing rights organizations can be found by scrolling through http://www.kohnmusic.com/.

The record company

In addition to the rights of the writer, there is the creative contribution of the performers to consider. In a live performance, the transaction is directly between the performers' management and the paying audience. Not so on a recording. So, for example, the rights to the original recording of 'Imagine' are owned separately by EMI Records Ltd. A different recording of the same song could be owned by a different record company. In a classical music recording, the copyright of the composer might have expired, but the rights to each recording are almost certainly still active and owned by a record company somewhere.

US broadcasting has grown up without an additional royalty fee for airing the recording of a song. This follows the market logic that playing a record on the radio is a direct promotion of that record and the more airplay it gets the more copies it is likely to sell. Remembering that US radio stations started small, local and commercial, it seemed wise at the time not to levy additional fees which might inhibit stations from playing and hence promoting records (Barnouw, 1966, p. 119–21). In the UK, by contrast, the early music copyright negotiations were with a single, centrally funded, national broadcaster, the BBC, at a time when the emphasis was still very much on live performance and the most powerful music industry interests around the table thought playing records on the radio *should* be inhibited (see, for a contemporary account, Reith, 1924, pp. 93–107). The result was that UK stations have, since 1934, had to pay an additional fee for playing the recording, collected and distributed by Phonographic Performance Ltd (PPL). Their website is at http://www.ppluk.com/.

Mechanical copyright

There is a third way a radio station is likely to use music, which is also regulated by copyright, and that is to copy or dub from the original disc onto another medium. The traditional reasons for doing this ranged from making a back-up taped copy to be played in full, to using a short excerpt in a trailer, advert or a sting. This again refers back to the composer owning the right to be paid for the use of any part of their work. In the UK, this kind of internal copying comes under the aegis of the Mechanical Copyright Protection Society (http://www.mcps.co.uk/). In the US, mechanical copyright is licensed through the Harry Fox Agency (http://www.nmpa.org/hfa.html).

For most of the Broadcast Century, the disparities between analogue copyright laws negotiated in different countries had little effect on the arrangements terrestrial broadcasters followed within their own countries. Recently, though, the accelerating globalization (a) of the demand for music and (b) of broadcasting/distribution, both of which have been greatly facilitated by digitalization, created the need for some form of global agreement (see Box 8.1).

Box 8.1   The International WIPO Copyright Treaties

Two international treaties have been negotiated through the United Nations World Intellectual Property Organization (WIPO), both adopted in principle in December 1996. The WIPO Copyright Treaty (WCT) applies broadly to authorship and songwriting, and the WIPO Performances and Phonograms Treaty (WPPT) to performers and the record companies. These currently form the basis on which national governments are amending their internal copyright laws, although interpretations of such complex definitions are likely to differ from country to country. The terms are drawn fairly broadly (WPPT is printed in full at http://www.wipo.int/treaties/ip/performances/performances.html).

While 51 nations originally signed the WCT and 50 signed the WPPT in 1996, the implementation remains patchy to date and not therefore fully in force. In March 2001 the US, most of Latin America, Japan and a scattering of Central European states had ratified them, while the European Union had not by that date (http://www.wipo.int/treaties/ip/copyright/index.html).

The EU member states are in the process of finally agreeing on the harmonization of certain aspects of copyright and related rights in the information society.

And, of course, the evolution of the digital technologies which gave rise to the WPPT is far from over.

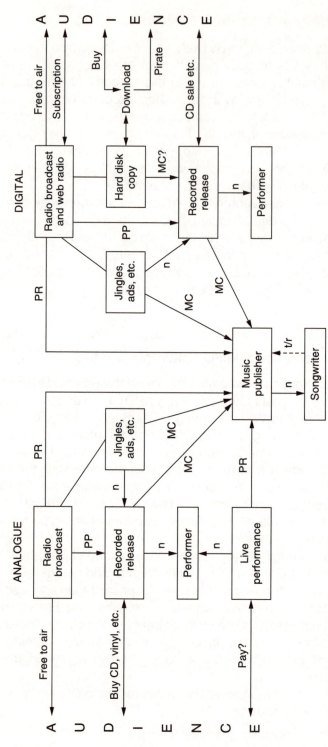

Figure 8.1 A schematic diagram illustrating the main routes for music copyrights (royalties). Key: MC = mechanical copyrights; PP = phonographic rights; PR = performing rights; 'n' indicates rights; 'n' indicates where some form of negotiated contract is typically involved; 't/r' indicates that the ownership of all rights to a song is sometimes transferred wholesale from the original songwriter to a publisher.

Music copyright in the digital environment

So, once the online personal computer came into contact with the music CD, words like 'broadcast' and 'copy' took on new and technically complex meanings – meanings beyond the previous legal definitions. For example, whereas 'to broadcast' a piece of music once meant putting a record on a turntable and transmitting the sound direct via radio waves, it now routinely involves digitally copying from CD onto a hard drive first and using the copy as the broadcast source. Transmission might then take place via any number of different analogue or digital routes. Should this add a third tier of mechanical copyright fees to every song that's played in this way? What if the station, sensibly, wants to make back-up copies of those same playlists to a second server in case the first should crash? Does each clone require a separate royalty fee? Does each parallel transmission?

The exchange of files in MP3 format has come to symbolize the cloning problem, but that is really only today's symptom of a much more fundamental shift for copyright owners and more particularly for the record companies. The US courts may be able to close down centrally organized companies like MP3.com and Napster for aiding and abetting copyright infringement, but, as many observers like UK copyright lawyer Mark Haftke (2000) have observed, the genie of music cloning cannot now be put back in the bottle. 'Peer to Peer (P2P)' exchange of music files or any other data looks, in all practical senses, impossible to police.

Nonetheless, a few visits to performing rights societies' websites show that they are confident they will be able to detect unlicensed distribution of music, whether as downloadable files or streams. Web radio stations are particularly 'visible' when they publicize their streams in a way that individuals using file transfer software like Napster or its successors are not. So web stations should assume that sooner or later the contents of their output will be scanned and checked for copyright compliance. Then the question for those policing the system is 'Who it is worth our while prosecuting?' The question for the web station is 'Are we certain we have copyright clearance for everything on our site?'

The first – globally significant – moves to interpret the WIPO treaties and reframe the copyright laws so as to make any unlicensed digital transfer of music illegal have taken place in the US through the 1998 Digital Millennium Copyright Act (DMCA). This was preceded by the closely related 1995 Digital Performance Rights in Sound Recordings Act (DPRA), and the combined effects of these two pieces of legislation are likely to be significant for all web radio stations, at least in the short to medium term. Strictly speaking, they are internal to the US and only apply to transmissions originating in the US.

However, this is complicated by the global nature of the technology. For example, a webcast from outside the US may be relayed by a server which is physically located inside the US and thus logically subject to US legislation. Therefore, as a guide to the legal trends affecting web radio, it is important for stations anywhere in the world to keep an eye on these American developments.

At this point in time, though, no significant court cases have been reported that test the application of these new copyright laws specifically to streaming as opposed to file sharing. That can only be a matter of time and powerful lobby groups, notably the Recording Industry Association of America (RIAA, whose website is at http://www.riaa.com/), will have taken heart from their recent success in halting unlicensed downloading of MP3s through Napster's servers.

The recording rights to the vast majority of records any mainstream radio station plays belong to one member or another of the RIAA. So we need here to be aware of the key points of these US Acts as they apply to web radio, and especially the definitions they apply to various uses of streaming. I will summarize these below in brief. I am indebted for my lay understanding of this complex area to the comprehensive and authoritative website 'Kohn on Music Licensing' (http://www.kohnmusic.com/), created by music copyright lawyers Bob, Al and Matt Kohn. I would recommend the site as an excellent resource for prospective webcasters.

It may be helpful to note here that these Acts do not themselves use the kind of language contained in this book: terms like 'streaming' or 'downloading'. Instead, they attempt tightly to define the end use of the copy by the listener and the intention of the person transmitting, in this case, a piece of music. The most important end use the legislation is aimed at outlawing is anything which might effectively substitute for the purchase of the original recording and hence the collection of copyright payments from members of the public. Although this is not the intention behind what I have defined as web radio, we have to acknowledge that web radio is being pinned down in the crossfire between the major record companies and the file sharers.

A rather surprising casualty of the crossfire is that, as a result, the 'loss of sales' argument has gained the upper hand over the 'promotional benefits of music radio' in the US, the home of the free market in broadcasting. The DMCA brings all digital radio transmissions originating from there, whether on the Internet or any other platform, into line with most of the rest of the world: royalties become payable for the first time to the record company as well as to the music publisher. The individual payments may be trivial, but this represents a significant shift in favour of larger broadcasters, with their deeper pockets (and the 'big five' record companies), where the playing of mainstream music is concerned.

Streaming versus downloading

Throughout this book I have laid great emphasis on the difference between streaming and downloading, because the intention behind each activity is very different. For most end-users at the moment this is a very obvious difference: the sound quality of streaming is inferior to the downloaded equivalent. For the music fan, this means copying a streamed track is not an acceptable substitute for buying the CD original, whereas downloading an MP3 version might be (even though each track can take an age to arrive and even though the MP3 format is some way from aural perfection compared to CD).

However, from a technical standpoint, that difference disappears as connection speeds get faster, as a quick glance at Table 3.2 reveals. With a reliable minimum connection speed above 128 kbps, an MP3 copy of a song or album can be streamed or downloaded in real time with no difference in the quality of its stereo sound. With minimum speeds above 1.54 Mbps, tracks at stereo WAV quality could be streamed in real time. (Indeed, if the promise of streamed high quality video is ever realized, the current need to buffer an audio-only stream will then be a thing of the past.) So it turns out that streaming versus downloading is not a helpful distinction as far as defining digital transfer of music for copyright purposes is concerned. Here the legislation is attempting to look somewhat ahead of the technology that is commonly available today.

For this reason, the DMCA includes stringent restrictions on several aspects of web radio: on how often playlisted tracks can be repeated within a 3-hour period, on prohibiting pre-announcement of which tracks are coming up next on a stream and on limiting the number of complete tracks from the same album that can be played in close proximity. The intention of the legislation – and this is the important thing to grasp – is obviously to make it difficult for a web station to provide a service from which a private individual with a broadband connection can obtain perfect copies of released singles or whole albums off air.

Subscription versus non-subscription

One way of recreating a point of sale in this digital environment is to turn yourself into an encrypted, subscription-based service. This is the way out that is currently being offered to Napster and being proposed by the major RIAA members for the MusicNet and Pressplay services (see Box 2.1). If, like today's satellite broadcasters, you charge people to access the audio on your site then you can incorporate copyright fees into the price. For web radio this is not an attractive proposition, because (a) radio is customarily free to air and (b) it would undermine many of the horizontal characteristics that make this new medium an *alternative* to the established terrestrial competition. One day we may all be paying for our media channels by subscription, but for now radio is one of the services online audiences are least likely to want to pay for – over and above the hurdle of the connection charges they pay already.

Nevertheless, the effect of the new US copyright Acts is to make the subscription route a very much easier road to travel, whether you are a web radio station or a virtual music shop, providing downloads on request.

Live streaming versus on demand

By now the drift of this summary should be becoming clear. At high bandwidth, an on-demand archived stream containing music or other copyright audio becomes very much like a searchable site for downloads. If that archived stream is available in the US it is subject to US digital copyright legislation. And because by definition archived files need to be permanently online for a period of days or weeks, they are far easier to screen for copyright compliance than a live stream. So for every piece of music on your station's archived streams you need in principle to obtain both a mechanical copyright licence and a performance licence to play the recorded track. Obtaining the first of these licences is usually straightforward. It is typically a small, standard charge, often paid as a blanket licence, which ends up with the music publisher. The second may be more problematic because it is non-standard, which means it has to be negotiated, either through an agency like PPL or directly with the record company, who have the right to refuse you or set prohibitive terms. On the other hand, the record company may decide to charge nothing. This is more likely (a) if your station is part of a non-profit-making organization and (b) if you are asking a small, independent record company.

The online phonographic performance licence is then something of an unknown quantity at present and should be investigated thoroughly before you start archiving music streams – in whichever territory you plan to base your streaming server. Potentially the most troublesome aspect of webcasting is archiving streams when they include music or other published recordings, especially for the unsuspecting, new web station with limited financial means at their disposal. Later in this chapter I suggest a number of alternative, precautionary approaches on the basis that, as yet, there are too many unresolved variables in this particular copyright equation to safely predict the outcome in any given jurisdiction. You may decide to take a risk of not being found out or hope that you are too small to sue, but on the other hand it would be advisable to know where you stand if your local copyright agency does decide to ask you to remove the majority of your playlist from your streaming server.

Simulcasting versus Internet only

A prime example of the way in which web radio has been caught up in the record companies' fight to protect their income is to be found in the situation where an analogue station simulcasts their terrestrial output as a live stream on the Internet. In the US, a terrestrial station, remember, pays no performance fee to the record company for playing their records on air. But the DMCA appears to have the effect of saying that the live stream of the same show, because it is now a 'digital transmission', does incur performance fees – even if that stream is at much lower sound quality than the parent analogue transmission and even though the online audience is a fraction of the size of the terrestrial broadcast. This anomalous conclusion was drawn in a ruling by the Official Register of the US Copyrights Office on 11 December 2000 in favour of a submission brought by the RIAA (see Box 8.2).

Box 8.2   US Copyrights Office's ruling finds broadcasters liable for phonographic performance copyrights for streaming their terrestrial signals on the Internet

The ruling has important repercussions for web radio based in the US, whether simulcast or Internet only. Firstly, its effect is retrospective. That is, it makes phonographic performance fees payable for all recordings that have been streamed since DMCA was enacted in October 1998. Secondly, it says that the sizes of those fees are yet to be negotiated and at the time of writing they have still not been set. In other words, all existing and future music streams are liable for a back payment of an as yet unknown amount. (It may either take the form of a 'per play' fee, or else a blanket percentage of a station's revenues, as is the case in the UK, for example.) Alarming as this sounds for any station, its retroactive effect is likely to be confined to the US, where simulcasting terrestrial stations have not previously paid fees to record companies, only fixed and fairly modest performing rights fees to the ASCAP, BMI and SESAC. As I write, the ruling is the subject of an appeal by the National Association of Broadcasters (NAB) and a number of US radio station owners. Further information can be found at http://www.nab.org/. Representing the Internet-only radio stations, the Digital Media Association (DiMA, http://www.digmedia.org/) agrees with the ruling on the basis that it is unfair for one set of web stations (Internet only) to be charged phonographic performance royalties by record companies if another set (simulcast) are not.

For a summary of the ruling's effects on web radio, see Ryan and Bingaman (2001).

In one sense, this effect of the DMCA is no more than one of the stranger effects of the attempt to harmonize music copyright arrangements internationally under the WIPO. In the US, it is a temporary anomaly in the move from analogue to digital transmission. But in another sense, it is far from clear what short-term implications the loss of the NAB's appeal might have for future webcasts. The piling of separate royalties onto web radio in different territories may prove too much for small enthusiastic outfits who haven't yet figured out where the profit is for them in this fabulous new form of niche music promotion. Such a pile of incidental expenses might well be enough to make them reconsider the value of their efforts. Watch out for further developments.

One further dimension of this particular legal argument is that, as noted above, the record company appears at this stage to have the right under the DMCA to refuse rights or else dictate restrictive terms for online transmissions of any recording they own. This could mean suspending an online simulcast – because of its global reach – where the station only holds a licence to transmit that same recording in their own territory. A parallel situation arose for the BBC's webcast of their Five Live coverage of the Sydney Olympics in August 2000. Although they had paid for the rights to broadcast the event within the UK on their terrestrial transmitters, they discovered – along with many other online services around the world – that this did not cover a separate right to transmit the same coverage online and therefore globally. As it was impractical to blank any feasibly contestable reference to Olympic coverage from their live streams, they had to suspend their entire online radio output for the whole fortnight of the Games (Dodson and Barkham, 2000).

So it's a messy legal situation at present and by no means resolved. It is therefore important for web stations to check precisely where they stand on all copyright material before they take the decision to put it online.

National versus international agreements

I should stress again at this point that the lead on music copyright is very much being taken in the US, for the reasons suggested above: they are the pioneers of the technology and generally have the highest use of the Internet there; establishing profitable commercial use of the Internet is widely seen as an integral part of the nation's economic future; the 'big five' transnational record corporations are worth billions of dollars to the US economy and constitute a powerful political lobby group in the RIAA; the RIAA are worried by what Internet distribution of music by any means might do to their members' viability; and the RIAA have been keen to correct the long-standing agreements by which US broadcasters do not pay phonographic performance fees, while most of the rest of the world's radio stations do.

The DMCA does not, though, constitute international law for web radio and the WIPO treaties will not necessarily be interpreted so strictly for web radio elsewhere. So we should expect variability between territories. (Look out for specialist servers setting up in countries which take a more lenient view.) Nonetheless, the Internet is no respecter of national borders. We will have to wait for the first test case to see how US courts will decide to regard web radio transmissions that penetrate their borders from different jurisdictions whose copyright terms are more lenient.

If the major record companies make it too difficult or expensive to use their recordings on web radio stations (which typically generate very small profits or none at all), they may leave the way open for other smaller, competing labels to encourage web stations to act as alternative promoters of their signed artists. In other words, one future scenario would envisage two parallel global music systems: one in which five or fewer large, vertical, global record corporations promote their artists to mass audiences through the digital terrestrial and satellite transmissions of national and international, vertical broadcasters plus the labels' own online subscription channels; and an alternative, lower cost, more horizontal network of web radio stations playing the music recorded by smaller record labels and unsigned acts for niche audiences. We can see some seeds of such a division already. The owners of performing rights, the representatives of the songwriters, have generally negotiated their fairly modest standard fee rates to accommodate web radio with broadcast and webcast representatives (such as the Digital Media Association (DiMA), whose website is at http://www. digmedia.org/). Similarly, smaller independent record labels have shown themselves much keener to see web radio stations as allies rather than a threat – in a re-run of the 1920s, when the fledgling radio and record industries began their symbiosis. For example, the Association of Independent Music (AIM) has been set up explicitly to represent independent labels in exploring online methods of distributing their products and working with web radio stations over royalties on recordings. AIM's website is at http://www.musicindie.org/.

The precautionary approach

This all sounds very intimidating, not to say confusing, to the newcomer to copyright issues. How can a web radio station be safe from charges of breach of copyright?

The first rule is to ask the legal experts where you stand with your particular type of webcast. Use a search engine to find the specialist copyright advice sites on the Web. Browse through their Frequently Asked Questions pages. Some now offer free advice via email as well, though you should verify any information you receive by these means by cross-checking several sources. And look up the music copyright information pages on the streaming software sites, like Real, Microsoft WMP and QuickTime. They are all in close negotiation with the copyright agencies (see p. 171). Bear in mind though that any discrepancies between sources are just as likely to arise from differing but valid interpretations in this uncharted legal territory as from the kind of unreliable information for which the Internet has become well known.

The second safety rule is to be open about what you are doing: write to the relevant performing rights and phonographic performance agencies, tell them what you are planning for your streams and ask them what royalty fees you should expect to pay. Depending on where you are, how big or small your operation is and when you write they may or may not be in a position to answer your questions. But, should you get no reply, the fact that you have officially asked is important in legal terms, because it provides evidence that you are not deliberately trying to evade copyright.

Beyond those two somewhat vague initial guidelines, there are some sensible precautions a station can take based on understanding a little more about the potential sources of conflict over the way it presents recorded copyright material. We need to think in terms of the value, both for the radio station and the record company, of the music or copyright material on that stream. The major factors that determine this can be summarized as follows.

Sound quality

CD sound quality is the benchmark as far as the record company is concerned. On current compression formats there is no question of anything streamed at less than 56 kbps being burned onto a disc and passed off as the original or a fair substitute. For many web stations nominal streams of 56 kbps are perfectly adequate, but a specialist station that sells itself on high quality music reproduction may well want to offer MP3 streams at 128 kbps and above. Popular music streamed at these higher rates can be seen as potentially yielding copies of high enough quality to substitute for CD sales. (As we have seen, compression formats are improving all the time, so that the minimum bit rate will gradually move downwards.)

The live radio model

For a station whose content is mainly or entirely music (or other published sound recordings), a live stream is easier to clear for copyright because it is very close to the familiar terrestrial radio model, whether analogue or digital. However, there's a trade-off here because an archived, on-demand stream is usually much cheaper for the station to maintain than a live one (provided it has relatively modest simultaneous audiences).

Completeness of tracks

The cheapest method of getting a 'radio station' online is to encode your own 'unique' playlist of favourite tracks onto a basic server, and enable the whole sequence to play out on demand, back to back and with no DJ presenting (what I describe in Chapter 2 as a 'music channel' rather than a radio station). When complete tracks are streamed in this way, they can easily be an acceptable substitute for the original if the sound quality is good enough. This makes record companies nervous, whereas segues and presenters talking over beginnings and endings protect against such substitution. When domestic cassette recorders first went on the market, the same solution was offered by radio broadcasters to protect against the threat, as it was perceived then by record companies, of 'home taping'. How our expectations of sound quality have changed since then.

Proportion of music on an archive stream

Where an archive, on-demand stream comprises mainly recorded music it can self-evidently be used as a searchable source, the more so if the stream is identified with a popular music style on the website or player. The majority of web stations arrange their stream(s) like this to attract audiences looking for particular types of music. These stations are also more likely to attract the attentions of copyright agencies than those whose archives contain relatively little music (or other published recordings, like readings or dramas on tape or CD).

A copyright checklist

So web radio stations need to take account of these factors when they plan the content of their streams and consider the trade-offs they involve. The kinds of questions they should be asking themselves are outlined below.

Is the station predominantly a music station?

If so, its managers should research the rules of music copyright thoroughly as they apply within the station's home territory. Use of previously unreleased original music should be negotiated with the writer and musicians – most of whom will be only too glad to get their work to a (potentially) global audience. Most truly independent record labels are also taking a constructive approach to web radio because they recognize the publicity value (see, for example, the AIM website mentioned earlier in the chapter). Don't forget that the rights to the songwriter are separate from the rights to play the record. If, on the other hand, you want to play music released by the major record companies you ought to approach your region's performing rights and phonographic performance agencies. The information you get from them may lead you to consider the next two questions.

Does the station have the resources to run a live stream?

It is noticeable that since the arrival of DMCA in the US, more web radio stations have dropped their archived music streams. This is for the reasons outlined above. From a copyright point of view, live streams are certainly cheaper and easier to negotiate. But, of course, a live stream implies either a continuous live human presence or automation. If this is a radio station with a live presenter, that raises questions of how long you expect to be on air and how often. Remember that a great strength of web radio is that there is no obligation to be on air all day like a licensed terrestrial broadcaster. The more specialist the programming, the more quality counts over quantity (see Chapter 10). It is also true, though, that a live transmission need not in fact involve a live human presence at all . . .

Can the station automate a live stream instead of archiving?

Automation software and additional server memory can turn an archived stream into a live stream and for music stations is probably the best solution to the copyright problems associated with archiving. Depending on the sources of a station's music, the price of some suitable automation software should be offset against the difference between live and archive copyright fees. Stations can set this kind of software up in a number of ways: it may be music only or include pre-recorded presentation; there is the option to segue between tracks or not; the rotation of tracks can be in a set sequence; or else a random play function will usually let you set 'rules' which can select for tempo, for example, and impose a minimum time between repeats of the same track. These rules for playing out a randomized live stream can easily be set to comply with particular copyright terms, such as those defined in the DMCA as the 'sound recording performance complement' (Kohn, 1998, p. 11). Simply put, this is the number of times tracks from the same published CD can be played within a 3-hour period.

Can the archived streams afford to be at lower quality?

An alternative solution is to downgrade the sound quality of the music by providing archived streams only at lower maximum bit rates – say a nominal 28.8 kbps. This is likely to be more appropriate for mixed speech and music stations, where the content of the speech is the reason for archiving particular clips or programmes. Occasional music tracks may be integral to the clip, but this is unlikely to be a station which has much use for a fully automated play out system. Here performing rights or mechanical copyright fees would still be payable, and permission to archive the recordings would still need to be sought. But the fact that this use would clearly not threaten to substitute for a CD sale would usually make that permission easier to obtain. And as we've seen, there are other good reasons to stream speech at lower bit rates: it saves on server memory and bandwidth; and it also does not exclude listeners with older modem connections.

Would 'library' or 'production music' serve the purpose?

If a programme to be archived uses music for mood or effect, rather than playing specific recordings of songs, there is usually a piece of production music available through one of the music publishers to suit the situation. Radio stations can access these libraries with the payment of an annual blanket licence fee. For example, in the UK, registration with MCPS gives automatic access to more than 70 libraries of production music CDs. Fees for the use of any of their contents are payable according to one of a number of production categories (e.g. for broadcast, non-broadcast, radio advertising or online use), but the arrangement is simple, covers comprehensive rights and is relatively inexpensive.

What in-built copyright protection does our streaming server software have?

Streaming software companies have had to develop their own protection against accusations of abetting the avoidance of royalty payments. And being based in the US, the leading, highly visible brands have to offer their services in such a way as to comply with the terms of post-DMCA copyright law. This is doubly important with the spread of broadband delivery across the US. So you will find mechanisms for copyright compliance built into the encoding, server and client software of Real, Microsoft WMP, QuickTime and SHOUTcast.

At the introductory level, these companies' websites offer comprehensive advice about how anyone using their product to stream can comply with the terms of (US) copyright. Secondly, the server software provides the means for your station to prevent your stream being captured or 'ripped' within the receiver's computer and saved as a digital copy. This is done in a simple check box when you are setting up the server. If the listener wants to record 'off air', they have to take a line from the analogue output of their computer's sound card and so step down in quality. (However, you should also be aware that other software programmers are producing 'fixes' which get around this part of the player's codes.) At the third level, the encoder software asks you to input the copyright details of each track you put into the system. This text information is then attached to the audio file as part of the stream and automatically displayed on the receiver's player.

Making full use of these measures on a station's live stream does not make it immune from royalty payments within its own territory. But they do provide evidence that it is not seeking to evade its copyright obligations during this legally ambiguous period while the governments of the world work out how to interpret the agreements they have negotiated under the WIPO.

Should I seek the protection of a streaming host?

If you are planning to stream copyright protected recordings on a small web station and find the whole prospect of organizing your own copyright arrangements just too daunting, there is another solution. Some of the major streaming hosts have announced recently that they will include clearance of all music copyright licences, both from songwriters and record companies, as part of their overall service package. These moves are again by US-based companies in line with the US Copyright Office's interpretation of the DMCA (but in advance of a settlement of what the phonographic copyright charge might be). Most have paid performing rights fees to songwriters all along, but, for example, Stream Audio was the first to announce in January 2001 that it would also include the royalty payments for the phonographic performance of sound recordings as part of its monthly $395 charge for unlimited simultaneous streams. Other hosts have followed suit and it's worth checking the copyright terms of the host your station intends to use (reported in *RAIN*, 30 January 2001).

Ownership versus consumption models

Web radio practitioners can only hope that the new paradigm created by Internet publication leads to a simpler, more practical system of rewarding the creators of music and sound recordings wherever their work enters the public digital domain. We should anticipate any change taking a long time to settle because there are so many competing financial interests involved in the negotiation. In the wake of the recent Napster judgement, there has been much discussion of the need now to replace the old ownership model – as in owning the hard copy of a work, for example the CD – with some form of subscription or consumption model. At the moment, such a model is hard to envisage precisely, because it would need to be workable across so many different ICT platforms. As I've already discussed, we cannot expect listeners to subscribe to web radio stations while the competition is free, but this is much more than a narrow debate about royalties on web radio: it is about a funding model capable of supporting an entirely new, multichannel, narrow-cast relationship between music making and radio.

One alternative to watch for will be some method of wrapping up an allowance for copyright fees within a 'one-stop' monthly connection fee covering all Internet services on a broadband, 'always on' connection. Distribution of those fees to the appropriate individuals in some kind of proportion to the use of their work remains a difficult problem. But then the automation of the process of tracking such information across the net also continues to move on apace.

Non-musical copyright

Although I have spoken in terms of music copyright throughout this chapter so far, much of the above is applicable to any published sound recording. So a recording of poetry reading or a drama production is protected by copyright in broadly similar ways: there are the rights of authors, performers and recording labels to consider. The major difference is likely to be that you may only need to find one copyright holder, in the form of the publisher of the recording. They are more likely to have bought the right to record and publish the work from their original author or their estate (if the term of copyright has not expired) and have paid the performers for the appropriate reproduction and publication rights. However, it is rather *un*likely that either contract says anything about rights for rebroadcast by anyone else – least of all a web radio station. The terms of any such contracts are very specific and, unless they are very recent, will not incorporate the concept of 'Internet rights'. So a web station would need to negotiate terms directly with the publisher of the recording. This might turn out to be straightforward, particularly for the use of an extract of the recording, or it may be long and complicated. In any event, as a station manager you would need to allow plenty of time for negotiating such arrangements. To take contrasting examples, it is usually a straightforward matter to buy the right to use 'library' sound footage from a BBC News programme, but negotiating to use passages from a BBC Drama recording – even one commercially available on tape or CD – is far more complicated and specific. In the latter case, it would be easier for the station to negotiate directly with the author's agent to create a new version of the extract (provided they have not sold the audio rights outright). The terms could then be based on the maximum size of Internet audience that could be expected to hear it.

On the other hand, a station may want to commission their own project with a writer and cast. That is clearly a matter of individual negotiation. However, it should take account of prevailing agreements between the national unions representing writers and performers (see Box 8.3). To take the UK example, you can find information about the rates the Writers' Guild has negotiated on their website (http://www.writers.org.uk/) and about actor's rates and repeat fees from Equity (http://www.equity.org.uk/). Both organizations are beginning to agree rates for Internet presentations with their major radio employer, the BBC, and these make a helpful starting point from which to negotiate smaller productions.

Box 8.3   A second rights blow to US web radio simulcasters

Interestingly, to reinforce the complexity of individual actors' repeat fees, as this book goes to press, parts of the US web radio sector have been hit for a second time in 3 months by a new claim for additional Internet rights fees. On 12 April 2001, a majority of US commercial stations closed their simulcast webcast streams until further notice, following the announcement by the American Federation of Television and Radio Artists (AFTRA), who represent the voice-over artists behind most US radio ads, that they were now asking for supplementary payments when any of their clients' ads appeared on the Web.

The options for the simulcasters were (a) automated substitution of Internet-only ads for all ad breaks on simulcast streams, (b) a move away from simulcasting by terrestrial stations to separate side channels or (c) getting out of web radio altogether, because they don't make any profit on those streams anyway. The dispute, which does not affect US web stations who contracted voice-overs specifically for streaming ads, had not been settled by July. However, the first of the affected companies, Clear Channel, have now decided to go down the automated ad insertion route.

Sources: various headlines at http://www.radioink.com/ and http://www.kurthanson.com/, 10–11 April 2001; Snyder (2001).

Quoting from a written text is typically covered by the 'fair dealing' clauses contained in copyright laws around the world. This is usually taken to allow for quotations of up to 400 words in total from a substantial text, as long as they are acknowledged – although not for several complete poems which 400 words might encompass. It is a good idea to check with the publisher if you want to use anything more than a passing quote.

Protecting your own copyright

Finally in this complicated chapter, we should remember that a web radio station is also a publisher and as such owns rights to any material it originates itself, from a presenter's voice to the contents of its web page. It is entirely up to the station how it deals with those rights but, now the shoe is on the other foot so to speak, we can view some of the above issues from a different perspective.

Let us assume that you have created the entire content of a small webcast yourself. You may decide generously to adopt the 'open access' spirit of the Web and 'donate' your work to the world, in which case you ought really to make clear to the visitors to your site that that is your intention. For example, you could display a prominent notice on your web page to that effect. Technically, whether you display such a notice or not you are still the owner of the copyright on your original material. When you are starting out this may seem unimportant and you will probably just be grateful for any visits at all to your site. But suppose your programme starts to gain a reputation and become popular, and suppose then that you visit another site and happen to find an inferior copy of your programme included on it – unacknowledged. If you are just happy to hear it out there then, yes, you have the open access spirit of the Web.

You may, on the other hand, feel cheated by this discovery. So OK, you do own the copyright, but can you do anything about it? The first thing is to add a copyright notice to your website, with the universal copyright symbol, ©, along with your station's name and the date you first put that page or radio stream on the Web. Most sites do, in fact, display some form of copyright notice, usually linked from somewhere near the bottom of each page. Have a look at a range of examples from other sites. Some are long and complicated, others really do little more than tell the impressed visitor to the site who to contact to request permission to reproduce or link to any of the work it contains. And make sure your server software is set to deny receivers the means to save your audio stream directly to their hard drive.

Having announced your copyrights, how can you protect them? That really depends on their value to you. Just like terrestrial radio, a high proportion of web radio content is either 'disposable chat' or someone else's copyright. For those original programmes that are worth more in terms of your investment or reputation, there are a number of strategies you can employ – but all involve time, money or both:

- *Join a copyright protection society.* To take one example, a UK songwriter or composer should investigate the benefits of registering their work with the PRS (http://www.prs.co.uk/). They can advise how best to protect your copyright.

- *Investigate 'digitally watermarking' your work.* Huge investment is being pumped into developing software that will add a secure, indelible electronic tag to any digital recording. See, for example, Digimarc's site at http://www.digimarc.com/. The technology is not failsafe at the time of writing (because 'counter-watermark' software, which detects tags and removes them, is also a potentially lucrative field). But so long as a watermark remains attached to your files (which for radio may not need to be long before the programme goes out of date), they can be automatically searched for across the Web by matching 'copyright spider' software. You can find out more about the current position by entering an online search for 'digital watermarks'.
- *Make your own periodic searches.* The current generation of powerful Internet search devices can be useful in some circumstances. They cannot yet search audio streams, but they do search text on websites in various ways. So, for example, if the value of your programme is that it contains an interview or performance by a well-known 'name', then a search for that name should reveal whether anyone else is promoting your interview on their website. Try, if you haven't already, http://www.google.com/, http://www.ixquick.com/ or http://www.vivisimo.com/. All search in different ways but they all explain what they do best.

Summary

Some reflection on the difficulty of trying to protect your own 'micro' copyright on the Web does indicate the scale and complexity of the macro problem faced by the major publishers and recording companies. They know for sure that routine infringement of their existing copyright is occurring on a large scale. They have also shown that they can successfully close down or restrict the activities of companies who profit from the infringement of their copyright – where those companies have a commercial identity and material assets. What we do not know yet is how successful symbolic cases like RIAA's fight with Napster will be in retaining the status quo of the ownership model of copyright in the face of infringements that are (a) cross-continental and (b) in the dispersed sphere of semi- or non-commercial, peer to peer, Internet activities like small-scale web stations. That will be a story for another book.

It's going to be important to remember, though, that technically, as soon as we achieve 'end to end' broadband delivery, the distinction between streaming and downloading is not a helpful one so far as copyright is concerned. However, for web radio practitioners the critical difference lies in the intention behind the transmission. If your aims are clear that your station is there to communicate with an audience through speech, music and sound, you can fairly easily take precautions to protect yourself against accusations of copyright piracy, as suggested above. The further a station moves in the direction of a plain, non-subscription music channel – and there are good financial incentives for doing that – the greyer the copyright issues become.

By contrast, the more speech content a web radio station's output contains, the more they need to consider the other legal and ethical issues which form the subject of the next chapter.

Further reading

Carter, M. E. (1996). *Electronic Highway Robbery: An Artist's Guide to Copyrights in the Digital Era*. Peachpit Press.

Creech, K. C. (1999). *Electronic Media Law and Regulation*. Focal Press.

Kohn, B. (1998). *A Primer on the Law of Webcasting and Digital Music Delivery*. Published at http://www.kohnmusic.com/articles/newprimer.html.

Law Research Website – http://www.lawresearch.com/v2/practice/ctcopy.htm.

Merriden, T. (2001). *Irresistible Forces: The Business Legacy of Napster and the Growth of the Underground Internet*. Capstone.

USA National Research Council (2000). *The Digital Dilemma: Intellectual Property in the Information Age*. National Academy Press.

9 Free speech on web radio

Where the previous chapter concerned itself chiefly with the musical side of web radio and the legalities of copyrights, this one focuses on the spoken word and the messages and information contained therein. (The message can, of course, also encompass song lyrics, banned in one country or another.) It may be easy to imagine – living in a liberal democratic country – that web radio stations have nothing to worry about in this regard. It is certainly a very much freer environment than terrestrial broadcasting, but the history of the mass media tells us that free speech is a not a right we can ever take for granted.

If copyright law is difficult to formulate and police on a global network, how much more complicated a matter is it for media regulators to apply their own internal broadcasting laws to this international soapbox? For, however else we describe it, anything that is printed, pictured or spoken on the World Wide Web is a form of publication by most legal definitions, and as such web radio streams and pages are already subject, in theory at least, to individual nations' laws and broadcasting regulations. The effectiveness of those laws and regulations in this new environment is just beginning to be tested in courtrooms around the world.

Sitting at home, listening to – or eavesdropping on, might be another way of putting it – a voice which is actually talking live to an audience in *their* homes or cars 10 000 miles away remains a fairly extraordinary thing to do. Or we might happen upon a lone voice from nowhere in particular which has decided to offer itself up exclusively to the world online. The extraordinariness by now lies less in the distances involved than the fact that we are hearing people speaking for themselves on their own terms from their own lives and thoughts. It is in the horizontal, phone-like nature of web radio. We are, after all, very likely to be familiar with musical sounds from most parts of the world by now, since they have become absorbed into the universal pulse of global entertainment, and those of us with TV are used to being armchair tourists to other people's countries and houses, carefully mediated and interpreted for us through the filters of our own national broadcasters.

We know too that radio is a powerfully intimate medium, in which the listener can have the simultaneous sensations of being talked to as a private individual but paradoxically also of sharing the experience with a very public audience (Hendy, 2000, p. 186). Governments have naturally always been sensitive to the broadcasters' power and have usually succeeded in exercising some control over the limits of what can be said on their nation's airwaves. But what happens to laws of defamation, privacy, incitement or official secrecy when the transmission is coming from another country?

Transnational broadcasting has, of course, been with us since the earliest days of radio. But the contents of long-standing 'external services' like Voice of America, the BBC's World Service, Radio France Internationale, Deutsche Welle or Radio China International have always been firmly under the control of their home governments and carefully calculated not to offend the broadcasting sensibilities of friendly nations. Hostile nations, especially during the Cold War, would often succeed in jamming incoming radio frequencies to prevent their own citizens from picking up overseas broadcasts. In more recent times, direct satellite transmission has further eroded national broadcasting boundaries and this time brought commercial corporations into negotiations with national governments over the rights to broadcast into their countries – though mainly on TV. However, the infrastructure of satellite TV is such that it is perfectly possible for governments to deny them licences (as, for example, China did to Rupert Murdoch's Star TV in 1993; see Herbert, 2001, p. 29). It is relatively easy to police the presence of satellite transmissions or the import of the necessary dishes and set-top decoders, but not so easy to stop imports of multimedia computers or trace all their connections to phone lines.

Thus, web radio is an altogether different proposition in the field of international media relations – apparently uncontrolled and in the hands of unlicensed, private individuals or else those influential licensed broadcasters who thrive on airing deliberately controversial, inflammatory or xenophobic opinion. To take a crude example, the verbal venom typically aired during a licensed phone-in show of a 'shock jock' like a G. Gordon Liddy or a Rush Limbaugh may be acceptable under US rights to freedom of speech, but it often goes beyond the legal constraints that apply to UK broadcasters, let alone those working under more restrictive regimes in countries whose citizens will, from time to time, (certainly) be the subject of deliberately offensive comments from the jock or one of his callers. (You can find the actual Rush Limbaugh radio shows on the Internet, but CBS have forbidden the rebroadcasting of Mr Liddy's on the Web.)

So, do presenters of a web radio station need to concern themselves (a) with their own national broadcasting laws and codes of conduct or (b) with any international agreements or attempts to regulate the Internet? Or, put the other way around, how far are national broadcasting controls being applied to web radio?

And running alongside those questions of strict legality are the wider considerations of personal ethics and the kind of reputation a station wants to acquire for itself. An absence of legal controls on published speech does not mean freedom from the consequences of speaking freely. Libertarians who oppose any attempt to regulate content on the Internet argue that a truly open communication system evolves its own mechanisms for dealing with those who abuse its power. So if a site gains notoriety for expressing offensive views it must expect to be vigorously challenged by those who oppose those views – and on an equal, unregulated footing. The history of the Internet already contains many examples of techniques for 'getting even' or challenging perceived misinformation. To mention two for the time being: concerted email campaigns are easy to initiate where a modest supporter base exists online and they may be used to clog and crash a targeted site or throw a spotlight on a dark corner of the Net; or any disgruntled individual can create a 'counter' website, give it a name very similar to yours and register it with the keywords to bring it up close to or next to your own on the major search engines. And, of course, there is no shortage of hackers on the Internet, capable of gaining access to even well-protected sites and modifying their pages. Precisely as long as the Internet remains such a horizontal medium, the argument goes, it can be used to mobilize opposition or support far more widely, directly and immediately than could any of its predecessors – whether that opposition or support is directed at a lone maverick, a rogue company, a global corporation or a government. The advocates of this 'wild frontier' attitude to life on the Internet argue that it makes it the first truly democratic medium – for those who have access to it (see, among many examples, international campaigns like the Electronic Frontier Foundation at http://www.eff.org/ and their web radio page at http://www.eff.org/radioeff/). The implications of 'free speech', then, need to be considered in tandem with questions of the regulation of content on web radio in this chapter.

Reasons for regulating radio

The kinds of regulation that have been applied to terrestrial radio can be categorized broadly as follows:

- Regulations about ownership and control – both within the national radio industry and across the other mass media, print and TV.
- Regulations setting conditions on licences to broadcast – technical questions about frequencies, the power of transmitters, etc. and terms of the licence, such as the application/bidding procedure and the length of tenure of the licence.

- Laws of the land that apply to what may and may not be published in any public medium – laws like defamation, obscenity, incitement, contempt of court, official secrecy and copyright (though these may be interpreted differently as between print and electronic media).
- Regulations that are specific to the content of broadcasting – matters of impartiality and balance in news reporting, special conditions of the coverage of elections, taste and decency, fair treatment and other things under the banner of broadcasting standards.

Each category has been treated differently in different countries according to their own long-standing constitutions and the policies of successive governments which more easily adapt with the times. How do these categories apply to web radio and how far should stations take note of them?

Ownership and control

In Chapter 1 we looked back to the heady days of the 1920s, when radio seemed to promise so much as a force for democracy, enlightenment and equality between peoples. Hidden not far beneath that idealistic optimism though was the anxiety that, in the 'wrong' hands, such a powerful mass communication technology could equally be used as an agency of oppression, disinformation and divisiveness. Very quickly, two fundamentally opposite views emerged as to how to regulate against radio falling into the 'wrong' hands, one on each side of the Atlantic. Put simply, the European way was to keep radio out of irresponsible, self-interested private hands, while the American way was to keep it out of irresponsible, self-interested government hands. The ideological foundations of these strategies run very deeply indeed and, although both approaches to regulation have been modified by the experiences of the Broadcast Century, they remain much in evidence today. It turns out that the major weaknesses in both models, as far as the listener is concerned, appear when either allows too much media control to fall into the hands of too few individuals. The content of programmes and the diversity of views presented can be curtailed equally effectively by heads of governments for political reasons or by heads of dominant private corporations for commercial reasons.

Such are the characteristics of the vertical broadcast technologies. But on the multichannel Internet, centralization of power is by definition much more difficult in practice. This is not to suggest that governments – especially authoritarian governments – would not feel much more comfortable with more say about ownership and control, nor that old and new media corporations are not busily working to win dominance and profitability on the Net. These are long-term considerations which web radio strategists need to keep in sight. Some stations today have problems with their national governments, as I discuss later in the chapter, and there's a big financial question mark over the commercial profitability of many web stations, but for the most part web radio is not yet subject to any rules of ownership nationally or at any other level.

Licensing

Happily, no-one needs a government licence or permit to run a web radio station. This means the content of web radio stations is not bound by the legal terms and conditions operated by any broadcast licensing authority, such as the Radio Authority in the UK or the FCC in the US. The threat of suspension or permanent withdrawal of licences is one of *the* major sanctions that ensures terrestrial stations keep within the rules that specifically govern broadcast content, so the absence of licences effectively frees web radio from a whole range of legal restrictions on content (see 'Regulations specific to the content of broadcasting' below).

There remains, though, a potentially significant grey area. Can web content published under the company banner by an existing broadcaster infringe the terms of their terrestrial licence? I am not aware that we have an answer to that right now. We do know, though, that this is likely to be a temporary loophole – if indeed it is a loophole. Many governments are in the process of re-framing their broadcasting laws to fit the new ICT environment. The UK government, for example, signalled some medium-term intent on this kind of crossover in their 2000 White Paper, *A New Future for Communications*. Talking about existing licensing arrangements under the heading 'Broadcast material on the Internet and via telephony' it briefly says:

> 'Aside from basic laws and the current good practices of self-regulation, which will of course continue, we would expect to see public service broadcasters applying the same high standards and high quality in their services on the Internet and via telephony as they do on their traditional broadcast businesses. The BBC's high quality and distinctive Online service, which enjoys page impressions of around 200 million a month, is an excellent example.'
>
> (Department of Trade and Industry/Department of Culture, Media and Sport, 2000, p. 56)

The next two of our four categories of regulation do apply, at least in part, to web radio stations. As with copyright, it is for the station to assess its own particular situation and decide how it intends to comply with its national regulations in these areas, but it is essential for all involved to find out where they stand in relation to their country's law. And as with the previous chapter, the guidance here is not intended to be comprehensive nor could it be in any way legally watertight: it is meant as a checklist of the kind of things to take into consideration.

Laws of the land that apply to all published materials

After a period of some uncertainty, governments, the courts and the police across Europe and the US, and doubtless elsewhere, are beginning to demonstrate that the Internet is not beyond criminal or civil law – as perhaps appeared to be the case before around 1998. Chapter 8 noted how the US in particular is moving against companies who provide the means for the evasion of copyright. As I write, the (civil) legal case against Napster is being won in the courts by the RIAA, though in the longer term it is not clear how many more distributors of similar MP3 file-sharing software could in practice be dragged through the same lengthy legal process. That said, any such company (or perhaps eventually private individual) who has to defend this kind of civil case had better be ready to bear some hefty legal expenses.

A recent UK court case has created a landmark ruling which simultaneously shows that civil laws of defamation and the criminal law of contempt of court can be enforced on the Web. There are a number of aspects of the case of 'Totalise plc v. Motley Fool Ltd and Another' that anyone involved in webcasting should take careful note of (see Box 9.1).

Box 9.1 'Totalise plc v. Motley Fool Ltd and Another', outlined in *The Times* Law Report, 15 March 2001

Totalise is a UK ISP which claimed that it had been repeatedly defamed by an anonymous person who used the name Zeddust on discussion boards hosted by Motley Fool and Interactive Investor. In order to bring a libel action against that person, Totalise brought its case against Motley Fool and Interactive Investor to see whether the courts could force them to disclose information that could identify Zeddust. The defendants argued that they did not exercise any control over the words other people posted on their sites and therefore were not liable for them. They also argued that they had undertaken on their sites to protect the privacy of contributors within the terms of the law as they understood it. The court ruled that the defendants must disclose what they knew of the identity of Zeddust, otherwise anyone could use such sites to defame with impunity. At the time of writing, the consequent libel case has not yet reached the courts.

For publishers of online content, the ruling in this case means that in the UK:

- You are legally responsible for anything posted anywhere on your website, whether by you or a third party, which includes the contents of a chat room or bulletin board or, presumably, their audio equivalent, such as a publicly accessible voice message or phone-in comment.
- As an operator of a website which hosts a chat room or bulletin board, you cannot protect the identity of contributors whose remarks are potentially defamatory – you can be forced by the courts to reveal any information by which they may be traced or else face criminal prosecution. In other words, if you do not exercise editorial control over content, you cannot claim the customary protection given to newspapers (and broadcasters) under the UK's Contempt of Court Act to protect the sources of their information.
- The case confirms that a civil case of defamation can be pursued anywhere on the Web – which of course includes web radio.
- These rules can be applied across national borders. Motley Fool is, by definition, a worldwide site, but its US owners decided to defend the action in a UK court to protect their own viability within this country – and lost. So they have the choice of complying with the order or facing sanctions within the UK. Exactly what those sanctions might be is an open question for now.

We should remember, though, that bringing civil defamation cases is a very expensive business, well beyond the means of most private individuals. Thus, a small webcaster would have difficulty using the libel laws to protect the good name of their own operation from a campaign to undermine its reputation.

The high-profile cases of international co-operation to crack down on other illegal activities on the Internet, such as fraud, malicious hacking, conspiracy to commit crimes and pornographic abuses against children, are directed at very different uses of the technology than web radio. However, they illustrate two important points that are applicable right across the Net.

One is that the clandestine operator of even the smallest web station should not reckon either on being untraceable or, however small their niche audience, that they are immune from laws that apply to any other publication in their country. Similarly, the precedent is being established that ISPs can be held responsible for illegal content which reaches their clients, as for example demonstrated when the Bavarian regional government succeeded in forcing German CompuServe to impose restrictions on certain sources of illegal content in 1998 (Gold, 2001). So an ISP might, for example, be served with injunctions to block or report a webcast originating from a particular IP address (see Box 9.2). The exercise of laws relating to content is far less automatic than terrestrial broadcasters have been used to. On the Web, it is more a case of who notices and then takes exception to the illegal content. So the more successful you are at projecting your controversial message to the world on the Web, the higher the risk those you offend will try to initiate some form of court action to stop you. Hence the importance of not discounting the possibility, even though web radio stations have so far not been the subject of such legal action.

The second consequence of legislation beginning to catch up with the Internet is precisely that the focus is on activities which are internationally recognized as illegal – as opposed to trying to impose national broadcasting regulations on the Web. In this sense, the signs are that web radio will, for the time being, remain a much less restricted environment than terrestrial radio – at least in Western democratic states. Therefore, web stations will be treated more like magazines and newspapers than broadcasters. So, for example, the UK government's recent White Paper, *The New Future for Communications*, has a revealing section on how its proposed new regulator OFCOM (the Office of Communications, possible successor to the Radio Authority, among others) will deal with Internet content. Section 6.10 in the chapter on 'Safeguarding the interests of citizens' acknowledges that the Internet content cannot be regulated in the same way as terrestrial broadcasting has been. Instead, their policy is to rely on a watchdog, the Internet Watch Foundation (IWF; see Box 9.2) to collect evidence of illegal activities on the Net, and on voluntary actions by users to filter undesirable content:

> 'The Government sees enormous benefits on promoting new media, especially the Internet. But it is important that there are effective ways of tackling illegal material on the Internet and that users are aware of the tools available, such as rating and filtering systems, that will help them control what they and their children will see on the Internet. Research suggests that this is what people want in relation to the Internet, rather than third party regulation.'
>
> (p. 67)

Note the use of the words '*see* on the Internet': there's nothing in this section about hearing, because it is explicitly aimed at allaying well-publicized fears about unwanted access to pornographic images and text-based messaging.

Box 9.2   The ISPA and the IWF

The drift of the approach being taken, for example in the UK, suggests two latent subdivisions amongst the users of the Web. On the one hand, there are the 'respectable' users – perhaps the majority – who want to be protected from some types of content and, on the other, there are those who don't, who want access to the Web uncensored. In response, the ISP industry in the UK has set up its own voluntary association, the ISPA, and published a set of guidelines by which its members agree to be bound (http://www.ispa.org.uk/html/code_of_practice.htm). Most of the code of practice refers to fair trading with customers and abiding by them is a condition of membership of the ISPA. Section 7, though, contains *recommended* best practice and abiding by these guidelines is voluntary. Among them are the following:

> '7.2   Members should provide guidance to Customers about the availability of tools which may assist them in filtering content which Customers deem unsuitable ("Filtering Software").
>
> 7.8   Members should include on their websites the ISPA logo, with a link to the ISPA website.
>
> 7.9   Members should include on their websites the IWF logo, with a link to the IWF website.
>
> 7.10 Members should develop an Acceptable Use Policy and require their Customers to adhere to it.'

(The IWF website at http://www.iwf.org.uk/ makes clear that they see their main role as monitoring the Web for evidence relating to child sex abuse.)

The fact that compliance with these four guidelines is optional suggests that, while the ISPA is keen to maximize membership, it is also aware that a sizeable section of their client market would seek alternative ISPs which reject this kind of control and surveillance over the content that passes through their servers.

The US equivalent body to the ISPA is the US Internet Industry Association (http://www.usiia.org/).

Why is all this relevant to web radio? Well, consider the situation in which a web station wanted to organize a serious debate about what might be done about child pornography on the Web – as many a terrestrial current affairs broadcast has done before now. Part of the programme invites email or phone-in contributions from listeners. However innocent the intentions of the programme producer, the situation could easily become complicated for them. They should certainly seek legal advice before going ahead, rather than imagining that, because this is the Internet, the discussion in the studio could automatically be more open or the editorial control less cautious than would be the case for their terrestrial cousins. In this particular instance, as illustrated above, pre-publicity for such a debate on a website could trigger automated surveillance in response to key text words, and contributions which might be interpreted as promoting exploitative images of children in some way might legally result in the station being asked by police to reveal the IP addresses of contributors from its server log.

Regulations specific to the content of broadcasting

Programme makers on a terrestrial station know more clearly where they stand on sensitive or controversial subject matter, because the codes of practice they have to observe as a condition of their licence tell them quite precisely about their editorial responsibilities (plus they would usually have access to a legal department, steeped in well-established media law). In the UK, for example, all terrestrial radio broadcasters are bound either by the BBC's copious Producers Guidelines (which can be found at http://www.bbc.co.uk/info/editorial/prodgl/index.shtml) or by the Radio Authority Programme Codes: 1 covers 'Violence, Sex, Taste and Decency, Children and Young People, Appeals for Donations, Religious and Other Matters'; 2 covers 'News Programmes and Coverage of Matters of Political or Industrial Controversy or Relating to Current Public Policy' (http://www.radioauthority.org.uk/Information/Publications/index.html). These codes incorporate conditions laid down in the 1990 Broadcasting Act which specifically govern broadcasting, as opposed to any other area of public entertainment or publishing. So section 90 of the Act includes, among others, particular obligations not to 'offend good taste and decency' and to present all news with 'due accuracy and impartiality'. The US equivalent, the legally binding Fairness Doctrine, was repealed in 1987 (Douglas, 1987, pp. 298–300).

No such obligations or regulations apply to web radio originating or being received in the UK. So a web station may decide to ignore them completely. As the new Communications White Paper says, the government do not favour third party regulation of Internet content – other than for that which is illegal beyond the world of public broadcasting. It is important to register and understand this distinction. Other national governments take different views on the freedoms of the broadcaster (see, for example, Herbert, 2001, Chapter 4; Hilliard and Keith, 1996, Chapter 6). We will return to how effective they can be at blocking Internet transmissions later in the chapter.

On the other hand, such codes and regulations do stem from real ethical questions about broadcasting in the public arena, which we enter into every time we make a piece of radio available on air. As such, they provide a useful starting point for the first-time webcaster. Whether the audience is large or small, programme makers do not know exactly who may be listening. They may decide to select against a particular audience simply by the station's content, but that choice does not make those social and ethical considerations disappear. One rather narrow view of the Internet is that it transfers editorial responsibility from the producer to the audience. Well, yes, this is certainly much more true of the Internet than any previous mass medium, but if we take that idea too far down the road of 'If you don't like it, go somewhere else', we eventually negate the very point of making radio and return to something which more resembles a private phone call. Making radio is a social activity which only comes into being when it has an audience. Otherwise, there's little point in going to the expense of streaming. So although we are truly in the realm of self-regulation here, in this next section we need to consider the kind of ethical questions that bind a web station into a social relationship and determine its reputation.

Problem areas

Thus far then, the content of web radio remains relatively free from official interference – apart from the exceptions I have indicated above, which arise from generally applicable 'laws of the land', not specifically media law. It is certainly more free than terrestrial radio. The relationship between listener and producer is self-regulated, on both sides. As well as having a liberating effect, this simultaneously returns us to the potential problems associated with the power of radio. In a sense, whether or not they realize it, listener and programme maker are back at ground zero: they have to 'sound out' a new relationship to one another. Should the listener trust what the web presenter has to say more or less than they did on regulated, institutionalized terrestrial radio? What should the presenter assume or presume of the listener?

For a large internationally established radio brand like the BBC, the groundwork has already been done; its reputation has been cemented by its long history as a terrestrial broadcaster. At the opposite end of the spectrum, the micro webcaster is both absolutely free from preconceptions but also needs to establish a reputation and a relationship with an audience.

To help the process of starting to think about the web radio producer's responsibilities, I'll refer back to the major areas regulators have typically identified as problems through the Broadcast Century.

News and factual programming

More or less centrally controlled in authoritarian states and elsewhere during times of war. In liberal democracies, the emphasis is towards regulating for accurate reporting and a balanced representation of opinion and party political views. On web radio there are no such obligations. However, the competition in reputation as a 'trusted source' is dominated by some very well-established, well-resourced international players. The choices for news editors on a small, self-regulating web radio station are either to win reputation for accurately, ethically presenting alternative angles and stories within a mainstream news agenda or to specialize outside the mainstream in under-reported, geographically or culturally specific areas. In news, of course, accuracy and reliability are what create reputations.

Expression of political opinion

Officially forbidden or else unofficially inadvisable in some states. Web radio has much more distinctive scope in this area, a continuation in fact of the long tradition of analogue radio being used as a tool of underground resistance against oppressive regimes. This, of course, can cut both ways and equally provide a flow of propaganda against enlightened government. Broadcast regulations in democratic states promote neutrality between the main political parties. Again, web radio can make its own editorial decisions about and, for example, represent a deliberate bias in favour of views it believes are excluded from a consensual news agenda.

State secrecy and freedom of information

A routine area of conflict between news reporters and government officials, yet it has often gone unnoticed by countries' citizens. The Internet has proved a powerful mechanism in helping to erode state secrecy in many important areas, because it makes information that is available under regimes with effective freedom of information policies available across the online world. Web radio is ideally placed to exploit this mechanism for importing a wealth of knowledge and insight into more restrictive jurisdictions from those that are more open. However, publishing your own state's secrets on the Web when they are not available elsewhere remains one of those illegal activities that is very likely to be of particular interest to your country's security services.

Religious and cultural difference

An extremely sensitive area for anyone working in a public medium, which really highlights the question of individual ethical responsibility in the media. We should remind ourselves often that radio has proved to be a particularly effective tool for inflaming lethal hostility towards minority groups, from 1930s Europe to 1990s Rwanda (see Kellow and Steeves, 1998; Hendy, 2000, pp. 200–214). Most states today have general laws against incitement to racial or religious hatred and, to varying degrees, against discrimination on those grounds. But it is within and through the mass media that 'difference' can be so powerfully magnified. Web radio can have an important role here. For one thing, it can help remove some of the obstacles to minority groups gaining access to and representation within the public media (see Chapter 11). For another, it means they can do this without observing regulatory obligations to balance their own perspective against that of the majority population. That said, such a web station faces an ethical choice: whether to adopt a policy of openness and inclusiveness towards wider audiences or to become exclusive in the way they address their particular audience and thus distinctly separate. As ever, it can be a short step from identifying strongly with a niche audience and expressing hostility to another religious or cultural group. At the extreme, that free expression can turn into criminal incitement to hatred, which is another of the Internet activities courts have shown their willingness to block or prosecute, for example in relation to Nazi literature in Germany and France. (For example, the well-publicized block on web pages from a Canadian neo-Nazi by the German ISP T Online in January 1996.)

Contempt of court

The rules surrounding court proceedings differ from country to country and, so far as the media are concerned, have traditionally only been applicable within national boundaries. In practice, this probably remains the case, but the Internet poses very real problems in this important area of law. In the vast majority of cases, it is unlikely that a small webcast with a small audience would be seen as prejudicing the outcome of a trial. (The ethical reasons for doing so are another matter.) But if, for example, a web reporter managed to get an interview with a key witness about an exceptionally high-profile case, transmitting it during the trial would be serious contempt of court in many countries, though not in others. So the technicalities of the relevant national law cannot safely be ignored by any web station which intends reporting or campaigning in any area of a criminal justice system.

Taste, decency and exploitation

Traditionally, this area of regulation, as it's applied to radio, has been to control swearing, sexually explicit talk and sounds or the occasional particularly vivid representation of extreme violence. Such broadcasting regulations do not apply to web radio – though, of course, incitement to commit illegal acts remains a criminal offence in most countries, as noted previously. So here the question is purely what sort of audience you are playing to and what kind of reputation you want your station to have – and with listeners in which parts of the world.

Defamation

In territories with strong defamation laws, this can potentially be a danger area, though there are also signs that the Internet is eroding its force. In a country like the UK, where the threat of libel action is ever-present for broadcasters and newspaper editors, there are some important risk factors to note. Firstly, there are plenty of overtly libellous websites out there, evidence that there is less of a risk of legal action than through an offline publication. Secondly, it depends who you are libelling: some public figures are more ready and able to go to court than others. Thirdly, a libel on web radio is more likely to pass unnoticed than in text on the Internet, unless it is archived, repeated persistently or reaches a significant audience – as, for example, at a well-publicized live event with a 'star' presence.

Privacy and fair treatment

Again, different countries exercise different kinds of regulation over the way broadcasters and the press can report on their citizens' private lives. For example, while the UK has very strict defamation law, it has no legal privacy regulation, although for licensed broadcasters independent adjudication of complaints about fair treatment (by the Broadcasting Standards Council) does form part of the conditions of their licence. Neighbouring France, on the other hand, does have a legal statute to protect its people from media intrusion into their private lives. However, the recent incorporation of European Union Human Rights legislation into domestic law has opened the door for people in the UK and the other member states to bring civil cases to stop unwanted press intrusion. At the same time, though, we have a fairly potent counter-current of gossip on the Web. It is too early to say which will gain the upper hand in web radio practice. So while the situation under this heading remains unclear, it is as well to know whether there is a privacy law in your home country and also to take note of the same risk factors as I've suggested under defamation above.

Advertising/promotion

Conditions about advertising and promotion often form part of terrestrial broadcast licences, but no such controls apply for web radio. It is entirely for the station to decide which products and firms, if any, it wants to associate itself with and in what ways. These associations can be a potent part of the mix that creates a site's reputation.

Data protection

Whichever server is running your streams has the potential to collect very detailed information about your audience, such as IP addresses, post codes, email addresses, even credit card numbers. This opens a whole Pandora's Box which may contain unfamiliar legal and ethical issues, even for the experienced terrestrial broadcaster. These are not issues you can ignore online. They overlap with technical questions of server security on the Internet (see Chapter 4 and http://www.w3.org/Security/). Many countries now have Data Protection laws which are formed around common sense ethical principles. One is that if I give you information about myself, for one purpose I am not thereby giving you permission to use it for any other purpose. The second is that I have a right to know precisely what data you are storing about me. (For more information about the UK's strong Data Protection law, see 'Data Controller's Brief Guide' at http://wood.ccta.gov.uk/dpr/dpdoc.nsf. For the US voluntary guidelines, see http://www.usiia.org/legis/privacy.html and the recently passed US Consumer Internet Privacy Enhancement Act.) To take an obvious example, a collection of email addresses of listeners who have entered a particular online competition is a valuable commodity which might be sold for a good price to an online marketing company. Direct marketing is seen as the advertisers' most powerful tool and it requires detailed knowledge of individuals' lifestyle preferences. Alternatively, a third party might be willing to pay for the list of your listeners' IP numbers if they know how to trace them and convert them to saleable lists of names and addresses. Selling such information is not usually, in itself, illegal, but under the UK Data Protection Act the first step, passing on any data about someone without their permission, is. This is another area where legislation is running to keep up with the technology. From an ethical standpoint, the important basics to remember are:

- if you are collecting and storing any metrics data, convert it quickly and directly into the anonymous statistics it's supposed to provide, like audience numbers, and then delete the raw data;
- treat any raw IP data as confidential – never leave lists lying around in hard copy or on unprotected computer terminals and certainly don't be tempted yourself to pass it on;
- treat any email addresses you receive with respect, which means letting senders know in advance if you intend to keep them on a database for your own future use, telling them if you have a policy of selling or passing on email addresses and giving them the option in advance to say no;
- store as little personal information as you can;
- take full responsibility for protecting any personal information you do gather from listeners by installing relevant encrypting security software and firewalls to stop anyone else getting into your server online and copying from it.

In any area of the Internet, data protection is a minefield. From a legal and a reputation point of view, it is your responsibility to take active measures to protect client information. Any web users worried about the implications of their online connections can find software which claims to make IP numbers harder to trace (see http://www.freedom.net/).

Zoning and filtering

Technical solutions are being evolved month by month with the aim of making the Web a safer place for those users who are worried by its anarchic tendencies. For web radio, three technical fixes are worth mentioning here because of their possible longer term effects on web radio.

At the server end, it is possible to control who receives your output, if you decide you don't want to expose it to the whole online world. For large institutions who want to run an internal web radio station for the benefit of their members, there is the option, mentioned in Chapter 4, of making transmissions available only on their own *intra*net. An extension of a similar principle, but applied to the Internet as a whole, is known as 'zoning'. It is possible to organize this yourself by establishing a geographically dispersed network of relay servers, which receive the original transmission and retransmit it only to registered receivers. However, zoning is also now much discussed on the Net as a controversial future mechanism for regulating or corralling Web content into controllable categories and creating zones of access to them. Each zone could then, for example, form the basis of subscription-only access. Watch this space for developments which may affect the distribution of web radio.

Downstream at the consumer end of the Internet, as mentioned in the earlier quote from the UK government's Communications White Paper (see p. 185), is an increasing array of filtering software: the personalized equivalent of signal jamming. Different filtering software works in different ways, but broadly speaking this is either blocking named sites or by detecting particular key words, phrases or combinations of words and images – especially those which suggest 'adult' content. Either can be quite a blunt instrument as far as the innocent author of web text or moderator of a chat room/bulletin board is concerned (see, for example, http://www.we-blocker.com/). The only reason for mentioning filtering in relation to web radio is that it may influence a station's use of text language on its website. The available choices, then, are: deliberately to select for the kinds of phrases guaranteed to trigger widely used filters, and thereby exclude the station from young or sensitive audiences; or to take care not to place too many trigger words on the site; or else to ignore the whole filtering audience because it's too difficult to second guess what the triggers might be. Similarly, a site which gets a reputation for explicit talk on air can quickly be added to lists of 'unsuitable' sites. It is for the station to decide whether this suits their aims or not.

Horizontal media and centralized control

As noted earlier in the chapter (see 'Ownership and control' section), restrictions on the independence of the public media and the diversity of voices and opinion heard thereon can equally be imposed in law by government edict or de facto by commercial imperatives. The characteristic in either regime is towards a small collection of media organizations with large, vertical structures headed by a handful of controlling individuals. So the process of regulating the Internet, whether to make it 'safe' for Commerce or for Society, can be seen as necessarily changing its character away from the confusing horizontal medium it is today and towards the more orderly, vertical organization we recognize in today's traditional media. Of course, we have been in this position before, in the earliest days of radio before national or commercial ownership models established it as the predominantly vertical broadcast medium it has become. We in the politically stable West perhaps need to remind ourselves of the value of having a horizontal mass medium when we contemplate repeating the exercise.

Radio B92 has become something of a *cause célèbre* in the recent history of radio being used to combat oppression. It demonstrates, as has often been demonstrated before, that it is very easy to close down vertical broadcasters, by law or by force. There are obvious targets, such as transmitter sites and broadcast studios. But, more important, it shows how horizontal media, where the routes to air are diffuse and lack obvious centres, are much harder to close down – at least in the short term.

Case study: Radio B92, Belgrade

Radio B92 was an independent station, licensed in Belgrade from 1989, which broadcast a mix of urban pop music, irreverent humour, non-partisan news and a certain good-natured, defiant attitude towards the totalitarian regime of President Milosevic. The station's studio and transmitter were threatened or physically closed down on a regular basis, only to be allowed back on air when public demonstrations attracted the attention of international governments. While B92 increasingly became a focus of opposition to the regime, it was also useful for Milosevic to be able to point to this 'free' and 'independent' media as a token of his 'democratic' republic.

When the plug was pulled on the transmitter yet again on 3 December 1996, B92 staff were able to switch their broadcast onto a newly available piece of software called RealAudio. Their signal, travelling via an ISP in Amsterdam (xs4all.com), now became available all over the world. It was quickly picked up by the BBC in London and beamed via satellite back into Yugoslavia, where small radio stations around the whole country began picking up the satellite signal and rebroadcasting it on low powered local analogue transmitters. So the net effect of the closure of a local Belgrade station at the end of 1996 was to precipitate a national independent radio network, which 6 months later comprised more than 30 stations. The network become known as the Association of Independent Electronic Media (ANEM). A further cautionary lesson was to follow. The Yugoslav authorities closed the B92 studio once more, as NATO began its bombing campaign against Belgrade, and then reopened the B92 website, sounding very much like the original station but with their own people behind the microphones. When news of the deception got out, a new website was established in Amsterdam with the name helpB92.com. It now carried at the top of its front page the slogan, 'Don't believe anyone, not even us'. Having played its important, perhaps vital, role in the overthrow of the Milosevic dictatorship, the station changed its URL once again to http://www.freeB92.net/, which is where you can hear B92 in RealAudio back on air in Belgrade. The site has a very large text archive of its eventful history.

Sources: Veran Matic and Drazen Pantic article, 'War of words. When the bombs came Serbia's B92 hit the Net'; Matthew Collin (2001); the freeB92 website.

Summary – is freedom of speech safe on web radio?

For the time being and for the most part, yes it is, compared to the vast majority of radio broadcasting. And that is an important, though volatile, asset. The influence of the First Amendment of the American Constitution has some leverage on the culture of the Internet here.

However, it is important for a station to keep itself well informed about how its own national jurisdiction is applying its national laws on the Internet. The signs are that the pressures to regulate in some areas and in some form are increasing. Web radio is certainly not in the immediate front line in this regard. But that does not mean it has no role to play in the arguments. In his impressive book, *Code and Other Laws of Cyberspace*, Lawrence Lessig (1999) warns that we cannot take the freedoms of the Internet for granted. There is nothing automatic, he says, about the technology ultimately defying regulation. Quite the reverse. New software codes continue to be devised which make surveillance of traffic on the Web ever more powerful. On this basis, he argues passionately against the widespread libertarian philosophy of the Internet and for a framework of regulation to put the use of such code firmly into democratically accountable hands. Otherwise, he argues, the Internet could be killed off as a medium of free expression and become instead a tool of oppressive surveillance.

In this context, it is important for web radio practitioners to demonstrate that their technology is being used to some overall ethically constructive purpose. This is not an argument for censorship or self-censorship of free speech. It is to say though that, because of its apparent freedoms, web radio must guard itself against becoming merely a playground for the aimless and irresponsible (though they will surely be a part of it). Freedom of speech is not the same as freedom from the consequences of how we use or abuse it.

Further reading

Braithwaite, N. (ed.) (1996). *The International Libel Handbook. A Practical Guide for Journalists*. Butterworth-Heinemann.

Collin, M. (2001). *This Is Serbia Calling*. Serpent's Tail.

Creech, K. C. (1999). *Electronic Media Law and Regulation*. Focal Press.

Data Controller's Brief Guide – http://wood.ccta.gov.uk/dpr/dpdoc.nsf.

Departments of Trade and Industry/Culture, Media and Sport (2000). *A New Future for Communication*. London: The Stationary Office Limited (online at http://www.communicationswhitepaper.gov.uk/).

Frost, C. (2000). *Media Ethics and Self-Regulation*. Longman.

Hendy, D. (2000). Culture. In *Radio in the Global Age*, Chapter 5. Polity Press.

Herbert, J. C. (2001). *Practising Global Journalism*. Focal Press.

Lessig, L. (1999). *Code and Other Laws of Cyberspace*. Basic Books. Plus Lessig's website – http://cyberlaw.stanford.edu/lessig/content/index.html.

McQuail, D. and Siune, K. (eds) (1998). *Media Policy. Convergence, Concentration & Commerce*. London: Sage.

The World Wide Web Foundation – http://www.w3.org/Security/.

10 Redefining radio content

Having considered the technical, legal and ethical considerations thrown up by web radio, I move on in the next two chapters to look at their implications for what we can hear on web radio: the nature of the content of programmes; the organization of programmes into schedules; and the part the audience plays in this dynamic. This book has shown already, I think, that web radio is something other than merely another distribution mechanism for radio. Yes, we can hear the same programmes through both terrestrial and Internet receivers, but web radio also allows us to tune in to a great quantity of other listening if we want it. But what precisely does or can the programme maker do to create web offerings that are different to terrestrial radio? I am returning then to the two questions posed early in Chapter 1: 'What new strengths does web radio add to pre-Internet radio?' and 'What established strengths of radio does web radio supplant?'

We know from the history of radio that questions of what to put into a programme, how to schedule it in relation to others and how both communicate with a listening audience – or not – are all intimately intertwined. As Hendy (2000) points out in his introduction to *Radio in the Global Age*:

> 'No one aspect of radio can be fully understood without some reference to three interrelated aspects of the medium: first, the ways in which it is produced, secondly the form and content of its programming . . .and thirdly the interpretations and reactions of its consumers, the listeners.'
>
> (p. 7)

Accepting that those relationships are dynamic and not frozen, in this chapter I intend to focus on the nature of the content. Or I should say the possibilities in the content as they are apparent at the moment. We must, of course, keep reminding ourselves that web radio is in its infancy: we don't know what it's going to turn into or quite whether it will survive as a medium we recognize as radio at all. That will depend on how the new makers of web radio decide to use its freedoms and how the listeners will choose to use it.

The ingredients that go into creating radio content can be grouped into the following loose categories, admitting again that they overlap:

● Music presentation radio.
● Factual speech radio, including news, current affairs, educational pro-grammes and sports coverage.
● Audience participation speech radio, including talk radio formats.
● Non-factual speech radio, including comedy and drama.
● Radio experiments, which have been tried by programme makers from time to time to test the boundaries of what radio can do.

I have listed these roughly in descending order of the proportion of total global radio output they presently represent – judging by the kind of semi-systematic search of stations around the world the Web now makes available. These loose categories provide the framework for the chapter.

Chapter 1 pointed out how today's conception of what web radio content can be tends to be framed in thinking distilled from lessons of the Broadcast Century – with its own particular history of the relationships between media and the societies they serve. The majority of web radio transmissions are either simulcasts of terrestrial radio broadcasts or else variations on the American model of format music radio. They are looking for the business model that can repeat that commercial success story on the Internet. Does web radio have any more to offer its users than this duplication?

In suggesting the approaches web radio practitioners might take towards the categories of content below, I am acutely aware of how little we yet know about each of them in this new context and how much research and experiment needs to be done in it. To make the content that works for web radio, we must understand more about narrow-casting and indeed about what studying this offspring of broadcast radio can tell us about the parent(s). Just as in the early infancy of radio, there was nothing automatic about the directions in which it developed: real people had to keep coming up with the ideas of what to put into the ether: day after day, year upon year.

Music presentation on web radio

Chapters 2 and 8 have looked at radio's relationship with the music industry in some detail already. But as web radio and much of its content are poised at the moment, I don't think the importance of this relationship can be over-emphasized. This is where the economic spotlight is shining, at least in affluent countries, where the Internet is most used and music sales are highest. Much fascinating data are already being collected and interpreted by the US audience research specialists, Arbitron, Edison Media, Jupiter, Nielsen, recently Measure-Cast and doubtless many others. Where is the commercial model of web distribution that will work for both parties? No answer has emerged in the short term, but we can be certain that the search will continue to be backed by huge financial investments.

So far as the musical content of web radio is concerned, the lessons that seem to be emerging for the radio industry as a whole are:

1 That the radio industry has almost perfected the fully automated music channel as the most efficient means of playing music to an international public, 24 hours a day, 365 days a year. The economics of this are compelling. After a modest capital investment in reliable hardware and software, a single station can serve any definable musical taste, based on instantaneous, invisible and 100 per cent accurate audience research using server logs (e.g. which tracks or combinations of tracks make more listeners tune out, which rotations result in better sales). Technical and support staff costs are modest and the equivalent of 'on-air' staff costs can be confined to a single playlist programmer. Voice-overs and on-air ads are optional. The main ongoing costs are in marketing the station. With the right 'click-through' deal with a retailer for downloads or hard copies, over time the company should be able to show a healthy profit. Better still, they can work more closely with the major record labels to minimize royalty fees, on the basis that the station can demonstrate their role as a branch of retail as well as of entertainment.

2 That this music channel model can be applied to any analogue or digital radio platform, in principle, if local regulation permits. And mobile Internet technology can now link any radio platform directly into sales with click-through links. However, of all platforms this is a concept particularly suited to the Web, because of its global audience and the accuracy of the metrics from end to end of the listener to sales chain. Whether the streams are technically live rotations or archived rotations is immaterial to the listener, though in practice the copyright rules indicate that on-demand music channels are more likely to be pushed towards becoming subscription channels if the music they carry is mainstream.

As I have said, I classify the music channel as being on the margins of web radio, overlapping more fully with music sales than radio has done before. This is emphatically not to say it will be marginal in any other sense: the investments of the record companies in web distribution/promotion tell us that much. And the same technology has made it possible for non-commercial sites to bring minority music services to new audiences online while keeping their running costs manageable. The question that follows though is: where does the growth of the music channel leave the rest of us – in web radio or indeed any other form of radio – who regard the medium, including music radio, as a form of human communication?

The – as yet – unknown factor in this equation is how the majority of radio audiences will respond over time. How many will prefer music channels over presenter-led music radio? Did listeners, all along, really only want radio as a means of hearing their favourite music, uninterrupted by DJs' chatter ('more rap less chat', as one UK commercial station used to put it) or low budget local advertising?

The evidence from the terrestrial, DJ-orientated music stations simulcasting on the Web is perhaps comforting for radio practitioners for now. For one thing, many simulcasts have become popular over the Web for listeners within and beyond stations' transmission ranges (as any month's figures from Measure-Cast at http://www.measurecast.com/ will show). For another, we have the invention of the side channel – the radio content additional to the terrestrial broadcast that is only available from the website either on a live or archive stream. Whether or not these side channels are offered alongside or instead of the simulcast, the important thing is the difference in what they have to offer. This may include in-depth interviews with artists about their music and/or latest release, news features from the worlds of music or entertainment, DJs' audio diaries, spot the voice or other aural competitions: typically speech-based items that don't fit into the station's routine schedule because they would hold up the music flow and hence create 'tune out' points. In other words, side channels can increase the total of speech content that's available on free to air music radio *for those who want it*. The two can coexist, serving the same audience in two ways instead of one, without jeopardizing the headline broadcast listening figures.

This looks potentially important for web radio. If, in the medium term, established stations can increase their overall audience or strengthen loyalty to the station through side channels on their websites, this does create a new, additional dimension for the medium as a whole. It provides evidence that music radio audiences – who may not choose to listen to speech radio in any other context – do respond to more than the music. The difference is that the music provides the broad, continuous appeal, while each individual item on the side channel will interest a much smaller proportion of broad audience at any given time. The aim then should be to offer a range of programming on the side channel that will, over time, appeal to each of the different individuals that make up the main audience.

Web-only radio stations need then to make crucial decisions about where they envisage the spoken voice fitting into their music station. Presumably, they have some kind of music policy if they've decided to go on stream. But is the intention just to 'spin' the discs, or is it the enthusiasms and knowledge of the real music fan(s) presenting them that's going to carry the station's personal appeal? What are the options?

One is to present it just like a broadcast station. Learn from their playlisting techniques and adapt it to your style of music. Make your jingles and idents and decide how often to fire them in any given hour. Learn from your favourite presenters, their style, their pace, the amount of talking they do, their intonations – quite possibly with the (conscious or unconscious) intention of sitting in their seat one day, talking to a broadcast-sized audience (see some of the classic radio production texts under 'Further reading').

But hold on. If you're a presenter on a web radio station, who are you talking to? (If you can't answer this tricky question it might be an additional argument for keeping the presence of the DJ to a minimum.) I need to come back to discuss audiences in the next chapter, but a station can't plan the content between the music without knowing who it's for. A golden rule of good radio presentation is to talk to a real person and not into a void. This is very unlike many of the text 'announcements' adorning websites, which typically address 'anyone out there in cyberspace'. Radio is a much more personal affair than that (McLeish, 1994, p. 65).

A simulcast station has a hidden psychological advantage in this respect. As listeners from outside their transmission area, we understand that we are eavesdropping on a more localized 'conversation'. We unconsciously recognize the context of what the presenter says; we may even feel privileged to be doing so, while not getting the references to local news or personalities or whatever. This can be the next best thing to travelling abroad. But listening to a web-only station we know that geographical context is absent. The presenter of web radio has to create that context for us by talking to *someone*. Who? Where does he or she live?

- Is s/he a member of a self-consciously global audience, united in their appreciation of the music you are playing? Therefore, probably of a particular age group, with common interests in activities common in most countries like clubbing or fashion? We may increasingly be able to identify within this category the young, relatively affluent 'global citizen' who travels regularly to international holiday spots to join in with a global 'club culture'.
- Is s/he in fact part of a geographically local population after all? One not currently addressed by the prevailing licensed radio broadcasters. Does this mean you, the presenter, actively ignore or turn your back on other potential listeners who happen to like your choice of music but live in another country?
- Is s/he a member of a geographically dispersed cultural group – a diaspora – which shares a particular musical heritage distinct from the global main-

stream? Does this involve decisions about what language you use? Are you excluding some second and third generation members of that audience by sticking to a native tongue? Can you mix languages within programmes or between programmes?

- Does s/he identify with a particular system of beliefs that is international and identifies itself through a style of music? Is the purpose of the station to talk to a particular age group within that belief, or indeed one sex or another? Again, what assumptions do you then make about what language(s) to speak in?

In answering these kinds of questions, we are beginning to think ourselves into the concept of the niche audience. To some extent, some terrestrial broadcasters in some parts of the world do try to address audiences in this highly targeted way, but in order to retain ratings they tend to go for an inclusive approach. They can achieve that to a degree through a shared local or national identity. If web radio is to play to its distinctive strengths though, it has to start from the opposite perspective: building outwards from an exclusive audience initially.

Having identified who you are talking to, you have several options as to how. Again, web radio offers many more options than the traditional concepts of a broadcast radio station.

- Is it a live stream? If so:

  - How long is each programme slot?
  - Is it a 24-hour, 7 days a week transmission or are shorter transmissions scheduled at regular times?
  - How many programme slots does it have or is it a single programme?
  - Are you trying to hold on to listeners using broadcast scheduling techniques, or are you expecting a rapid turnover of listeners?
  - Is all the presentation live – in which case you need to make that an obvious feature of the presentation – or are programmes recorded 'as live'?
  - How often can you repeat or rotate recorded programmes?

- Will you offer archived streams – bearing in mind the copyright implications (Chapter 8)? And having weighed up how effective DJ presentation is when it doesn't feel live to the listener? It tends to work better for a special interest programme rather than a regular music show. If so:

  - How many clips of what length can you afford to make available? (In terms of server storage; see Chapter 4.)
  - Is archive your only output? (That is, is that the character of your station?)

– How do you divide the clips in length? For example, the last half of a long show will be heard by many fewer listeners than the start when it's on demand, so is it worth the storage? Browsers like to have the choice and for the bit they're interested in to be clearly labelled.

These are some of the questions any web radio maker should be asking, but they are particularly pertinent for music radio presentation. The challenge for music radio on the Web is to fill the gaps between existing radio provision, to be different and take advantage of the characteristics of this medium. On the one hand, there is plenty they can learn and apply from experienced radio presenters, programme makers and scriptwriters about the timeless, personal, intimate qualities of radio – across one or a thousand miles – but on the other, a whole set of assumptions and accumulated wisdom about the generality of the broadcast audience need to be cleared away, because web radio is not broadcasting.

To this extent, we are re-running the experiments of the very earliest radio pioneers, before regulation caught up and before the industry became dominated by vertical broadcasting institutions. We are not reinventing the wheel in this – though we may suspect that many large media corporations may be trying to. For the web radio pioneer there is a fundamental difference in the medium we are dealing with: there is no shortage of transmission space and therefore no technological – or, so far, regulatory – reason why anyone with the energy and passion for music can't have a go and see what they can do with it.

Factual speech on web radio

News and current affairs and the Internet

It's difficult to talk about how news and current affairs reporting changes on web radio without also considering how much the Internet as a whole is changing all news and all current affairs journalism. The Internet is first and foremost an information medium: and news is information. There are many excellent texts on the changing theory and practice of journalism (I've listed a few under 'Further reading'), but for now there are a few salient points about the shifting relationships between the different news media we cannot avoid mentioning.

After the rise of TV in the 1950s, the three main news media – print, radio and then TV – learned to coexist on the basis of what each technology did best.

- Radio was fast and first to break stories. It usually ran hourly bulletins. A couple of phone calls were enough to sketch the early facts of a story. Cheap, lightweight recording equipment allowed radio reporters to get to the scene quickly and turn around an on the spot report before the next bulletin or two.
- TV was second, usually working on a cycle of deciding where the crews were going at the start of the day in order to bring back the edited picture report in time for the main evening news bulletins.
- Newspapers were 24 hours behind, but made up in depth, detail and analysis of what lay behind the events.

Satellite technology brought us 24-hour TV news, so national TV could catch up with national radio (though local radio could stay ahead of local TV and print). Now the Internet changes that dynamic again – for those who have access to it – with text-based news sites being updated, in some cases every 5 minutes, or more usually hourly. These sites are either run or supplied by established newspapers and news agencies, by TV and radio broadcasting organizations or now by online-only news sites. The major news sites typically provide examples of the Internet at its most overtly converged. Here it's now the text that arrives first, followed by stills, and then radio interviews and video as soon as they can be gathered.

The Web is a natural second home for established news organizations around the world and all of them are now accessible by anyone online. Established news names like Reuters, the BBC or the *Washington Post* are joined there by a host of alternative news sites – ranging from the genuinely accurate alternative to the thoroughly inaccurate, scurrilous and malicious.

The second enormous change Internet technology brings is the personalization of news selection. All the major browser home pages and many others besides offer facilities for searching out 'my news'. You, the viewer, are invited to become your own editor, choosing to receive only stories that fit the categories you specify. However, this search function is text based and cannot, yet, make each listener the editor of their own radio-only bulletin.

Is web radio the best place for news?

What does this tide of globally available news mean for web radio programme makers? That depends very much on why you want news in your programmes and who you are addressing it to. A simulcast station, of course, is already running its hourly bulletins, compiled to be relevant for their home transmission area. Some simulcast stations also hold their bulletins over for an hour as an on-demand stream on their websites. But how does news fit into a web-only station? Some factors to take into consideration are the following:

- Hourly news has, for a long time, provided a structure for music radio stations. In many parts of the world it was imposed as part of the public service remit of commercial radio as a condition of their licences, so it's become ingrained in radio thinking. Bulletins are often bought in from outside providers (like IRN in the UK), so they are not particularly connected to the station's location. This needs rethinking on the Web because there's so much news out there – as up to date and relevant to the listener as they want it to be, geographically or in any other way. Why will the listener wait for the next radio bulletin if they can be viewing it at any time on the screen?
- There may be little point in trying to compete directly with the major news organizations by offering something similar. They have their well-established, extremely powerful infrastructures for collating, writing and distributing the main news of the day, across the Net as well as anywhere else. Thinking now purely in terms of hard news, how is your station going to offer something different than is already extremely widely available?
- Where some independent web stations may be able to compete is (a) by being very local or in areas poorly served by the big organizations and (b) by providing a specialist or alternative perspective on the mainstream news agenda. But even then you should ask, given that most listeners will be at or close to a computer, why create radio bulletins and not write news updates straight into (searchable) text on the station's website?
- In the case of reporting local news, a web station which both serves and grows from within a particular community is doing something different: niche news reporting. If it also earns a reputation for reporting and interpreting effectively, it is certainly filling the gaps between mainstream broadcast and print. This concept is at the heart of the ethos of the well-established community radio sector outlined in Chapter 1. In hard news terms, location reporting using mobile phones can be extremely effective. But radio's other great strength is in people talking about the news: interviews, discussions, commentary, explanation – in this case from the local point of view.
- In less localized terms, a station's own interviews, discussions, commentary and interpretation around the mainstream news agenda can also provide something different – and very important. The oft-repeated criticisms of the news agenda provided by the mainstream broadcast organizations are (a) that it too often shares a consensus of what the main international and often national stories of the day should be, and (b) that it is too readily sourced and interpreted from the perspective of those in positions of authority (see, for example, Allan, 1999, Chapter 3). This again is where small independent stations can fill the gaps for particular audiences, as long as they have the resources to commit to doing so.

Having considered these points and decided, yes, our web station does need to include news programmes that offer something different, and then having identified which audience on the planet it's to address, there's still some thinking to do: how best to make those programmes available?

News bulletins

Is the hourly, live news bulletin the best way of putting news across on web radio? If you anticipate the audience using the station exactly like a terrestrial station and staying tuned in for sustained periods (for example, at work), then some form of bulletin can provide a way of imposing a framework we know works on radio to fit the other programmes into. This would make sense, for example, in a multicast environment, once you've taken the above factors into consideration and worked out who the news is for.

The alternative is to offer bulletins on a regularly updated archive stream. The thinking behind this decision applies equally to other factual speech programmes. As in the case of Radio Netherlands, which specializes in news and current affairs, one strategy is to offer very short term and then longer term archive bulletins and clips to give the listener maximum flexibility in how they listen. On the home Dutch language pages, a range of Dutch-oriented bulletins are offered on demand, from the most recent back through the day. Elsewhere, in other languages, longer news programmes are kept available on a 24-hour rotation. And then for those less time-critical current affairs features, there is a much longer term archive.

The principle of time sensitivity and the programmes whose live value very rapidly fades can, of course, be applied to any speech-based programme on web radio.

All factual speech programmes on web radio

As a listener to a terrestrial radio broadcast, how often have you tuned in half way through a programme and thought 'I wish I hadn't missed the beginning of that'? A familiar, mild annoyance which illustrates three timeless truths about listening to the radio.

1 If we really, really want to hear a programme we, most of us, have to reorganize our personal schedule to be by a radio at the right time.
2 Radio is made to be dipped into and out of. We may have missed the start, but – if the programme was well made – we weren't so completely baffled that we couldn't make sense of the rest of it.
3 Once it's gone, it's usually gone for good and we're onto the next item or programme. We may be lucky and find it's repeated (back to point 1) or if it's important news we can rely on the station to bring it around again.

The interactive side of web radio can abolish that tyranny of the clock – if we, as the programme maker or the listener, want it to (in multicast it cannot). I'll say more about that from the listener's side in the next chapter, but for now consider some implications of on-demand availability for the factual programme maker.

They may say:

- Great! No-one need ever miss any part of one of my programmes or my news packages again.
- And I don't have to worry about getting buried in a lousy slot in the schedules.

Does this mean the station should plan a live stream with a live schedule or not? Perhaps, but what's the character of the radio station? If it only has archive streams, that might make it a station people only visit when they know what they've come for: for example, a current affairs feature about X or Y's interpretation of yesterday's controversy. Could this have the effect of encouraging them to visit less often? Does that matter?

These questions are merely a way of pointing out that the attractions of an on-demand technology run counter to a great strength of radio, which is its ability to surprise us with things we didn't know we wanted to hear, precisely because it is a medium we drift out of and back into with our full concentration. It can introduce us to a new piece of music we would not otherwise have heard of, or it can catch us up in a story or discussion we didn't know we'd be interested in. And if it didn't do that for us today, it might do tomorrow. Surprise and anticipation produced by the programme maker versus search and precise selection by the listener.

So there's a tricky balance to be struck between offering live and archived streams. The art of scheduling live programming is what keeps regular listeners tuned in (the 'push' side of radio). On the other hand, if you've spent time and money putting together a really interesting programme, you want people to be able to hear it whenever they have the time or interest (the 'pull' side again).

There are merits in both. The ideal solution is probably therefore to offer both if you can manage it. Aim to build your relationship with your audience through the live stream, even if it's only for a few regular hours a day. And keep a limited archive of shorter self-contained features, package or highlights available on demand, for example an edited version of a live studio discussion. Most need to be replaced very regularly to save resources, probably from material that has gone out on the live stream. The convinced station manager may ask:

● OK, why don't we transfer all our great live output onto archive and double its audience?

You may or may not double your audience. That's what your server's metrics are there to tell you. But the main question is whether you can afford the memory on the server.

'As live' speech

And if you're a small station or a solo enterprise and you don't have the resources to mount any live programming? The alternative is to create something that's a hybrid between live and archived. That is a show that feels live, but plays on demand. To make it feel live, a programme or a sequence of programmes needs to be recorded live and contain the usual ingredients of, for example, a current affairs programme. In that case, it needs a variety of topics and voices, live discussion, several short packages, but obviously not the details of time or references to today's news. Perhaps you could manage to record once a week, perhaps an hour per programme. The programme or sequence would then sit on the archive stream until the next week. This approach is ideal, for example, for a regular specialist radio feature starting its life within a text-based website – or an online newspaper or magazine.

   This is the speech-based equivalent of the 'as live' music programme suggested above. For a music programme, it probably makes sense to record a longer sequence and run it as a loop on the server feeding a live stream. In this speech radio case, because your programme will be more structured with a beginning, middle and end, the more 'user-friendly' approach is to offer the stream on demand. This approach to radio programming is certainly not a new invention from the producer's point of view: 'as live' recording is a well-established method in terrestrial radio. The difference, of course, lies in the way the audience experiences it and that's something to return to in the next chapter.

Non-factual speech on web radio: drama, comedy, entertainment

Decisions about programmes versus programming lead neatly into this next area of radio, which, in production terms, stands somewhat apart from the routine flow of live broadcasting. Although it represents a small proportion of total radio output around the world today, there is a strong tradition on both sides of the Atlantic of 15-, 30-, 60-minute and, occasionally, 90-minute pre-recorded radio drama, comedy and entertainment programme making. (And, of course, before audio tape came along, these were all broadcast live as well.)

So although such programmes typically again have the live feel (comedy and entertainment are often recorded with a live audience), they are crafted or 'built' in rehearsed production and post-production. So having invested the time and resources in making the programmes, why would we not want to make them available on demand? These are, after all, precisely the type of programme that corporations like the BBC and ABC (US) have made available as tapes for sale sometime after they have been broadcast. Indeed, there are now many sites on the Web offering one-off dramas or series on demand. For example:

Independent Radio Drama Productions	http://www.idrp.co.uk/
Shaun MacLoughlin's	http://www.soundplay.co.uk/
Yuri Rasovsky's	http://www.irasov.com/
Various Sci-Fi on	http://www.scifi.com/
Various US work on	http://www.virtuallyamerica.com/

For a web station interested in including this kind of content, once again the new possibilities radio on demand has to offer raise some interesting dilemmas.

1 *Built programmes within the schedule.* On terrestrial radio, the scheduling of popular programmes within this category has formed distinct 'tuning in' points for their fans, habitual listening appointments around which personal schedules across the reception area have often been organized. For example, the BBC's Comedy Hour on Radio 2 (Saturday lunchtime), the Sunday Play on Radio 3 (movable within Sunday evening) or the Archers (7.02 p.m. weekday and Sunday evenings on Radio 4, with repeats). These kinds of slots provide a permanent (or at least durable) frame around which other parts of the schedule can be constructed. Tuning in points ideally then carry a high proportion of their listeners over into the next programme in the schedule. Is this concept transferable into the context of web radio? It depends how you expect listeners to listen (see Chapter 11).

2 *The risk of ghettoization.* If these kinds of programmes do not form part of a continuous schedule, will they benefit from a move to on-demand streams? Although they are constructed and self-contained, are they in fact meant to be heard sandwiched between other, different kinds of programmes? That's certainly where they originated. As I've said, a traditional strength of radio has been to introduce its listeners to new things they would not pick out from a radio listings page. This 'happy accident' effect may of course work on a specialist web radio stream – as long as it is streamed live or as part of an 'as live' sequence. Thus, a station dedicated to outrageous comedy might make a good job of scheduling unknown acts between big names. If that's the decision, the question is then how long the station intends the keen listener to listen. Does outrageous comedy lose any of its comedy outrage value after an

hour of similarly outrageous comedy? Or if a station decides to set itself up as an on-demand library of new radio plays, would listeners, knowing they could visit any time, in fact make the time to do so? These are genuinely open questions. Though they may sound like discouragement, I do not intend them in that way.

3 *Niche interests*. On the other hand, is this not the very property that distinguishes web radio from its terrestrial parent? Its strength is exactly *to* define pockets of niche listening and make them available to larger but more dispersed audiences worldwide. Having this new aural space allows the freedom for dedicated and passionate writers and programme makers to have a go at producing great pieces of drama or entertainment that work for them in sound and to get reaction from a public. It provides opportunities that simply cannot be offered by the relatively few broadcasters who have created and continue to nurture this rich tradition for radio. Experiment is, by definition, not a commercially viable proposition until you can prove it works, and so can be difficult for public service radio broadcasters on tight budgets to justify. The problem for the creators is that you cannot productively experiment in radio without doing it in public for radio listeners. Web radio makes this possible.

Audience participation and talk on web radio

On-demand streaming represents one example of audience interactivity on radio. A more traditional example is the radio phone-in. This form of audience participation in radio has grown prodigiously in the last quarter of the Broadcast Century, so that today it has become a station format all its own. Try searching the simulcasts on any of the major web radio tuners to get a sense of how these stations work in the US context, where the Talk/News format claimed a 16 per cent share of the listening audience in 1999 (Hendy, 2000, p. 27). At one extreme, radio phone-ins are associated with the 'shock jocks' – opinionated, aggressive, male hosts verbally abusing a succession of callers willing to try their hand at radio jousting. At the other, a mild-mannered presenter chats and coaxes stories from gentle callers who have rung in to answer an on-air quiz. Somewhere between the two, an impartial journalist figure fields public opinions on the important issues of the day or questions to experts.

A range of critiques of the radio phone-in emphasize the unequal power relations between host and caller. The interactivity, they argue, is only on the host's or the programme producer's terms. Calls are screened in advance for their suitability within their overall scheme for the programme, when on air the inexperienced caller is confronted by a practised controller of the medium, who anyway has their hands on the fader should the caller threaten to tip the balance too far onto their own terms (see, for example, the excellent summaries in Douglas, 1999, Chapter 11, and Shingler and Wieringa, 1998, Chapter 6). Although the phone-in claims to let the listener speak, in doing so it can also serve to emphasize the vertical relationship between audience and institution.

That said, we should acknowledge that phone-ins *can* also reinforce a more horizontal relationship between caller and station where it exists, for example in a community station like Kothmale (see Chapter 6). So what place can this form of radio interactivity have on the Web? As I have said, it is well represented on simulcast, especially if you are keen to hear Americans talking to American hosts. So here's an obvious problem. It plainly could work as a live programme on a geographically local station, but for a global audience the cost of phoning in presents something of a barrier. Maybe a well-financed station could manage to strike some kind of deal with a telco for favourable international call charges in return for advertising. After all, web radio transmission runs in parallel with the international phone network, not to say intimately bound up in it. So it surely makes little difference to a telco if sound travels down its lines as a phone call or an audio stream. Put like this, an interesting line of thought emerges.

We do know that email-based, international chat rooms have been one of the major success stories of the Internet. And text-based bulletin boards, forums and chat rooms are important parts of many radio station websites (also see the next chapter). The technological means is here to put all these forms of interactivity together – the radio phone-in, the text chat room, the web station – and produce something which is uniquely a sort of global web radio phone-in. Indeed, Lycos have recently initiated a 'Voice chat' service: a software download which allows you to speak into a microphone in your computer and use it to talk via streaming to anyone else connected to the same service, or else email voice messages as attachments (http://www.uk. lycos.de/service/mediaring/service). Several companies also offer various forms of audio and video web conferencing services for business (for example, eVoke at www.evoke.com/). The international chat room with real voices replacing anonymous text and in real time cannot be far behind, especially over broadband connections.

Granted, this is now swimming far to one edge of our web radio current, but it does produce some very interesting, and I think significant, paradoxes for web radio practitioners to wrestle with. Leaving aside the practicalities of managing such an event for a moment, this image of a globally connected conversation in which collections of participants could speak to each other as well as be heard takes us straight back to Chapter 1, to what I described as the forgotten sector of analogue radio, ham radio, and to Brecht's thwarted vision of:

'the most wonderful public communication system imaginable, a gigantic system of channels . . .capable not only of transmitting but of receiving, of making listeners hear but also speak, not of isolating them but connecting them.'

(quoted in Lewis and Booth, 1989, p. 186)

I could also add one more comparison to the pot for good measure and describe such a system as a global variation of two-way Citizens Band (CB) radio, which also has its own long-standing, dedicated following in those countries where it is licensed. Like ham radio, it also has many websites (which are easy to locate with online searches for 'ham radio' or 'CB radio').

Another well-documented aspect of the terrestrial radio phone-in is that most of its collective audience never ever phone in; a minority of, often regular, callers provide the entertainment for the mass. Could we imagine a spontaneous phone chat room turning into its own web radio station as word spread via email that this or that evolving discussion/debate/shouting match was a terrific listen? There may be a few technical congestion problems along the way, but ultimately I can't see why not.

The serious underlying point here is that the convergence of technologies raises another question of definition about what we mean by radio – not the technology, but the public medium. If the talk radio phone-in is by now a great radio institution – filtered as it is through a station's switchboard and faders – is a web-based voice chat forum – spontaneous, anarchic, but nevertheless creating its own group dynamics, its own 'host' figures – is this not a new version of the same old format? An even more literal manifestation of what Rehm (1993, p. 69) describes as the 'voices over the electronic backyard fence'? Time will tell.

For the web radio station, thinking in terms of organizing a phone-in, that question should provide some food for thought. Some kind of web phone set-up would make the costs manageable, and it would certainly add a new dimension to the old radio phone-in. But what else would the producer need to do to make it *this* station's phone-in? Because that is the decision which separates radio as a public medium from radio in the private or semi-private worlds of CB or ham radio. Again, on the Web the physical, technological divide between these old classifications is not there to help us any more, but a public medium has to be consciously constructed for an audience, even if the intended niche makes it very narrow-cast indeed. (And, in fact, many of the most popular text forums are discretely managed and channelled into coherent 'threads' of discussion.) Radio for a listening public does involve production and it does involve shaping. In the case of a phone-in, that does mean a host figure to guide, clarify and keep participants to the point, and it does mean some strong producer figure to steer the conversation into a coherent form that will be intelligible and engaging to the listener. It could presumably also benefit from some kind of moderation of calls (like most radio websites' chat rooms).

So this is now beginning to sound like the way the broadcasters have been running phone-ins for years. Up to a point, that is so. The difference is that the web radio environment would enable such a show to become a far more open forum than the average, tightly controlled terrestrial phone-in. The addition of special guests, again matching a common feature of email chat rooms, could turn the occasion into a high-profile event – and because on web radio it could sit outside a traditional schedule it could be allowed a reasonable time to develop.

Experiments in horizontal radio on the Web

Such an open-ended web radio phone-in would indeed be something of an experiment. We would expect its appeal to be limited, and therefore not broadcast material. That is precisely what web radio is for: minority audiences pursuing their own interests and enthusiasms. (There might even be the bonus of such an experiment paying off and yielding some great edited highlights that would precisely fit the brief for a broadcast slot.)

So a tremendously important section of radio on the Web is the play area, for experiment and learning about what radio can be if it's not broadcasting in the established sense. It is interesting to see how similar technical methods are beginning to be applied to achieve very different radio uses. The concept behind Pulse Radio and to some extent the VSF event in Chapter 6 follow indirectly from two earlier experiments in hooking up parallel radio events to create a sense of web radio as a global conversation. Soon after RealAudio appeared on the Web, the Austrian broadcaster ORF and the European Broadcasting Union (EBU) staged a one-off 'Kunstradio' event which they dubbed Horizontal Radio. This was a free-form day of communication between radio stations and sound artists, really just to see what the new medium could do with live streaming and sharing audio files. The experiment is documented at http://gewi.kfunigraz.ac.at/~gerfried/horrad/. In a similar vein were the Radio TNC experiments, which were based around connecting different dance parties around the world on live links so they could all listen and talk to each other (more details are at http://www.aec.at/residence/radio-tnc/). These kinds of experiments began way back in 1995, and in some ways it is surprising how little new radio has yet developed along such lines since then. There certainly are sites today which usually class themselves as 'sound art' or 'radio art', and continue to explore (see as an introduction, for example, the links collected at http://www.swr2.de/hoerspiel/audiohyperspace/index.html). But we rarely yet find anything as radical or technologically ambitious as a VSF event.

That might tell us that the technology hasn't yet developed far enough for new uses of web radio to emerge in a very public way. Although they are growing fast, audiences for Internet-only web radio are still relatively small and geographically concentrated. This may mean that it's too early for us to have really turned our gaze around from Marshall McLuhan's rear view mirror, in which each newly invented media technology can at first only be comprehended in the terms of the one that went before. It may indeed tell us that these experiments are the wrong ones to be trying and that when it comes down to it, we can't actually see how this long-cherished dream of radio as a global conversation can work in practice. Maybe the national and local terrestrial broadcast is radio's only natural home. We won't know until we try and web radio gives us the freedom to do just that.

Summary

We can, then, treat web radio simply as an alternative distribution route which either:

1 Gives broadcasters an extra global dimension to their local or national audience, as is the case for the many simulcasts in evidence.
2 Allows unlicensed local stations to spring up in order to narrow-cast to a particular audience, previously poorly served by analogue stations. In these cases the stations are already or behave like broadcast radio stations, applying the kinds of methods and techniques outlined in some of the classic production texts below.

Both have the very important function of filling in with different voices the gaps between the provision licensing authorities allow in different parts of the world.

Or, alternatively, we can begin to take advantage of the new properties web radio adds over and above the familiar broadcast models. The new possibilities these create can broadly be summarized as follows:

Live streams (unicast or multicast)	– Start small if necessary with much shorter schedules, because you don't need to prove how efficiently you can use a transmission frequency any more.
	– Play 'as live' sequences, either singly or in 24-hour rotation. Especially suitable for music radio.
Archive streams (unicast only)	– Offer single, self-contained programmes 'as live' though on demand. More suited to structured, speech-based programmes.

	– Offer short, clearly signposted clips, typically extracted from the live stream or from a longer 'as live' programme.
	– Either or a combination of the preceding two can form the basis of a distinct 'side channel', offered alongside and signposted from a live stream.
	– Availability of clips may be for very short periods like an hour (closer to 'live' radio), a week or months (more like a radio library).
Other interactive audience involvement	– As in broadcasting today inclusion of email responses within programmes can quickly heighten content, especially where it emphasizes live interactions.
	– Text-based chat rooms, bulletin boards, etc. are additional website features but may also help provide content or ideas for programmes.
	– Experiments in audio two-way interactions. May include web phone-type contributions or 'hook ups' with other webcasters.

The web-only station really needs to experiment with these ways of offering content – and the medium makes this far more possible than did broadcasting. There are many valuable lessons to be learned from the history of radio and the communication techniques that have evolved in response to new technologies and social attitudes. At the same time, web radio offers individuals who have the ideas, the energy to put them into practice, and the passion and enthusiasm to communicate them with an audience to have a go and see what they can make of the new narrow-cast environment. We have the challenge here to enrich the variety of radio content in ways which proved not to be possible within the finite limits of the frequency spectrum of the radio wave. How today's web radio stations rise to that challenge will determine the future viability of radio online and will also have its influence on radio offline. What relationship they can manage to build with a listening – or participating – web audience is the flip side of the same coin and is the subject of the next chapter.

Further reading

Allan, S. (1999). *News Culture*. Routledge.

Ang, I. (1996). *Living Room Wars: Rethinking Audiences for the Postmodern World*. Routledge.

Giffard, C. A. (1998). Alternative news agencies. In *The Globalisation of News* (O. Boyd-Barratt, ed.). Sage.

Herbert, J. (2000). *Journalism in the Digital Age*. Focal Press.

Levinson, P. (1999). *Digital McLuhan. A Guide to the Information Millennium*. Routledge.

MacLoughlin, S. (2001). *Writing for Radio. How to Write Plays, Features and Short Stories That Get You On Air* (2nd edn). How To Books.

McLeish, R. (1999). *Radio Production* (4th edn). Focal Press.

Scannell, P. (1996). *Radio, Television & Modern Life*. Blackwell.

Shingler, M. and Wieringa, C. (1998). *On Air*. Arnold.

11 Scheduling for redefined audiences

'I expect the day will come when, for those who wish it, in home or office, the news of the world may be received direct from the mouth of the radio reporter in any quarter of the globe. With this there may be mechanical devices for permanent record when the set is unattended.'

(John Reith, 1924, p. 113)

The broadcast radio scheduler's craft involves connecting together the two ends of the transmission chain: the way audiences listen and the content created by programme makers. It has evolved over time in response both to technological changes in the receiving equipment and social changes in the lifestyles and attitudes of the listeners. In the industrialized world at least, the reverberations from digitalization of the mass media industries are producing a new set of challenges, the implications of which we are only just beginning to comprehend.

In the very earliest days of radio, the most pressing need was to develop the skills of making *programmes*: creating content using whatever resources were to hand. The novelty of receiving anything through this magical device meant that the audience's critical expectations of what they heard were not sophisticated by today's standards. Listeners in the 1920s were in the position of giving their full concentration to the act of listening and they had far fewer competing distractions than today. Hence the focus was on the programme at the time rather than the flow of programmes across the (much shorter) broadcasting day. The above quote from the then managing director of the British Broadcast Company, John Reith, emphasizes the point. He envisaged the time when technology would transmit radio content, in this case news, to reach the listener's home as and when it was produced, but allow everyone to access it individually according to their own personal timetable. The complexities of *programming* a station in order to satisfy diverse tastes and in competition with so many other calls on the individual's time had not yet been realized. Over the years of broadcasting it became apparent that, in fact, programming a radio station's output comes first, with the right kinds of individual programmes then being commissioned to fit into that schedule.

Today, the programme is shaking itself free of the programming once again. In many parts of the world, we now have a multichannel broadcast environment and the 'mechanical devices' which allow us with increasing ease to store the programmes we want until we are ready to watch them. This trouble has been brewing in the schedulers' offices for some time, but powerful domestic hard disk recording technology like the TiVo (for one somewhat prototype example), which gives the TV viewer far-reaching control over their own order of watching, is now revealing the extent of their problems.

Over on terrestrial radio, maybe things aren't quite so threatening yet. Yes, we may have multichannel competition in privileged parts of the world, but the way we use the radio has not changed substantially since the transistor took the radio away from the fireside: it still accompanies us as we get up in the morning, when we drive to and from work, probably last thing at night and to fit into the rhythms of domestic life. Above all, we turn the radio on, often to our habitual station, and leave it on while we get on with whatever else we are doing. We are not so much in the channel zapping frame of mind as we tend to be in front of the TV. Routine and habit like this are music to the scheduler's ears. As we've seen though, web radio is not entirely like that. For one thing, it is a hybrid of programming and individual programmes; for another, it involves targeting the habits and preferences of much narrower audiences; and for a third, the physical surroundings where people can be to listen to web radio are for now rather limited.

So this chapter is about attempting to bring together the technological aspects of web radio of Chapter 3 with the content options in Chapter 10 in order to communicate with an audience. Again we, as practitioners and students of web radio, along with the whole of the broadcasting industry, are staring into an unknown future. We can though, as web radio *listeners*, begin to appreciate the issues of programmes versus programming we will need to be exploring through the next 10–20 years.

Programmes versus programming

At first glance, the obvious divide on web radio is between the programming carried on a live stream and the programmes on an archive stream. But, as suggested in Chapter 10, the permutations are a little more complicated. A live stream may be carrying a repeating rotation of a single pre-recorded programme or a short sequence of programmes, or it may be carrying a live output from a radio studio. An archive stream may conceivably carry the same pre-recorded sequence but without the automatic rotation. So the question we need to ask here is, irrespective of our definitions of live and archive streams, 'How does the listener encounter the options they are presented with?'

Here again, the ideas of the push and the pull sides of web radio are helpful. *Programming* is at the heart of a *push* medium: how do we, the station, keep delivering the content that will keep the audience with us while they have the radio on and give fewest of them reason to tune onto another competitor? In the niche medium of web radio, we have less of a need to keep such a broad range of listeners interested or satisfied – and we certainly shouldn't stake our financial prospects on that broadcast scale of audience within one territory. Nevertheless, the aim is still to keep individual listeners with you because they like your programming and away from opting to try your nearest similar competitor.

The *pull* side is diametrically opposite. Here you fully expect listening habits to be promiscuous, that audiences probably will not be tuning to your programming on a daily basis: they'll come and visit your site when you have a *programme* they want to listen to. They'll find that programme through the online grapevine (email, search engines or well-placed hyperlinks), maybe through offline promotion, or else they'll learn that it's in a regular slot – say once a week. And what's more, they are very likely to tune out again after it's finished or indeed as soon as they lose interest. The more these visits are part of listeners' routines, the more like conventional radio usage they become; the more occasional they are, the less any notion of programming matters and the less the station has its singular identity.

Listening habits

From a slightly different perspective, consider the habits of two listeners. Listener A might want his/her favourite radio station always to be there for him/her to drift into and out of at different times of day according to what s/he is doing. Whereas Listener B might like a station because s/he knows it's generally where programmes of interest can be found and so s/he would sometimes (or even often) modify his/her drifting in and drifting out to coincide with known preferences in the schedule. Listener A sounds as if s/he is more likely to be tuned to a music-orientated station or perhaps a phone-in talk station (with or without music as well). The programming, including the playlisting, is important to this person. Listener B is probably more of a speech-orientated radio listener, a follower of more structured and concentrated listening, who usually likes the way the schedule fits around his/her day or perhaps is occasionally frustrated at missing particular items or programmes. Whether s/he would go so far as to search them out on another platform is an open question (and a significant one for online and offline schedulers alike), but it will depend very largely on how convenient it is to do so in comparison to their usual method of listening. But s/he is certainly *potentially* more likely to listen to an archived stream than Listener A.

Cost of listening

As I've suggested, both listeners are constrained by the shape of their daily routines and I'll return to those effects on programming and programmes shortly. On web radio, we also need to take into consideration the factors of (a) the cost of connection to the individual and (b) the convenience or where physically they need to be to tune in. At the moment, for the majority of web radio listeners, the two places they listen are at work or on a domestic computer. If they are able to listen at work the connection is not costing them per minute, but if they're listening at home it might well be. Therefore, scheduling a station's output over eight or so hours is likely to be relevant for the listener at work. Whereas for the home listener – and especially if they're paying by the minute – individual programmes or short clips from programmes are much more likely to fit their pattern of use. These constraints will certainly change as the technology improves, but they are the reality for now.

It is worth re-emphasizing the point that web radio gives us unprecedented levels of feedback about how listeners like to listen either across programming or to individual programmes or sections of programmes. This comes both from server metric data and, if a station cultivates it, email feedback from a higher proportion of listeners than broadcasting has previously been used to. A station should use this feedback to gauge whether it is offering the right variety of listening options.

Patterns of listening

Our Listeners A and B above represent the kind of audiences the terrestrial radio schedulers recognize and whose daily listening patterns they have studied exhaustively. The shape of the daily audience graph is well known and discussed in many radio texts: the biggest peak across all terrestrial radio stations and spanning the breadth of each station's demographic is during the breakfast show (getting up and driving to work or the school gate), followed by an abrupt decline into the mid morning, a modest increase over lunchtime, a second lull through the afternoon until 'drivetime', after which listening loses out in a big way to the evening's entertainment before a slight pick-up around bedtime. Through the weekend, overall listening is more evenly spread out and lower. Some slots do particularly well for some stations; for example, older listeners are rather more likely to tune into a favourite relaxing station as they get ready for bed, despite the total audience across all radio being low at this time. How do these patterns compare with the times people are most likely to tune in to web radio?

At this point, we really have to stop thinking about web radio as competing for listeners directly with terrestrial radio and look to other times of day, when *computer* use is highest. A very interesting dimension of the new mosaic of radio platforms is that, precisely because of its current lack of mobility, web radio is likely to be more popular at times when terrestrial listening is lowest. People are perhaps least likely to be near a computer between getting up in the morning and going to work. If they work in an office, they are most likely to be in front of a computer during the working day, from 8 or 9 a.m. to around 5 p.m. (This is certainly supported by MeasureCast, 2001, and the Virgin Radio and Radio-Valve case studies in Chapters 5 and 6.) Many of those workers will then tune back from web to analogue for drivetime on their car radios or their personal pocket radios. And if they have computers at home, the US trends show they are rather more likely to be in front of them in the evenings and weekends, as Web activity competes with TV more than it does with radio (UCLA, 2000, p. 18; Arbitron, 2001, p. 5; Scarborough Research, 2001). So scheduling programming specifically for web radio in any given territory needs to try to take account of this new pattern of listening.

Furthermore, we can say with confidence that listeners at work – because they are not personally paying – are using web radio like traditional radio and thus are more responsive to programming over longer periods of time rather than switching between specific shorter programmes (although we can't rule that out altogether for a minority of listeners at work). Similarly, we can say that patterns of domestic computer use indicate that a high proportion of those listeners are (a) going to be mentally in 'search mode' anyway if they are using the Internet and (b) will be connected for much shorter periods of time, especially if they are paying for their connections by the minute. Therefore, across evenings and weekends especially, web radio listeners will be more receptive to individual web radio programmes than to the programming. We should also add into the equation that web radio is in more direct competition with CDs or MP3s among younger audiences in this setting, and also with whatever programming terrestrial radio has to offer at these times.

So far as the scheduling goes, then, a web station which targets workplace listeners should definitely be thinking in terms of programming over at least 8 hours. A web station targeting domestic listeners may want to look to tailoring a live schedule to an interrupted pattern of listening, but in addition should think about offering a selection of shorter programmes or clips gathered together as on-demand options. In this latter case, the linear schedule is broken up and offered instead in segments.

However, the dismembered schedule should still feel to the audience like it has a coherence they can recognize as a dynamic part of a living station: living stations have a 'house style' and the constant promise of something new to listen to. That feeling may have a lot to do with the website (and therefore grow less like conventional radio), but it may equally be in the sound of the programmes. An interesting test of the effectiveness of a house style is to play to a group of regular radio listeners 15-second unidentified extracts from the range of a station's programmes and see how many clips it takes them to correctly identify the station.

Time shifting

For the time-based media, then, the point at which the technology makes it just as easy for audiences to create their own schedule of programmes as turn the TV or radio on is a highly significant one. It really tests what audiences want each medium for, the programmes or the programming. This is the point at which the programme potentially takes over as *the* currency for a station, more like the article is in the newspaper or the page on the website. The combination of affordable hard disk storage with efficient audio and video compression formats – located either at the producer's end of the transmission chain or on the user's receiver – means that we can increasingly watch or listen to the programmes we want in the order and at the time we want. The technology is one thing, though: how much of a *want* that time-shifting power will turn out to be for viewers and listeners is quite another.

In the previous chapter I have already raised some of the ways this ability to time shift should be fed into the web radio station's planning in relation to different types of content. How useful is it for the *listener*? What difference does it make to their listening experience?

Again a complex question. A few technical distinctions should help towards an answer.

- Although storage capacity is the mechanism for time shifting, for the user time shifting a programme is not the same as storing it and the less like storing it can appear the better – in most circumstances. Most of us have had the experience of accumulating videotapes of TV programmes we've recorded and never got round to watching. If we transfer that experience into the context of radio, it tells us (a) that we don't need another growing pile of things we haven't yet got around to in our lives, (b) that most radio programmes actually lose much of their appeal when they are taken out of the programming context in which we would have enjoyed them on first hearing, and (c) that a few radio programmes do turn out to be worth hearing again.

- The best place to disguise the storing activity involved in time shifting is therefore at the producer's end of the transmission. For the majority of radio programmes (those in the (b) category of the previous paragraph), the more accessing them can feel like tuning into a living section of radio programming the better (reinforcing the point made in the previous chapter that music presentation and most talk shows work better as live streams in rotation – quite apart from the copyright considerations raised in Chapter 8).
- For this reason, it is probably going to be important to most listeners that a web radio station's website doesn't look like a permanent archive site – that is, that they're not going to see the same set of programmes on offer this week as they did last week. A minority may want to search a more permanent archive deeper into the website (as, for example, in the Radio Netherlands case study in Chapter 5). That's one option, but the front 'listen' page needs to look more like a choice between living, dynamic sub-stations or channels within the web station as a whole. The rate of turnover of programme options should aim to reflect that.
- At some point in a radio programme's life, whether it's transmitted live or on a temporary archive stream, it may become apparent that either the whole of it or parts do deserve permanent storage. This might be because it is a programme that people evidently do want to hear again or because it has acquired some classic entertainment or historical value. This is something of a cleft stick for web radio. How much to keep just in case? What can we safely erase? This needs building into the station's policies. Many terrestrial stations have been required by their regulators to keep log recordings of all their transmissions for set periods and this has usually allowed enough time for any real highlights on air to be extracted for permanent archive. Web radio, of course, has no obligation to keep a log copy at all – but the system has its value quite independently of any regulation. Many, if not most, of analogue radio's most precious moments have happened spontaneously live and unscripted: there is no reason why that cannot be equally true for web radio.

So time shifting is undoubtedly useful for some listeners, those interested in specific content. The risk – which will apply just as much to TV – is that the more time shifting of programmes we do as listeners, the less we enjoy that part of the experience of radio which has to do with joining in, in the moment; of being part of a live audience. The effect of placing scheduling in the hands of the listener is an enormous subject in its own right and the effects of time shifting real-time media will need a great deal of research in the next few years. But it is not a factor makers of individual programmes can ignore as unimportant in the way they relate to an audience. I'll come back to it again a bit later in the chapter.

The locality of the listener

Following hard on the heels of the topic of time shifting comes the question of time zones and the consequences of playing to a global audience. If you are a station which is using the Web to reach a local or regional audience then this section is irrelevant. If you are a licensed terrestrial station with a web radio simulcast this is also likely to be irrelevant – although quite possibly worth thinking through in relation to your 'graveyard shift' just in case the web audience comes to make up a significant proportion in comparison with the small insomniac or night working offline audience. Or if you are an archive-only station, it has only the limited relevance of helping you decide at what hour of the day to change the content over. For example, if you have a daily programme on archive, when does your 24-hour cycle begin and end? Or do you consider operating an overlap between two staggered streams of the same content?

Time zones really become important on a live stream – which demonstrates the principle in all cases well enough. What you are obviously working out is where the daily cycles of radio listening begin and end in different parts of the world. The first thing to do is stick a world map showing time zones on the office wall.

The Internet convention is to measure global time against Co-ordinated Universal Time (UTC or sometimes UCT) – which is the same as Greenwich Mean Time (GMT). Decide when the day begins for your primary target audience in relation to UTC and then work out what part of their day your secondary audiences will be in at that time. (Remember that many temperate countries also change their clocks twice a year between Summer time and Winter time.) So a station aimed first at a UK audience begins its work day at 8 or 9 a.m. UTC between October and March and 7 or 8 a.m. UTC between March and October. Listeners on East Coast Time in North America, Canada and the Caribbean start their working day 5 hours behind at 1 or 2 p.m. UTC – a typical lunchtime in the UK. And West Coast Americans are starting their work day as Britons finish theirs. Western Australia and Hong Kong are just on their way home from work as Britons struggle in.

This is familiar ground to international broadcasters, but not for most radio practitioners. If you want your station to communicate with Seattle or Tokyo audiences, you need to think about building that audience not only into the programme schedule, but also into what you say on air at the right times. Some web stations have taken the decision to carve up the 24-hour clock into three equal blocks and run their global programming on an 8-hour cycle. For example, RadioValve (see Chapter 6), based in west central Mountain Time in the US, records 8 hours of live programming per day and repeats it twice more on a live stream roughly to coincide with listening cycles across Europe and the Asia Pacific region.

Similarly, there is the opportunity to think about multilingual broadcasting in these time-zoned terms. Again, this is a familiar idea to existing specialist global broadcasters, but something a new station may want to take into consideration. To take the example of a station targeting a particular cultural group, say a Malaysian diaspora, it might make sense to speak only Malay on a live stream during early evening hours Kuala Lumpur time (UCT − 8 hours) and then increase the proportion of English spoken during the South East Asian night and early morning in order to address second generation communities living in England and America. Or perhaps a proportion of German and Dutch could be included in parts of the cycle as well.

The Web is proving a powerful medium in this kind of multilingual communication, because it is so straightforward to offer many language options in text on a website's home page. With careful scheduling and/or the use of alternative archive clips, there is no reason why this principle cannot be extended more widely into web radio (see, for example, Radio Netherlands in Chapter 5).

Global communities

Radio, of course, gains much of its communicative force from being a spoken, non-literary medium. In this, it has tremendous power to bring together very specific groups of people on the basis of some interest they share in common. As Susan Douglas reminds us in her chapter on The Zen of Listening (1999, pp. 22–39), radio listening has provided a means for uniting nations across divisions of class, race and gender at various points in history, but it has also frequently worked in the opposite direction: 'we must remember that people also used radio to tune in on difference' (p. 24). In the essay, Douglas draws together a wide range of research and writing about the psychology of listening in order to discuss the ways in which this particular medium communicates so directly with a person's individual idea of themselves and themselves in relation to others like them:

> 'Listening to radio also forged powerful connections between people's inner, thinking selves and other selves, other voices, from quite faraway places. Inner speech is, of course, an almost continuous aspect of our selves, as we think and talk silently to ourselves throughout the day. It accompanies all the rest of our experiences and is the inner thread of continuity to our sense of being in the world. With radio, this interior "I" began oscillating with the voices of those never met, never even seen.'
>
> (p. 31)

The communities of like-minded 'selves' may be very large, diverse communities or very small and particular. They may be united by a type of music, a style of humour, a regional culture and right down to a very specific geographical location, a few blocks of streets or an institution like a college or university. Each one of us potentially belongs or relates to many such communities of shared interests at the same time. It is the permutations of these differences that the notion of niche broadcasting, i.e. narrow-casting, tries to address. As has been the theme of this book, web radio is an excellent instrument for providing that variety of stations, appealing to smaller but more intense communities of interest, filling in the gaps between licensed broadcasting.

Meanwhile, widening use of the Web has also been generating the notion of 'virtual communities', based so far on the text contained on Internet bulletin or message boards. Howard Rheingold, among others, has tracked the development of such communities in order to study their potential for creating positive, supportive networks for real people separated by distance or isolated within supposed 'real' geographical communities. His website at http://www.rheingold-.com/ contains useful links, discussions of his findings and an online version of his trail-blazing book, *The Virtual Community,* which he first published in 1993.

Rheingold's emphasis on direct communication between 'real people' on the Net chimes clearly with Douglas's description of the radio community, and if anything rather better than we might imagine with purely text-based communities. Radio, when practitioners turn their minds to it, can be about nurturing audiences, drawing disparate individuals into a sense of relationship for the time they are listening. Rheingold has drawn the same lesson from his experiences:

> 'Over the years I've learned that virtual communities are not the norm, but the exception; that they don't grow automatically but must be nurtured. Any groups that are thinking about adding chatrooms or message boards to their Web pages, expecting a community to blossom without much forethought, design or commitment of ongoing resources, is headed for failure.
>
> In order to succeed, a virtual community has to have an affinity – the answer to the question: What would draw these people together?'

> (2000b, p. 173)

Redefining the radio audience according to shared interest more than or instead of shared geography is a new challenge in this niche, targeted sense.

Terrestrial radio's historic external services have been broadcasting to global communities for years, but still fairly firmly on the basis of where the target audience lives. The history of most radio to date has been in the form of either national or geographically local stations (although we can argue that music format radio has been with all of us as a generic global sound for decades). But here we are once again defining radio in the way it speaks to its listeners and the way it demonstrates that it shares their interests by:

- its selection of news stories;
- local/national weather reports;
- the area it covers in traffic reports;
- local/national advertising;
- a well-known building displaying the station's logo as its base;
- special events it stages or participates in to present a public face.

Addressing a community of interest

To address a global community, we need to establish different points in common. This does not mean, for example, abolishing all talk of where the station's studio is, but it does mean consciously framing that as talk *between* two or more locations on an equal basis. It means downplaying the 'one to many' relationship. It almost certainly means covering news very differently, in ways that define the station's community of interest (see previous chapter). And, of course, the station's website becomes its immediately accessible public face. The target audience needs to be able to recognize something of themselves in the whole image the station presents of itself in its talk, its programmes and visually on its web pages. Perhaps most important from the listener's point of view, web radio provides the mechanisms for the listeners' input to shape the station, the better to fit the niche it has chosen (see next section).

A live stream powerfully reinforces the sense of togetherness amongst those who listen. Up to now, this has been a strongly defining feature of the way audiences relate to radio, as indeed to any live event. The apparent paradox of individual members of a radio audience listening to a station, often alone yet having the sensation of being part of a mass of others tuned to the same station, has been pointed out by many who've studied it (for example, Sunstein, 2001). In this respect, the feel of tuning into a live stream of programming remains important – even if it is in fact on a rotating loop. But in the age of niche audiences and of time-shifted listening and viewing, we may be having to adjust this understanding of literally live togetherness. (Or else, in fact, the logical alternative is for audiences to reject this multiplication of choices and decide they prefer being part of the communal mass consumption of live broadcasting.)

Individual programmes for specific communities

A web station that is targeting a particular community of interest through speech needs to balance the value of liveness with convenience for the listener, whichever time zone they may be in. If a listener is attracted by the interests the station is dealing with, the relationship won't last long if they are forever missing the programmes that look most interesting to them. Keep in mind the idea that web radio can also serve that community like an audio bulletin board – I don't mean just for posting voice messages but for researched, built radio programmes or packages. Back to the pull philosophy: the reason the listener is visiting that station is because it's providing something they have not found elsewhere and they will keep moving in their search if they are disappointed.

So long as the producer of the on-demand programme manages to create for the listener the sensation of immediacy in its sound, there is no reason why they won't be drawn into its story in almost exactly the same way as a pre-recorded item on a genuinely live output. (In other words, a well-made, creative radio feature works for its audience wherever it is placed.) Here the connections from and back to the website are very important in reinforcing the listener's relationship to the contents of the programme. Many, many terrestrial broadcasters and newspapers have demonstrated the importance of providing follow-up information and links relating to specific stories on their websites. In many ways, the website on this type of station can go some way to replacing the sense of continuity of a live schedule. The website can also bring new dimensions to the relationship, should the listener want to use them, which are the subject of the next section.

We cannot ignore the fact that on web radio we are inviting the listener to put more into the listening relationship than conventionally has been the case in radio. But if they have found your station and it is genuinely filling an unmet need in their listening there's a good chance of them investing that effort.

Feedback and the effects of accurate audience measurement

As well as being offered a choice of programmes and programming, the web radio listener has a number of other mechanisms for furthering their relationship with a station should they want to. It's up to the station to reciprocate and make full use of them (assuming, of course, the station is hoping to build an audience).

I've previously mentioned the ways this feedback can happen:

- on a technical level, the station can get very specific information about each request for a stream if they are on unicast, such as the country they're listening in, when they tune in and out, what connection speed they are on;

- direct contact with the station through email, perhaps web voice mail;
- indirect contacts between listeners via the station's bulletin board, forum or real-time chat room.

Because web radio is narrow-casting, the more a station builds this kind of feedback into their routines the stronger the sense of community they can facilitate amongst their audience. As Rheingold points out (above), this community has to be actively nurtured and encouraged by its focal point – the station. It may be that you use these feedback mechanisms simply to solicit listener's views on a technical matter like sound quality (see the Virgin Radio case study in Chapter 5), it may be a place for them to express a deeply held opinion, or it may enable them to contribute an item or programme to the schedule. Whatever the level of involvement, it all contributes to the feel surrounding the station for everyone who visits it.

This level of interaction – or at least the loyalty it engenders – is something some terrestrial local radio stations have striven for for years. Web radio has two fundamental advantages over them in this: firstly, interactivity is there as a built-in feature of the technology and, secondly, it is not chasing broadcast-sized audiences so it can make its appeal more specifically to individual interests and worry less about leaving very different sections of a broad audience out by doing so.

Summary

From a listener's point of view then, we can begin to draw some early conclusions about which are the most useful aspects of web radio.

In some situations, the fact that we are likely to listen to web radio through a computer is a positive advantage – especially for office workers whose job involves an online computer. As noted in Chapter 3, this may be a temporary state in the evolution of the technology, but for now it's crucial. In this situation, web radio listening most resembles habitual terrestrial radio listening.

At home, listening is likely to be in the evening or at weekends and more focused on shorter, specific programmes or clips – until broadband and unmetered access are significantly more widespread.

The ability to time shift our listening has its obvious pros, but potentially also some subtle cons. The web radio practitioner needs to work especially hard to keep the on-demand station from sounding or appearing like a 'dead' medium -- a collection of library clips with no sense of the real people behind it.

There are ways of compensating for this problem, which have yet to be fully explored and exploited. Most important is the sense of a community of interest a station can create around itself by making the individual listener the focus: by building the rapid responsiveness the technology allows into that relationship – on air and via the website – and by finding ways of making the audience 'visible' to itself. So their feeling of being a part of a larger group happens not so much in the real-time listening moment and more on accumulated – and more concrete – evidence.

And, of course, all this rides on the assumption that the station's programmes are well made. A web radio station needs to find its distinctive sound. Whether or not they are actually live or pre-recorded, programmes that are skilfully put together for radio have a live feel about them because they draw the listener into the moment. That is the essential quality of radio on which its continuation as a distinctive medium depends, through whatever technology it reaches the listener's ear.

Further reading

Ang, I. (1996). *Living Room Wars: Rethinking Audiences for the Postmodern World*. Routledge.

Dickinson, R., Linne, O. and Ramaswami, H. (eds) (1998). *Approaches to Audiences*. Arnold.

Mallapragada, M. (2000). The Indian diaspora in the USA and around the world. In *Web.Studies* (D. Gauntlett, ed.). Arnold.

Rheingold, H. (2000). *The Virtual Community: Homesteading on the Electronic Frontier* (revised edn). MIT University Press.

Scannell, P. (1996). *Radio, Television & Modern Life*. Blackwell.

Smith, M. and Kollock, P. (eds) (1998). *Communities in Cyberspace*. Routledge.

Sunstein, C. (2001). *Republic.com*. Princeton University Press.

12 So how is web radio different? A checklist

The aim of this book has been to provide an overview of what is involved in putting together a web radio station: firstly, getting used to a new way of sending and receiving radio; secondly, understanding something of the environment of the Internet through which it is transmitted; and thirdly, identifying the ways in which radio content on the Web can differ from radio broadcasting as it has evolved over the last century. In each of these three areas, the book is a guide rather than a set of definitive instructions. It is an invitation to explore as a listener and experiment as a producer, because we do not know where this road is taking us: an invitation to research the possible routes ahead. In the process of this research, we may find out almost as much about 'old-fashioned' analogue radio as about the nature of its upstart offspring. For those of us interested in the study of radio, the Web provides the most comprehensive toolkit:

- for comparing current radio practice internationally;
- the first widely accessible audio memory for radio contained on history and archive sites;
- the close proximity of competing media across new, leaky borders helps challenge our definitions of what we mean by good radio content;
- the absence of barriers to public transmission enables us to re-examine some fundamental assumptions that have survived generations of radio about, for example, media ethics and censorship, about intellectual property and what we mean by 'originality', and about the validity of the sources we rely on to tell us about each other.

For all the differences I have put forward in this book, web radio is still a continuation of the 80 years or so of radio tradition that preceded it. Many fundamental techniques, tricks and short cuts have been learned along the way about what works in sound for the listener. Those lessons learned are not restrictions, more of a kind of liberation in the hands of the skilled programme maker. They cover a huge variety of styles of radio and they shift around according to the ways listeners use it: there is no one right way of making radio programmes. But what that accumulated experience does tell us is that there are plenty of wrong ways to make any kind of radio: uninterested presentation; false intonations; badly researched content; convoluted scripting; lack of signposting about what's happening or what's coming next; obvious, jarring editing . . .the list goes on. Because it now seems technically quite easy to get 'on air' (i.e. online), there is a danger that we don't have to think enough about what we put out there – as testified by the wealth of stations on the Web who can count their weekly reach on the fingers of one hand. We don't need to relearn *these* lessons for web radio.

So there are the essential aural qualities and production techniques that both forms of radio share in common. And then, superimposed in broadcasting, are institutional customs and practices, regulations, and assumptions about audiences: limitations on the medium which have evolved over time and through very different eras than our own. These facets of established radio we can largely forget about in web radio. Time to rethink. Of course, we can decide to run a web station along the same institutional lines as a conventional broadcaster – and those also broadcasting their web output on the airwaves have no choice – but the potential of web radio is diminished if we treat it only as an imitation of what mainstream radio broadcasting has become. The mass audience characteristics of DRM, DAB and satellite are better suited to that role, if we are imminently to leave analogue transmission behind. Indeed, there is the real danger that the more we treat web radio as though it *were* broadcasting, the more it will become exactly like another (rather inefficient) form of broadcasting – regulated and organized along the same vertical lines. And for a second time in history we will have passed up the opportunity to find out what radio in its horizontal, interactive form could be for us.

In this brief chapter then, I'll draw together the main themes that have emerged from the book and attempt to summarize these distinctive ways in which web radio differs from terrestrial radio and from which its real value derives. In Chapter 1 I suggested two questions to use in order to do this:

1 What new strengths does web radio add to pre-Internet radio?
2 What established strengths of radio does web radio supplant?

I'll apply those across the general headings of:

● characteristics of the transmission technology;
● where web radio fits into the mosaic of radio platforms;
● ways of being a web radio station;

- regulation and control;
- content.

Each one of the tentative conclusions – or theories, call them what you will – on the following checklist seems to me to warrant its own research project.

Review of the characteristics the Web adds to radio

Web radio works best as a narrow-cast or niche medium

This is its advantage. Analogue radio found its most efficient use as a broadcast medium – even though it can be used to target small geographical areas. Web radio can be used in a 'broadcast' mode, but in the context of this comparison it cannot compete with the real thing, for so long as big enough concentrations of audience remain to justify free to air broadcast radio (Chapters 3 and 11).

Web radio is a 'non-zero sum' medium

This is shorthand for saying that the Internet's infrastructure is an elastic resource, whereas the spectrum of radio frequencies is a fixed resource within each geographical area. The Internet can continue to accommodate new stations and each station can continue to add new streams to make more than 24 hours of programming available in a day *without taking away* any existing services to make space. Analogue radio became broadcast and increasingly vertically organized because it is, in principle, 'zero sum' and hence requires some form of regulated system to function: for each new station added to a full radio spectrum, one must be taken away and for each new programme added to a 24-hour schedule the same length must be subtracted to make room for it (Chapter 4).

Web radio aggregates listeners' specialist interests

Combine the fact that web radio is a non-zero sum medium with its global reach and this further strengthens its advantage as a narrow-cast medium. There may not be enough fans of Celtic folk music in your part of the world to justify a local broadcast station for it, but if you add together listeners scattered around the world who are missing that kind of entertainment the potential audience looks a lot healthier. Each new niche is an addition to the sum of radio. Some niches may be well filled by simulcasts of stations who do have broadcast licences elsewhere, but many more can come from web-only stations (Chapters 3, 5 and 11).

The scalability of web radio cuts both ways

This makes all the difference at the entry level of radio, where audiences, and hence bandwidth, and hence costs are small, but becomes increasingly burdensome the more (thousands of) concurrent listeners a station attracts. Multicast can be a way around this, but excludes on-demand interactivity. The sums in this equation will continue to change with the technology, but in the longer term scalability will continue to go hand in hand with narrow-casting (Chapters 4 and 5).

Web radio is inherently interactive

Whereas terrestrial radio stations have to increase their identification with their broadcast by other means – especially now through the station website. But email forums or request lines or chat rooms don't look after themselves, and they require the investment of time and money to maintain. Ironically, the more portable web radio becomes and the further removed from a reasonable sized screen and keyboard, the less of this visually interactive edge it will retain. There is no reason though why such interactivity should be confined to text. Listeners can become increasingly more involved as contributors or makers of pro-grammes if a web station creates that opportunity. The tools to make and transfer high quality programmes are now widely available to anyone with the interest and the outlet (Chapters 6 and 10).

'On demand' transfers control to the listener

The ability of web radio to offer both live and on-demand listening streams is a unique asset. On-demand streams need to be used and organized with care by the webcaster, but both for simulcast and web-only stations they can build the total listening audience for a programme both in the short term (in a 24-hour or weekly cycle) or the longer term. This also has the effect of spreading demand, so audience figures for a programme accumulate over time. On-demand archives are also starting to create an invaluable, collective, global memory for all forms of radio (Chapter 11).

Web radio can measure audience preferences directly

A unicast server can collect data about most requests it receives for a stream. Correctly used, that data can be converted into the kind of listening statistics broadcast audience researchers can only dream of – even with allowances for streams left connected but unattended and the fact that IP numbers can be

So how is web radio different? A checklist

235

'concealed' by listeners if they choose. As with any set of statistics, these can be used positively or negatively. They can allow a station, for example, to respond to listening patterns, to test interest in a new programme, to relate airplay to click-through record sales or to provide advertisers with instant feedback on a particular campaign. On the other hand, their precision can encourage a relentless, instantaneous, morale-sapping measurement culture – to a much greater degree than is possible for terrestrial radio, with its less exact and retrospective audience measurement methods. Both makers of and listeners to new programmes need nurturing and time to develop their affections (Chapter 4).

Managing demand

The Internet's version of 'word of mouth' can spread implausibly quickly. So it is always possible that today's quiet backwater of web radio will tomorrow be deluged, should one visitor decide to email 20 friends at work, each of whom email 20 more, and so on. These powerful surges of interest can be positive or negative in terms of reputation (and a server's ability to cope). Whichever, the station will find out about it very soon – another dimension of instantaneous feedback that broadcasters never experience with such direct force. In broadcasting, swings in popularity happen over much longer periods and, perhaps more importantly, sudden surges will almost certainly never be registered accurately on broadcast audience listening figures (Chapters 3 and 4).

Web radio as part of the mosaic of radio platforms

The evidence at the moment is that the above characteristics mean that web radio can be complementary to broadcast radio in several ways, just as it cannot compete with it in others. There are areas of radio transmission it can cover more effectively than any other digital or analogue route.

Adding a global audience

A terrestrial station can reach beyond its transmission area to listeners in other regions and other countries via the Web. A web-only station can define its international appeal from the outset. While this capability is not unique to the technology of the Web (think of the highly resourced external services at one extreme or ham radio at the other), the way the industry is now structured web radio is proving to be the most practical and accessible way of achieving it (Chapters 3, 5, 6 and 11).

Adding highly targeted audiences

Similarly, at the other extreme, web radio can get itself into individualized spaces not easily reached by terrestrial broadcasting (although, of course, micro-power transmitters can cover very small patches). Thus, the Web can add audiences in particular locations *within* a terrestrial station's transmission area, notably office workers for whom FM or AM reception is poor within particular buildings (Chapters 6 and 11).

Simulcasting a terrestrial output on the Web

For an established station, this is a simple but effective way of achieving the above incremental, additional reach. However, this tactic is not without potential problems: the cost of additional bandwidth sufficient to cope with very large simultaneous demand can be prohibitive; tensions are likely to arise between local and global targeting (e.g. over news and advertising); similarity with other stations' playlists may make it a pointless exercise; music copyright issues need thorough investigation (Chapters 5, 8 and 10).

Adding side channels

Terrestrial broadcasters are experimenting with adding side channels accessible from their websites alongside their simulcast. Some are narrowly targeted music channels, some are archive channels for special interest content. This is a smart way of integrating the unique niche and on-demand capabilities of web radio and at the same time reinforcing the interactive attraction of their websites (Chapter 5).

Integration of tuners

For the listener, the transmission route is usually immaterial so long as they can tune in to a clear signal. On this basis, the pioneers of web radio receivers are demonstrating models that integrate an Internet band alongside FM and AM in the same tuner. Similar integration is being tried with DAB and digital direct satellite delivery (Chapter 3).

In-house radio stations

Again, in-house or internal radio stations are not unique to web radio (store chains have used satellite distribution of their in-house stations for years, designed to build the brand's customer relationship). But the Web now provides an easier way for any suitable institution to do this without occupying valuable

So how is web radio different? A checklist

237

transmission spectrum. Even geographically dispersed organizations can run their own flexible internal radio station on their intranet. It may, for example, only want to transmit for an hour or two a day (Chapters 3 and 4).

Web radio as a proving ground

Web radio has the potential to be a rich resource for broadcasters as a proving ground for new presenters and, we hope, daring and imaginative programme makers, prepared to think beyond the mind-set that has evolved in the process of chasing median tastes to maximize audience. Claire Condra (2000) suggests, for example, that a broadcaster with a website, who is looking to create some niche content for a side channel, might be able to find just the programmes or presenters already finding the target listeners on their own small sites. This approach could enrich the total mix of radio programming (Chapter 10).

Automated music channels

The global mass market in formatted music stations can now be most efficiently served by automated music channels – whether they appear on the Web or on satellite, digital or analogue terrestrial stations. The Web has at least three clear advantages in this trend:

1 It can offer an infinite number of niche formats and permutations of niches.
2 It can add or remove channels at will without reference to licensing agreements.
3 It is the one platform that can claim to be one click away from a direct sale – whether of a download or a hard copy.

The economics of automation make it almost inevitable that music channels will come to occupy a very substantial section of the total listening market. I have been keen to stress that this form of listening is very much on the margins of what we know as radio. However, I have little doubt that, on whichever platform, it will transform the pattern of radio listening (Chapter 2).

Ways of being a web station

For an *established terrestrial station*, as noted under the previous main heading, a *simulcast* web presence is the obvious first step, though not necessarily the most fruitful. *Side channels* can extend the station's appeal and target specific sections of the total broadcast audience, perhaps on a rotational basis (Chapters 5 and 10).

A *web-only station* can be either/or a combination of *live* and *on-demand streams* – according to their aims, their means and their ability to generate content. For music stations, the distinction between three types of streams is technical rather than aesthetic. The listener may not spot whether they have clicked onto a stream that:

- always starts from zero and runs to the end of the show (on demand);
- joins a live output from a live studio; or
- joins a live stream on a randomized, automated rotation, which may or may not include speech inserts, ads, news, etc.

Unless a station has copyright clearance though, it's often safer to avoid offering the first of these options for music (Chapter 8). On balance, unless an online-only station is in the rare position of having a live studio output for speech programmes, on demand is particularly effective for pre-recorded programmes or sections of programmes ('as live' or 'built'). This ability to time shift and indeed make more than a full day's schedule available to choose from is just not feasible on a broadcast frequency – which is why many speech-based broadcasters around the world have taken to on-demand archiving (Chapters 6 and 11).

Scalable output

Whereas broadcasters have to justify their licence with a full schedule of programming 365 days a year, the start-up station on the Web can choose to create only a short schedule of live and/or archive streams to test the water. The danger for archive streams in this situation is if they appear lifeless or, worse still, dated. Analogue radio tells us that a sense of 'liveness' or spontaneity or unexpectedness is crucial for drawing the listener into a piece of radio. The makers of speech-orientated programmes can compensate by applying the broadcaster's skills of programme making. For any short-form station, it is crucial to set the streams on offer in the right dynamic website environment – so that the website clearly has a living presence behind it (Chapters 6, 7 and 11).

Using a host service

For stations or private individuals without the time, inclination, technical ability or access to adequate bandwidth, there are a range of extremely expert host services. As a first step, this can be anything from the cheap and cheerful portal site to a completely customized site/station management deal. The latter are especially useful as a means of coping with rapidly increasing audiences or special events, where guaranteed bandwidth is usually essential. These options are very far removed from the way broadcasting has traditionally worked (Chapters 4 and 7).

Managing your own station's streaming server

This provides complete independence as a webcaster. It requires time and a certain amount of technical ability to do well, but in the long run can keep running costs right down. This kind of solo independence is rare in the world of broadcasting. Ham radio and CB, where they are allowed, have been set about with restrictions, which have meant they remained more like remote telephony than radio. Small-scale third sector radio has been closer to it – although maintaining (or evading) a licence is a constant struggle in most parts of the world (Chapter 4).

Variety of website strategies

The station website has opened a new route for dialogue between any radio station and its listeners. This is changing the way many broadcasters work, but web radio stations have more opportunity to respond directly to individual members of a smaller audience (Chapters 5, 6 and 7).

Regulation and control

Copyright

The painful process of adapting copyright regulation to cope with the Internet is a serious problem for many web radio stations, especially those who are simulcasting a broadcast output and especially those based in America. The copyright issue is mainly a threat to the future profitability of web radio more than to its creative potential, because it is about the playing of mainstream popular music to build audience. Web radio, as defined in this book, is not the same as music file sharing, but for now it has found itself considered guilty by association. This is part of a very complex set of issues that will certainly redefine the present relationship between the major record companies, their artists, the whole of the radio industry and the music fan. Although radio broadcasters currently have the advantage of holding clear-cut music licenses, on the other hand web stations stand to be beneficiaries of the confusion if they can forge positive working relationships with the minor record labels, and directly with artists. This small-scale approach again fits with the niche audience role (Chapter 8).

Licensing

This is only an issue between web radio stations and copyright holders. At the moment there is no prospect of any equivalent of broadcast licences applying to web radio. However – as with any other medium – if a station is effective in opposing an authoritarian government attempts will very likely be made to locate its source and to find a pretext for taking it offline (Chapter 9).

Content regulation

While it is a mistake to consider the Internet as a medium immune from the laws of the land in the long term, web radio stations are unlikely to find their output being subjected to regulations that apply to broadcast content. (Text and images will be the focus of attempts to regulate Internet content for the foreseeable future.) On web radio there are no obligations to exercise political impartiality, good taste, decency or restraint in opinions expressed – the kinds of restrictions that are applied to many broadcasters under liberal democracies. Similarly, web radio can also sidestep the need to adhere to a particular party line under more authoritarian regimes if they can manage to locate their streaming server safely where restrictions do not apply (Chapter 9).

Free speech and responsibility

On the flip side of freedom of speech lie the ethical and moral consequences of what a station airs. Here reputation is the governing factor in place of external control. Again, this is an important new area for many experienced radio makers, who are more used to knowing what limits they are bound by. The content they put out on a web station is more fully a matter of individual conscience and demands a framework of media ethics for which the maker takes responsibility (Chapter 9).

The consequences of free speech

The downside of working outside laws and regulations is that a station's site is also much more exposed to the actions of any opponents it may gather than broadcasters are used to. It usually takes a government (or a coup) to close a broadcaster down. On the Internet, a determined individual with a reasonable knowledge of computers can close a website down, if only temporarily. The chances of detection or redress are minute (Chapter 9).

So how is web radio different? A checklist

241

Content

Putting the elements of the above summary together suggests the following as answers to the twin questions I began with. The strengths that web radio has to offer over traditional radio are decidedly complementary to it rather than supplanting it: they add to radio's horizontal capability and do not challenge its broadcast position. Therefore, web radio content needs to cater to narrower sections of audience and minority tastes: it needs to offer the kind of programmes that are not available in any given area on broadcast radio. It can do this anywhere on a scale from a geographically extremely local basis out to a global, but dispersed, basis. Because its infrastructure makes web radio unable, so far, to compete with traditional broadcasters, it needs to explore and exploit these unique new niche characteristics, which means dividing content *between* live or archived streams rather than trying to create a traditional broad mix *across* a 24-hour live schedule.

This conclusion is slightly complicated by the fact that web radio is part of the overall digitalization of the radio industry. We need to make a distinction between content characteristics that are due to that digitalization and those that are due to the niche and on-demand properties of Internet distribution. The automated playout of genre-specific music channels is not confined to web radio: it is also present in the 100 channels now being offered on, for example, the XM direct digital satellite. To a lesser extent, it is part of the multiplex infrastructure of DAB, and automated random rotations are increasingly being used as a way of cutting costs on analogue music radio stations around the world. The extent to which listeners will respond to that choice and hence support advertising revenues has yet to be proven. It's early days. But if this approach does work, it will clearly become the dominant form for delivering mainstream – i.e. broadcast – music radio. It won't be so particular to web radio as it is at the moment.

So what can make web radio content different? Mainly, that it's potentially orientated towards people as individuals rather than as mass audiences – both as listeners and, crucially, as programme makers.

Broadcasters with a simulcast stream

The real questions here are (a) whether being on the Internet adds anything to the broadcast content, and (b) whether the combined presence of the website and stream really is in tune with the horizontal character of the medium.

Music stations can:

- Extend the appeal of their broadcast output into other territories (or to fill in locally poor reception, especially for workplace listeners). This is likely to be because its *DJ presentation* and *music policy* are distinctive.

- Add archived side channels that add depth but appeal to sub-segments of the broad audience.
- Add live streamed side channels – though with caution. A strong existing brand is probably required to carry committed listeners over.
- Work with advertisers and sponsors to develop much more targeted promotional campaigns online – e.g. through ad insertion, carrying offline listeners to the website and co-ordinating on- and offline activities.

Speech stations can:

- Most importantly, develop strategies for their archive streams. Such strategies need to take account of short-term time shifting (within, say, a 24-hour or weekly cycle) and longer term archiving.
- Make available material they otherwise don't have time to include in specialist programmes, e.g. extended interviews.
- Develop website links to other programme makers to provide depth in background to their existing programming (on the assumption that they don't have spare budget to create new material to develop their own online-only side channels).

(See Chapters 5, 10 and 11.)

Web-only stations

For these stations to survive this pioneering phase, it is more important for them to understand the creative spirit of the Internet than the business models for broadcasting. They may simply be motivated by the fun of getting something they've made out there in the public domain, or by a desire to make the programmes they don't hear on the broadcast stations they can pick up; they will probably need a combination of the two. But as a survival strategy, whether for music or speech, they need:

- First and foremost to understand how to make good radio programmes that communicate the passions and enthusiasms of the individuals behind them.
- To take full advantage of web radio's scalability and concentrate on quality above quantity of output. With careful use of archive streams, the investment in programme content lasts longer on the Web. The proven strategy so far is to build audience patiently by establishing reputation among a very small listener base. In web radio you can afford the time it takes to do that if you don't over-invest in equipment and bandwidth to begin with. So far, the broadcast model of spending heavily on creating a big 'noise' at the outset has proved extremely expensive and notably ineffective on the Web.

So how is web radio different? A checklist

243

- To learn how to work with their audience in ways that broadcasting cannot: by making intelligent use of what their server metrics are telling them about who's listening to their content; by being able to respond; by using the station website positively to open and maintain dialogue; by thinking of audiences as potential contributors more than as listening numbers.

Above all, can we come up with the content, the new style of programme, the public service, the distinctive entertaining mix, the community building station that we always felt was missing from our own local patch of the airwaves? Because if we, as listeners, can't think of what that station would sound like the whole of radio's future in the digital era will surely be the poorer. There is a fantastic opportunity here, but there's also nothing automatic to say that web radio, the technology, will provide us with content that takes advantage of its unique potential. Just as in the 1920s, the new radio technology is only going to become what creative people make it.

(See Chapters 6, 10 and 11.)

Appendix 1 Glossary

ADSL Asymmetric Digital Subscriber Line. A technology upgrade to a local telco exchange which converts a normal copper wire phone line to a broadband connection for domestic receivers. 'Asymmetric' refers to there being a higher bandwidth available for incoming signals than outgoing.

Airport Apple's wireless technology which allows multiple computers to be networked together over short distances using radio frequencies (RF).

Algorithm A complex mathematical formula which defines a sequence of steps or computations. In this context, any formula which compresses digitized sound data.

AM Amplitude Modulation: the first of the two technologies for transmitting analogue sound on radio waves.

Analogue Applied to radio, as opposed to digital. Adjective describing the carriage of sound in the form of continuously varying electrical current and/or continuously varying electromagnetic signals.

Archive In streaming terminology this is interchangeable with 'on demand'. However, it should not be confused with archive in the sense of keeping a permanent audio record, e.g. on CD.

Archiving Storing encoded audio on a server ready for streaming on demand.

ASF Microsoft Windows proprietary streaming file format for Media Player, Active Streaming Format.

Audion A software product developed by Panic for storing, sending or receiving MP3 streams on a Macintosh computer.

Bandwidth The capacity of an Internet (i.e. phone) connection. Measured in bits per second, or the SI multiples: kilobits (thousands), megabits (millions) or gigabits (thousand millions).

Bit The smallest unit of binary computer code: a one or a zero. In electronic terms, a command to switch micro-current either off or on.

Bit depth The resolution of a digital sample of sound. The higher the bit depth, the higher the fidelity across the full range of sound frequencies.

Bit rate An expression of bandwidth: the rate of bits transmitted or passing per second.

Bluetooth An 'open source' (i.e. non-proprietary) standard or version of wireless technology, which allows multiple computers or microcomputers to communicate together using radio frequencies (RF).

Browser A software application which gives you access to the Web, such as Netscape or Microsoft's Internet Explorer.

Byte The standard unit of stored binary data, equal to eight bits.

Circuit switching 'Old-fashioned' phone technology which 'engages' a route between two phones as a continuous connection for the duration of the call.

CODEC A name given to any proprietary software which *CO*des and *DEC*odes data. In the context of web radio, the major streaming CODECs are the Real, Windows Media and MP3 formats.

Co-location (or colo) A secure facility designed to house Web servers securely, with a regulated, backed-up power supply and dedicated Internet connections.

Compress 1. (Traditionally) To squeeze a sound signal electronically in order to reduce the difference in volume between the quietest and loudest parts of the signal. Typically applied prior to transmission to boost average analogue or digital broadcast levels, the better to 'cut through' noisy listening environments, especially the car.

Compress 2. (In streaming) To massively reduce the size of a digitized audio or video file for streaming, by applying a specialist algorithm or software CODEC, e.g. MP3.

CPU Central Processing Unit. The heart of a computer; its microprocessor or microchip, which processes binary data. The speed of the CPU (in megahertz, MHz) or multiple CPUs determines how long the user has to wait for anything to happen on their computer.

DAT Digital Audio Tape. One medium for storing recorded sound, usually at very high quality, in digital form. A professional format.

Data rate The same as bit rate or connection speed.

DAW Digital Audio Workstation.

Decompress The receiving side of definition 2 under 'compress', above.

Digital Audio Broadcasting (DAB) Both a generic term and the proprietary name given to a transmission system for radio which uses parts of the upper end of the VHF spectrum. Around eight stations are bundled together into 'multiplexes' of simultaneous transmission on a given receiving frequency.

Digitalization (As opposed to digitization, q.v.) Generally applied to the conversion of an entire production operation (e.g. radio broadcasting, or newspaper layout and printing) from analogue technology to digital technology.

Digital Millennium Copyright Act (DMCA or DM Act) An influential piece of legislation, which was passed into American law in 1998 in order to protect copyright holders from the effects of digitalization.

Digital Radio Mondiale (DRM) A transmission technology for converting radio signals in the AM spectrum from poor quality analogue into high quality digital sound (see also DAB).

Digitization The conversion of analogue signal information into digital data.

Direct Satellite Broadcasting As distinct from terrestrial broadcasting, the transmission of radio or TV stations via satellite, direct to domestic receivers, which typically incorporate some form of dish.

DSL Digital Subscriber Line. The generic term for a range of differing technologies for massively increasing the data capacity of phone lines, of which ADSL (q.v.) is one.

DSP Digital Signal Processor.

Edge services Specialist multimedia Internet services whose physical location close to the highest bandwidths at the core of the Internet allow them to guarantee the most reliable connection and high data rates.

Electrophone Earliest use of the telephone network for transmitting public sound narrow-casts via local exchanges, before the invention of analogue radio.

Encode Convert an analogue or digital sound (or video) signal into one of the streaming formats (e.g. Real, WMP, QuickTime, MP3), prior to distribution on the Web by a suitable streaming server.

Encrypton Scrambling a digital signal so that it only makes sense to receivers with the codes to unscramble it. The mechanism underlying subscription-based delivery over the Web.

Firewall A general term for security software that protects a computer network connected to the Internet. It prevents anyone gaining unauthorized access to the network from an outside computer – and therefore can present a barrier to streaming if not configured appropriately.

FM Frequency Modulation. The second of the two technologies for transmitting analogue sound on radio waves.

2.5G A tag given to the GPRS (q.v.) mobile phone system. (If WAP is the second generation and UMTS will be the third, then GPRS is half way between.)

3G A tag given to the third generation of mobile phones, UMTS (q.v.).

GPRS General Packet Radio System. The mobile phone protocol that aims to succeed WAP (q.v.). Because it is packet switched it is always on and can carry data much faster than the circuit switched systems before it.

html Hyper Text Mark-up Language. The main coding standard for creating web pages so they can be read by browsers. The file extension thereof.

http Hyper Text Transport Protocol. The coding standards which govern the transfer of web pages between servers and client computers on the Web.

Hub A type of junction box on a computer network. It is a passive device, as opposed to a 'switch', which can actively assign pathways.

IBOC 'In Band On Channel' A system for delivering digital audio broadcasting on existing AM and FM frequencies. Currently being developed for the US Market by the iBiquity company.

ICT Internet and Communications Technologies.

iDAB The name trademarked by iBiquity for their IBOC (q.v.) technology.

i-mode A mobile phone system capable of accessing appropriately coded web pages, developed by the Japanese telco, DoCoMo. Roughly equivalent to WAP (q.v.).

Internet The global network of computers made up of a collection of inter-connected sub-networks.

Intranet A network of computers within a business or organization.

IP Internet Protocol. Part of the universal system of standard protocols which are the basis of packet transmission. The other part is Transmission Control Protocol (TCP).

IP address The unique numerical address of a connection to the Internet.

ISMA Internet Streaming Media Alliance.

ISP Internet Service Provider.

ISPA The Internet Service Providers' Association.

kbps Kilobits per second. The usual unit in the measurement of the speed, or capacity, of an Internet connection.

LAN Local Area Network. A small network of computers.

Mb Megabit (see bit).

MB Megabyte (see byte).

Mbone A multicast (q.v.) enabled route through the Internet.

Mbps Megabits per second: the unit for measuring the capacity of fast Internet connections.

MD MiniDisc: a medium now widely used for storing digital audio. Uses heavier compression than CD or DAT, but provides excellent sound quality for routine radio uses.

Media Player 1. The generic term for any software plug-in which plays back streaming audio or video.

Media Player 2. A common abbreviation of the Windows Media Player plug-in.

Metrics data Audience data collected automatically by a server on each request for a web radio unicast (q.v.) stream, including its location, connection speed and time and duration of connection.

MHz Megahertz: millions of cycles per second. A measurement of frequency.

MP3 Abbreviation of one very widely used compression standard. Short for MPEG II, layer 3. Layer 3 refers to the complexity of the algorithm and is an indicator of the processing power needed to run it.

MPEG Moving Picture Experts Group. The general term applied to any compression algorithm for audio and/or video devised under their supervision.

m3u The name (or file extension) given to encoded sequences of MP3 files.

Multicast A mode of Internet distribution which allows a single output from one server to be repeatedly split by 'multicast-enabled' routers and hence available to multiple connections. Therefore, unlike unicast (q.v.), it can only be used to receive live streaming and not for on demand.

Net congestion The common cause of break-up of audio steams, which occurs when Internet traffic comes close to the capacity of regions of the telecoms network. Particularly noticeable when, for example, East Coast America wakes up and starts getting online *en masse*.

NMPA National Music Publishers Association. Influential body representing the US music publishers.

OFCOM Office of Communications: the UK government's proposed new multimedia and telecommunications regulator.

Packet The standard unit of data that is sent across the Internet. Typically comprises 1024 bits of data. This includes a section of the message plus a 'header', which details the destination IP 'address', the sender's IP 'address', a check digit which confirms the data have not become corrupted and the packet's position in the sequence of the message.

Packet switching As opposed to circuit switching. A digital switching technology which massively improves the efficiency of telecoms pathways by making them continuously available for multiple simultaneous connections. This is possible when data pass through such a system as packets rather than complete messages.

Portal An Internet site which acts as a gateway or guide to the Web. Inevitably, each portal specializes in particular kinds of sites that are likely to be popular with its regular users.

QuickTime Apple's streaming software.

Radio Originally the shortened form of radiotelegraphy, derived from radiant or radiating, and applied to its apparatus. Subsequently radio-telephone (point to point) and later the receiver for sound broadcasting (one to many).

RAM Random Access Memory. The measure of the amount of space available for storing files on a computer's hard disk.

RealPlayer The software helper application needed to receive Real audio and video streams.

Re-purposed An adjective often used for streamed content that was originated for analogue broadcast. This may be the same as simulcast or else refer to archived material.

Resolution The detail contained within each sample in the process of digitizing sound. Along with the sample rate (q.v.), this determines the limits of accuracy or fidelity of digital sound. Measured in bits, hence also called 'bit depth'.

RF Radio frequency. Describes the part of the electromagnetic spectrum used for transmitting signals – typically in connection with remote control wireless technology.

RIAA Record Industries Association of America. The highly influential body that lobbies on behalf of the major international record companies.

Ripping Digital audio extraction. Copying directly (i.e. digitally) from an audio CD format into a sound file format on a hard drive.

Router A specialized computer which selectively routes data to different destinations on a network. Routers are therefore the motors of the Internet (and the packet-switched phone system), receiving packets of data, reading their header codes and re-sending them on to the next available router towards their destination.

RTP Real-time Transport Protocol. An open standard file transfer protocol suitable for streaming. Used by QuickTime among other formats.

RTSP Real-Time Streaming Protocol. The request, on-demand side to RTP in a unicast streaming set-up.

Sample rate The number of times per second an analogue current (carrying a sound signal) is sampled in the process of digitization. Along with the resolution (q.v.) of samples, this determines the accuracy or fidelity of digital sound.

Server Any computer that distributes ('serves') data across a network. In the context of streaming, it is typically a specialized machine with one or more fast processors and plenty of memory.

SHOUTcast One of the major software products for streaming MP3 files, made by Nullsoft.

Simulcast Distribute radio (or TV) content through more than one outlet at the same time. Originally applied to radio stations which broadcast identical content simultaneously on more than one frequency (e.g. on FM and AM), it is now applied to analogue or digital broadcasts which are simultaneously webcast.

Standard A universally or widely authorized and freely available (i.e. non-proprietary) file format, computer code or language; e.g. WAV or MP3 are standard audio file formats, html is a standard language for building web pages.

Stream Verb or noun describing the process of transmitting digitized audio (or video) across the Internet so that it can be heard or viewed in real time.

StreamWorks An early, high quality audio and video streaming system based on MPEG files, developed by Xing Technologies, now part of RealNetworks.

Strip scheduling Regularized, fixed scheduling, which places the same programme or type of programme in the same time slot every day – in a strip across a 5- or 7-day weekly schedule. The framework of format radio.

Telco Short for telephone company.

Terrestrial transmission Broadcasting from a radio wave transmitter.

Time shifting Listening to programmes at a time determined by the listener, not by a transmission schedule. In web radio this is made possible by on-demand or archived streams.

Timed out An error message received when RealPlayer has repeatedly tried and failed to receive a stream. It is controlled by an option in the set-up of the RealServer which sets a time limit for a stream to be established successfully or else aborted.

TiVo An early proprietary example of a digital television which incorporates a high capacity hard disk recorder for storing hours of programming.

UDP User Datagram Protocol. An alternative, faster Internet file transport standard to TCP/IP (q.v.). Used by the QuickTime CODEC and other RTP/RTSP compatible formats.

UMTS Universal Mobile Telecommunications System. The transmission standard for the forthcoming '3G' global mobile phone network.

Unicast The usual mode of streaming, which involves maintaining a one to one dialogue between each receiver and the streaming server. As opposed to multicast (q.v.).

URL Uniform Resource Locator. The standard form of address for locating a web page.

USIIA United States Internet Industry Association.

VBR Variable Bit Rate. A software function which detects the end to end bandwidth available for a streaming connection and automatically adjusts the output from the server accordingly.

VDSL Very high data rate DSL (q.v.). Currently in development. Intended to offer TV quality data rates through phone connections over short distances, e.g. between a local fibre optic link and the subscriber.

WAP Wireless Application Protocol.

Webcasting Generic term for transmitting audio or video content (with accompanying website text) on the Web using streaming software.

Winamp Nullsoft's PC-based receiver for streaming MP3.

WIPO The United Nations World Intellectual Property Organization.

Wireless A word which has been used to describe successive technological revolutions in radio's history. Originally applied to analogue radio sets with internal speakers (though they were still wired to mains electricity), it now describes technologies which link computers and their peripheral hardware by means of remote radio signals instead of wires or cables.

Wireless broadband The marriage of broadband and wireless technologies to give high quality remote access to the Internet – a 'holy grail' for the Internet in general and streaming technologists in particular.

Wireless Internet Connection to the Internet via satellite or a terrestrial transmission network, instead of through a phone cable. Currently through WAP or i-mode (q.v.).

WMP Windows Media Player, the client software for Microsoft's proprietary streaming format.

World Wide Web The most widely accessed part of the Internet, unified by the computing standards laid down by W3C, the World Wide Web Consortium.

Xing A software company that developed StreamWorks, an early, high quality audio and video streaming system based on MPEG files. Now part of RealNetworks.

Zoning (As applied to the World Wide Web) A measure advocated by some for separating out Web content into clearly identifiable categories (zones) to make it more amenable to regulation or to enable entry barriers to restrict or charge for access to different types of content.

Appendix 2 Useful websites

This is intended to provide some starting points for further research into the subjects contained in this book. It does not and cannot claim to be a fully comprehensive guide to sites that have some relevance to web radio. My apologies to all those people who are working hard to contribute to the development of web radio and whose hundreds (or possibly thousands) of websites I have not included.

It is essentially a list of sites I've included in the text of this book, plus a few more I've come across in my research. See also Appendix 3.

Streaming software products and information

Apple QuickTime home page	http://www.apple.com/quicktime/
Apple QuickTime tutorial	http://www.apple.com/quicktime/ products/tutorials/
Audion 2 (Mac MP3 player/streamer)	http://www.panic.com/audion/
Freeamp (PC MP3 players)	http://www.freeamp.org/
Icecast (MP3 streaming) home page	http://www.icecast.org/
K-jöfol	http://www.sonicspot.com/kjofol/ kjofol.html
Live Channel streaming	http://www.channelstorm.com/
Macast (Mac MP3 player)	http://www.macast.com/
MusicMatch Jukebox (PC and Mac MP3 players)	http://www.musicmatch.com/
RealNetworks home page	http://www.realnetworks.com/
RealNetworks tutorials	http://www.realnetworks.com/ getstarted/index.html
RealPlayer home page	http://www.real.com/
SHOUTcast home page (MP3 streaming)	http://www.shoutcast.com/

Sonique (Windows MP3 player)   http://sonique.lycos.com/
Sorenson streaming products   http://www.sorenson.com/
StreamWorks (MP3 streaming)   http://www.xingtech.com/
Winamp (Windows MP3 player)   http://www.winamp.com/
Windows Media Player   http://www.microsoft.com/windows/
                                   windowsmedia/
Xaudio (Unix MP3 player)   http://www.xaudio.com/
XMMS (Unix MP3 player)   http://www.xmms.org/

Some other streaming-related products

Dedicated streaming hardware tuners

Akoo 'Kima' KS-110   http://www.akoo.com/site/products.cfm
iM Radio tuner   http://www.sonicbox.com/
Kerbango AM/FM/Internet radio   http://www.kerbango.com/
   (mothballed)
Penguin Radio   http://www.penguinradio.com/

Some commonly used Digital Audio Workstations

CoolEdit Pro (incl. Real and MP3   http://www.syntrillium.com/
   encoding)
Soundforge (incl. Real, WMP and   http://www.sonicfoundry.com/
   MP3 encoding)
TC Works Spark XL (for Mac incl. QT) http://www.tcworks.de/

DSP processing for streaming

eStream   http://www.audiovault.com/
                                   ProducteSTREAM/eSTREAM.html

Wireless technology sites

Apple Airport   http://www.apple.com/airport/
Bluetooth   http://www.bluetooth.com/
Wireless LAN   http://www.wirelesslan.com/

Relevant directories to web radio sites

Akoo (online tuner)   http://www.akoo.com/
Apple's iTunes tuner download   http://www.apple.com/itunes/
Apple's Quick Time tuner   http://www.apple.com/quicktime/qtv/
                                            radio/
Audio Hyperspace guide to   http://www.swr2.de/hoerspiel/
   experimental sites   audiohyperspace/index.html
ComFM tuner   http://www.comfm.com/live/radio/
Cyberradio online tuner   http://www.cyberradio.com/
Live-Radio (all radio online)   http://www.live-radio.net/
MIT Radio-Locator (all radio)   http://www.radio-locator.com/
Penguin   http://www.penguinradio.com/
                                            stations.html
Radio4All alternative tuner   http://www.radio4all.org/
Radio Free World alternative online   http://www.radiofreeworld.com/
   tuner
RealPlayer tuner   http://realguide.real.com/tuner/
SHOUTcast MP3 tuner   http://www.shoutcast.com/directory/
Windows   http://windowsmedia.com/radiotuner/
                                            defaultalt.asp
Yahoo!Radio   http://radio.broadcast.com/

Streaming news and information

Current (the NPR journal)   http://www.current.org/
Radio And Internet Newsletter (*RAIN*)   http://www.kurthanson.com/
Radio Ink   http://www.radioink.com/
Streaming magazine   http://www.streamingmagazine.net/
The Standard (Internet industry news)   http://www.thestandard.com/
Whatis?com   http://WhatIs.techtarget.com/
Wired   http://www.wired.com/
ZdNet (Internet technology news)   http://www.zdnet.co.uk/

Radio and Web industry and related organizations

Commercial Radio Companies Assn   http://www.crca.co.uk/
   (UK)
Community Media Assn (UK)   http://www.commedia.org.uk/
Digital Media Association (US based)   http://www.digmedia.org/

European Broadcasting Union	http://www.ebu.ch/
Ham Radio links	http://www.ham-links.org/
Ham Radio news	http://www.arnewsline.org/
International Association of Student Radio	http://www.iastar.org/
Internet Streaming Media Alliance	http://www.isma.tv/
National Association of Broadcasters (US)	http://www.nab.org/
Radio Authority UK Codes of Conduct	http://www.radioauthority.org.uk/ Information/Publications/index.html
UK Hospital Radio	http://www.hospitalradio.co.uk/
UNESCO	http://www.unesco.org/webworld/ observatory/index.shtml
US College Radio	http://www.collegelife.about.com/ education/msub11.htm
World Association of Community Broadcasters (AMARC)	http://www.amarc.org/

Audience measurements and research

Arbitron	http://www.arbitron.com/
Edison Research	http://www.edisonresearch.com/
Jupiter Media Metrix	http://www.jmm.com/
MeasureCast	http://www.measurecast.com/
Nielsen Net Ratings	http://neilsen-netratings.com
NUA Internet surveys	http://www.nua.ie/surveys/
Scarborough Research	http://www.scarborough.com/
UCLA Internet Research	http://www.ccp.ucla.edu/

Streaming host services

High end, edge of Net services

Akami	http://www.akamai.com/
Coollink Broadcast Network	http://www.clbn.com/
Digital Island	http://www.digitalisland.com/
Level3	http://www.level3.co.uk/
Madge.web	http://www.madgeweb.com/
Perfect Technologies	http://www.perfect.fr/

ISPs and low end web radio host services

Demon (a UK ISP)	http://www.demon.net/
Live365	http://www.live365.com/
Silver (an Austrian ISP)	http://www.sil.at/
StreamAudio	http://www.streamaudio.com/
XS4all (a Dutch ISP)	http://www.xs4all.nl/uk/

Copyright-related organizations

ASCAP music publication (US)	http://www.ascap.com/
Association of Independent Music	http://www.musicindie.org/
BMI music publication (US)	http://www.bmi.com/
British Actors' Equity	http://www.equity.org.uk/
Harry Fox Agency (US mechanical copyright)	http://www.nmpa.org/hfa.html
Kohn Music (US) copyright advice site	http://www.kohnmusic.com/
Mechanical Copyright Protection Society (UK)	http://www.mcps.co.uk/
National Music Publishers Association (US)	http://www.nmpa.org/
Performing Rights Society (UK)	http://www.prs.co.uk/
Phonographic Performance Ltd (UK)	http://www.ppluk.com/
Recording Industry Association of America	http://www.riaa.com/
SESAC music publication (US)	http://www.sesac.com/
WIPO treaties (UN)	http://www.wipo.int/treaties/ip/copyright/index.html
Writers Guild (UK)	http://www.writers.org.uk/

Some sources of Internet-related information

Digimarc electronic watermarking	http://www.digimarc.com/
Electronic Frontier Foundation	http://www.eff.org/radioeff/
Freedom.net security products	http://www.freedom.net/
Google search	http://www.google.com/
ICANN Internet naming and numbering	http://www.icann.org/
Internet promotion service	http://www.virtualdomain.net/
Internet Watch Foundation	http://www.iwf.org.uk/

ISPA	http://www.ispa.org.uk/html/code_of_practice.htm
Ixquick search	http://www.ixquick.com/
Lawrence Lessig's site	http://cyberlaw.stanford.edu/lessig/content/index.html
Lycos Voice Chat	http://www.uk.lycos.de/service/mediaring/service
Search Engine Watch	http://www.searchenginewatch.com/
Submit-It Internet listing service	http://www.submit-it.com/
UK Data Protection guidelines	http://wood.ccta.gov.uk/dpr/dpdoc.nsf
US Internet Industry Association	http://www.usiia.org/
USIIA guidelines	http://www.usiia.org/legis/privacy.html
'Virtual Communities' – Howard Rheingold	http://www.rheingold.com/
Vivisimo search	http://www.vivisimo.com/
Web Developers' online journal	http://www.webdevelopersjournal.com/
We-blocker web filter	http://www.we-blocker.com/
World Wide Web Consortium (W3C)	http://www.w3c.org/
W3C's security advice	http://www.w3.org/Security/

Other digital radio platforms

Digital Audio Broadcasting	http://www.worlddab.com/
Digital Radio Mondiale	http://www.drm.org/
iBiquity	http://www.ibiquity.com/
OnStar in-car 'Internet'	http://www.onstar.com/
Psion Wavefinder (DAB receiver)	http://www.wavefinder.com/
Sirius digital satellite (N America)	http://www.siriusradio.com/
Worldspace satellite (international)	http://www.worldspace.com/
XM digital satellite (N America)	http://www.xmradio.com/

Some examples of web and/or broadcast radio stations

Those cited in this book (with apologies to all the others):

4ZZZ	http://www.4zzzfm.org.au/
95bFM	http://www.95bfm.co.nz/bfm.php
ABC's Radio National	http://www.abc.net.au/rn/
All India Radio	http://air.kode.net/live.html
Are You Sitting Comfortably (US archive)	http://www.rusc.com/

B92	http://www.freeB92.net/
BBC Online	http://www.bbc.co.uk
BBC Radio 4	http://www.bbc.co.uk/radio4/
BBC Radio 1 FM	http://www.bbc.co.uk/radio1/
CFUV, University of Victoria (case study)	http://cfuv.uvic.ca/
Freirad	http://www.freirad.at/
Horizontal Radio (archive)	http://gewi.kfunigraz.ac.at/~gerfried/horrad/
Independent Radio Drama Productions	http://www.idrp.co.uk/
Jazz FM	http://www.jazzfm.com/
KGNU	http://www.kgnu.org/
Kothmale Community Radio (case study)	http://www.kothmale.net/
KPFA	http://www.kpfa.org/
Livemusic.com (pay channel)	http://www.livemusic.com/
Miki FM	http://www.fm-miki.com/
Minnesota Public Radio	http://www.mpr.org/
National Public Radio (US)	http://www.npr.org/
Net Radio (music channel)	http://www.netradio.com/
Orange 94.0	http://www.orange.or.au/
Peoplesound (e-music shop)	http://www.peoplesound.com/
Pirate Radio	http://www.blackcatsystems.com/radio/pirate.htm/
Power FM	http://www.powerfm.com/
Pulse Radio	http://www.pulseradio.net
Radio Free Quebec	http://www.radiofreedom.com/
Radio Netherlands (case study)	http://www.rnw.nl/en/index.html
Radio TNC (archive)	http://www.aec.at/residence/radio-tnc/
RadioValve (case study)	http://wwww.radiovalve.com/
Sci-Fi radio dramas	http://www.scifi.com/
Shaun MacLoughlin's Soundplay site	http://www.soundplay.co.uk/
South Africa FM	http://www.safm.co.za/
Spinner	http://www.spinner.com/
Virgin Radio (case study)	http://www.virginradio.co.uk/
Virtually America US drama work	http://www.virtuallyamerica.com/
Voix Sans Frontières (case study)	http://www.amarc.org/vsf/
Yuri Rasovsky's radio drama site	http://www.irasov.com/

Appendix 3 Bibliography

Adams, D. (2000). Introducing 'The Hitch-Hiker's Guide to the Future'. BBC Radio 4, 4 October.

Allan, S. (1999). *News Culture*. Routledge.

Ang, I. (1996). *Living Room Wars: Rethinking Audiences for the Postmodern World*. Routledge.

Arbitron/Edison Media Research (2001). *Internet VI: Streaming at a Cross-roads*. Executive summary available as pdf file at February 2001 from www.arbitron.com/.

Barnouw, E. (1966). *A Tower of Babel: A History of Broadcasting in the United States*, Vol. 1. Oxford University Press.

Beck, A. (2001). *The Death of Radio?* Monograph published at www.ukc.ac.uk/sdfra/deathofradio/index.html.

Beggs, J., Thede, D. and Koman, R. (eds) (2001). *Designing Web Audio*. O'Reilly & Associates.

Berners-Lee, T. (2000). *Weaving the Web*. Texere Publishing.

Bingaman, M. (2000). The side channel study: extending your brand on the Internet. *Radio Ink*, 7 December. Published as at April 2001 at http://www.radioink.com/inkheadlines.asp?page=31.

Boyd-Barratt, O. (ed.) (1998). *The Globalisation of News*. Sage.

Braithwaite, N. (ed.) (1996). *The International Libel Handbook. A Practical Guide for Journalists*. Butterworth-Heinemann.

Briggs, A. (1995). *The Birth of Broadcasting 1896–1927*. Oxford University Press.

Carter, M. E. (1996). *Electronic Highway Robbery: An Artist's Guide to Copyrights in the Digital Era*. Peachpit Press.

Collin, M. (2001). *This Is Serbia Calling*. Serpent's Tail.

Condra, C. (2000). Stuck in the fast lane. *Radio Ink* conference provides a reality check and practical strategies for survival. *iRadio*, Vol. 6, no. 3 (December).

Covell, A. (1999). *Digital Convergence: How the Merging of Computers, Communications and Multimedia is Transforming Our Lives*. Aegis Publishing.

Creech, K. C. (1999). *Electronic Media Law and Regulation*. Focal Press.

Crisell, A. (1994). *Understanding Radio*. Routledge.

Crook, T. (1999). *Radio Drama: Theory and Practice*. Routledge.

Dean, D. (1997). *Web Channel Development for Dummies*. IDG Books.

Dennis, T. (2000). GPRS breaks its speed promise. *ZDNet UK IT Week*, published in January 20001 at www.zdnet.co.uk/itweek/analysis/2000/25/networks/gprs/01.html.

Department of Trade and Industry/Department of Culture, Media and Sport (2000). *A New Future for Communication*. London: The Stationary Office Limited (online at http://www.communicationswhitepaper.gov.uk/).

Dickinson, R., Linne, O. and Ramaswami, H. (eds) (1998). *Approaches to Audiences*. Arnold.

Dodson, S. and Barkham, P. (2000). Why the net is not invited to Sydney. *The Guardian*, 14 September.

Douglas, G. H. (1987). *The Early Days of Radio Broadcasting*. McFarland.

Douglas, S. J. (1999). *Listening In: Radio and the American Imagination, from Amos 'n' Andy and Ed Murrow to Wolfman Jack and Howard Stern*. New York: Random House.

EBU Webcasting Group (1999). *Practical Webcasting*. Published at www.rnw.nl/corporate/en/EBUWebcasting.99.pdf.

Engelman, R. (1996). *Public Radio and Television in America. A Political History*. Sage.

Flanders, V. and Willis, M. (1998). *Web Pages That Suck*. San Francisco: Sybex.

Fortune, D. and Adams, M. (1996). Radio and television on the Internet. In *New World Media*, Chapter 11. Published at http:/www.fortune.org/book/chapter11.html as at January 2001.

Frost, C. (2000). *Media Ethics and Self-Regulation*. Longman.

Gauntlett, D. (ed.) (2000). *Web.Studies*. Arnold.

Giffard, C. A. (1998). Alternative news agencies. In *The Globalisation of News* (O. Boyd-Barratt, ed.). Sage.

Gilliams, T. F. (1925). Radio service given over the telephone. *Radio News*, March, p. 1632. See White's URL.

Gold, S. (2001). End of the anonymous net. *The Guardian Online*, 22 March, p. 7.

Graham, G. (1999). *The Internet: A Philosophical Inquiry*. Routledge.

Haftke, M. (2000). Speech given at the Radio Academy 'Streaming 2000' Conference, London, 23 May.

Hashmi, Y. and Plumbridge, S. (1996). *The Internet for Broadcasters*. London: Sypha (http://www.mandy.com/2/sypha.html).

Helmore, E. (2001a). Chorus of confusion. *The Guardian Online*, 12 April, p. 7.

Helmore, E. (2001b). Net music strikes a bum note. *The Observer, Business & Media*, 28 October, p. 8.

Hendy, D. (2000). *Radio in the Global Age*. Polity Press.

Herbert, J. (2000). *Journalism in the Digital Age*. Focal Press.

Herbert, J. C. (2001). *Practising Global Journalism*. Focal Press.

Hilliard R. L. and Keith, M. C. (1996) *Global Broadcasting Systems*. Focal Press.

Hind, J. and Musco, S. (1985). *Rebel Radio: The Full Story of British Pirate Radio*. Pluto Press.

Holt, R. and Mandra, C. (2000). How NPR webifies its programming – and you can, too. *Current*, 30 October, published at http://www.current.org/stream/stream020npr.html as at February 2001.

Hoover, H. (1924). Opening Address to the 3rd Washington Radio Conference. See United States Department of Commerce.

Hoover, H. (1952). *The Memoirs of Herbert Hoover: the Cabinet and the Presidency, 1920–1933*. MacMillan.

IFPI (2000). World sales of recorded music – 1999. Published under 'Market Info' at www.ifpi.org/ as at February 2001.

Keith, M. C. (1997). *The Radio Station* (4th edn). Focal Press.

Kellow, C. L. and Steeves, H. L. (1998). The role of radio in the Rwandan genocide. *Journal of Communication*, **48** (3), 107–28.

Kohn, B. (1998). *A Primer on the Law of Webcasting and Digital Music Delivery*. Published as at February 2001 at www.kohnmusic.com/articles/newprimer.html.

Kosiur, D. R. (1998). *IP Multicasting: The Complete Guide to Interactive Corporate Networks*. Wiley.

Lake, D. (2001). Quick and easy. *The Standard Online* magazine, www.thestandard.com/, 26 February.

Lasar, M. (2000). *Pacifica Radio: The Rise of an Alternative Network*. Temple University Press.

Lessig, L. (1999). *Code: and Other Laws of Cyberspace*. Basic Books.

Levinson, P. (1999). *Digital McLuhan. A Guide to the Information Millennium*. Routledge.

Levy, D. A. (1999). Convergence. New approaches. In *Europe's Digital Revolution. Broadcasting Regulation, The EU and the Nation State*, Chapter 8. Routledge.

Lewis, P. M. and Booth, J. (1989). *The Invisible Medium*. MacMillan.

London Musician's Collective (1997). Retuning radio. *Resonance* **5** (2).

MacLoughlin, S. (2001). *Writing for Radio. How to Write Plays, Features and Short Stories That Get You On Air* (2nd edn). How To Books.

Mallapragada, M. (2000). The Indian diaspora in the USA and around the world. In *Web.Studies* (D. Gauntlett, ed.). Arnold.

Matic, V. and Pantic, D. (1999). War of words. When the bombs came, Serbia's B92 hit the Net. *The Nation*, 29 November. Published at http://past.thenation.com/issue/991129/1129matic.shtml as at April 2001.

McChesney, R. W. (1993). *Telecommunications, Mass Media and Democracy*. Oxford University Press.

McLeish, R. (1999). *Radio Production* (4th edn). Focal Press.

McQuail, D. and Siune, K. (eds) (1998). *Media Policy. Convergence, Concentration & Commerce*. Sage.

MeasureCast (2001). Press release: 'MeasureCast Releases March Internet Radio Report'. Published at http://www.measurecast.com/news/pr/2001/pr20010403m.html as at April 2001.

Merriden, T. (2001). *Irresistible Forces: The Business Legacy of Napster and the Growth of the Underground Internet*. Capstone.

Miles, P. (1997). *'Internet World''s Guide to Webcasting*. Wiley.

Milner, N. and Allen, N. (1995). *The Post Broadcasting Age: New Technologies, New Communities*. University of Luton Press.

Naughton, J. (2000). *A Brief History of the Future*. Phoenix.

Novak, J. and Markiewicz, P. (1998). *Web Developer.Com Guide to Producing Live Webcasts*. Wiley.

Patterson, J. and Melcher, R. (1998). *Audio on the Web: The Official IUMA Guide*. Peachpit Press.

Radio Authority (2000). http://www.radioauthority.org.uk.

Radio Netherlands (2001). Press release: 'Short-Wave of Publicity', 28 June.

Reese, D. E. and Gross, L. S. (2001). *Radio Production Worktext: Studio and Equipment* (4th edn). Focal Press.

Rehm, D. (1993). Talking over America's electronic backyard fence. *Media Studies Journal*, **7** (3).

Reith, J. W. C. (1924). *Broadcasting Over Britain*. Hodder & Stoughton.

Rheingold, H. (2000a). Community development in the cybersociety of the future. In *Web.Studies* (D. Gauntlett, ed.). Arnold.

Rheingold, H. (2000b). *The Virtual Community: Homesteading on the Electronic Frontier* (revised edn). MIT University Press.

Rudin, R. (1999). *Eureka 147 – Digital Diversity or Radio Restriction?* Available at April 2001 at http://members.aol.com/Soundsites/Radiocracy.html.

Ruggiero, G. and McChesney, R. W. (1999). *Microradio & Democracy: (Low) Power to the People*. Open Media Pamphlet Series, 10.

Ryan, E. and Bingaman, M. (2001). The death of streaming. *Radio Ink*, 11 January. Published online at http://www.radioink.com/inkheadlines.asp?page=26.

Sakai, D. (1999). *The Targeted Audience. Internet & Database Marketing Strategies for Broadcasters*. Washington: National Association of Broadcasters.

Scannell, P. (1996). *Radio, Television & Modern Life*. Blackwell.

Scannell, P. and Cardiff, D. (1991). *A Social History of British Broadcasting: Volume 1, 1922–1939, Serving the Nation*. Blackwell.

Scarborough Research (2001). Press release: 'First Scarborough National Internet Study Reveals Changes In How Online Consumers Use Traditional And Internet Media', 9 May. Published as at July 2001 at http://www.scarborough.com/scarb2000/press/pr_internetstudy1.htm.

Shingler, M. and Wieringa, C. (1998). *On Air*. Arnold.

Siegel, D. (1997). *Creating Killer Web Sites* (2nd edn). Hayden Books.

Smith, M. and Kollock, P. (eds) (1998). *Communities in Cyberspace*. Routledge.

Snyder, J. (2001). Radio returns to the Net. *The Standard*, 27 June. Published online at http://www.thestandard.com/article/0,1902,27564,00.html.

Spinelli, M. (1996). Radio lessons for the Internet. In *Postmodern Culture*, Vol. 6, no. 2 (January). Oxford University Press.

Sunstein, C. (2001). *Republic.com*. Princeton University Press.

Times Newspapers (2001). Law Report: Website operators must identify maker of defamatory comments. *The Times*, 15 March. Posted online at http://www.thetimes.co.uk/article/0,12–99112,00.html.

Tracey, M. (1998). *The Decline and Fall of Public Service Broadcasting*. Oxford University Press.

UCLA (2000). *The UCLA Internet Report: Surveying the Digital Future*. Available at February 2001 as a PDF file on www.ccp.ucla.edu/.

UNESCO (2001). *Final Report of the Kothmale Seminar on Integrating New and Traditional Information and Communication Technologies for Community Development*. Published at http://www.unesco.org/webworld/public_domain/kothmale.shtml.

United States Department of Commerce (1924). *Recommendations for the Regulation of Radio Adopted by the 3rd National Radio Conference called by Herbert Hoover, Secretary of Commerce October 6–10*. Washington. Government Print Office.

USA National Research Council (2000). *The Digital Dilemma: Intellectual Property in the Information Age*. National Academy Press.

White, T. (2001). *United States Early Radio History* website at http://www.i-pass.net/~whitetho/part1.htm.

Wilby, P. and Conroy, P. (1994). *The Radio Handbook*. Routledge.

Winston, B. (1998). *Media Technology and Society: A History*. Routledge.

Index

3Com, 67–8
4ZZZ, 24
95b FM, 20

ABC (Aus.), *see* Australian
    Broadcasting Corporation
ABC Inc. Radio Networks (US), 209
Ad(vert) insertion, 105, 115, 124, 174,
    242
Advertising:
    'on air', 80, 104–5, 113–5, 236, 242
    on the website, 80, 101, 105, 113,
        119, 191–2, 235, 241–2
    your station, 138–40, 151–2
    see also Radio industry sectors,
        commercial
AFTRA, *see* American Federation of
    Television and Radio Artists
Aggregating website, *see* Portal site
AIM, *see* Association of Independent
    Music
Akoo Kima, 70–1, 141
All India Radio, 18
Alternative radio, *see* Radio industry
    sectors, alternative
AMARC, 23–4, 126–30
Amateur radio, 10–11, 25, 211, 235,
    239
American Federation of Television and
    Radio Artists, 174
AM radio, *see* Radio transmission
    routes, analogue

Analogue radio, 244
    access to frequencies, 9, 23, 116,
        138, 155, 179–80, 233
    characteristics, 3–4, 8–9, 12, 26, 39,
        206, 214, 233
    perceptions of, *see* Public perceptions
    production:
        technology, 15
        techniques, 95, 232
    stations, 18, 20, 24, 101–13, 126–33,
        143, 151–4
    transmission, *see* Radio transmission
        routes
    see also Broadcasting
ANEM (Association of Independent
    Electronic Media), 195
Apple, 65
    Airport, 72, 244
    Mac, 60, 62, 64, 91
    QuickTime, 48, 56, 60–4, 91, 103,
        141, 168, 171
        Pro, 91
        Streaming Server Software, 91
Arbitron, 31, 51, 66, 113, 199, 221
Archives, *see* Station archives
Archive stream, *see* Stream, archive or
    live
ASCAP, 157, 165
'As live' techniques, *see* Radio
    programmes
Association of Independent Music
    (AIM), 167, 169

Audience(s), 82–88, 217–230, 233–6
  broadcast, 10–11,150, 202–3, 206,
    214, 220
  competition for, 3–4, 145, 151, 164,
    200, 221
  exclusion, 84–5, 149, 193–4, 202
  feedback, 104, 112, 120–2, 124,
    228–9, 235, 243
  finding, 136–54, 169
  fragmentation of, 14, 17, 22, 227
  interactions, 45–6, 147–8, 150, 207,
    215, 228–230, 239
  location, *see* reach
  niche, *see* Niche
  reach, 51, 64, 85, 103, 109, 124,
    173, 200, 214, 224, 228–9, 233,
    241
    international, 20, 25, 43, 114, 116,
     156, 178, 201, 211,
    local, 8, 21, 23, 27, 113–4, 132,
     201, 205, 236
    national, 1, 17, 18, 178, 233
  relationship, *see* interactions
  research, 88, 121, 136–7, 148,
    199–200, 208, 221, 228–9,
    234–5, 243
Audion, 64, 92, 244
Australia, 121–2,
  Australian Broadcasting Corporation,
    18
  radio in, 18, 23, 24, 40
Automated play-out, 29, 36–8, 104,
  170–1, 123, 199, 218, 237–8, 241
Automation, *see* Automated play-out

B92, 194–5
Bandwidth, 52, 57–9, 75, 244
  availability, 55, 85–7, 109, 164,
    238–9,
  calculating cost, 78, 93, 102, 128,
    234, 242
  see also Radio transmission routes,
    digital, broadband

BBC, 13, 17, 152–3, 158, 173–4,
    187–8, 195, 209
  Online, 101, 182, 204
  Radios 1–5, 18–19, 148, 166, 209
  World Service, 14, 106, 153, 179
Berners-Lee, Tim, 6
Bit rate, *see* Internet connection
  speed
Bluetooth, 72, 245
BMI, 158, 165
Brand, 47, 103, 152–4, 236, 242
Brazil, 129
Brecht, Bertold, 11–12, 211–2
British Broadcasting Corporation, *see*
  BBC
Broadband, *see* Radio transmission
  routes
BroadcastAmerica, 135
Broadcasting:
  digital audio, 25, 39–43
  financing of, 16–21
  history of radio, 231–2, 243
    institutions, 16–21, 181–3
    production, 15, 203–4, 217–8
    receivers, 14, 52, 68
    transmission, 8–14
    see also regulation of
    and Copyright history
  industry sectors, see Radio industry
    sectors
  licensed, *see* Licensed broadcasters
  regulation of, 14, 18, 20, 21, 178–91,
    194, 203, 223, 232–3
  see also Copyright standards, 181,
    191–2
'Broadcast' unicast, 86, 250
Browser, 52, 67, 148, 203, 204
Buffering, 55, 57, 129
Bulletin boards and forums, 7
  moderation, 100–1, 117, 150, 234
  responsibility for, 184, 193
  uses, 47, 125, 150, 211, 215, 226,
    228–9
Business models, 72, 121–2, 130, 135,
    172, 181, 198–9, 242

Canada, 109, 121, 129, 190
   radio in, 22, 23, 40, 143
Canadian Radio, Television &
   Telecommunications Commission,
   110, 112
Canary Islands, 20
Capturing sound, 81
CB radio, *see* Citizens Band
Censorship, 196, 231
Cerf, Vint, 5
CFUV FM, 109–14
Chat rooms, 211–13
   moderation, 100–1, 150, 213, 234
   responsibility for, 184,193
   uses of, 47, 49. 125, 148, 150, 215, 229
China, 179
Cisco, 65, 91
Citizens Band radio, 212, 239
Clear Channel, 174
Click through advertising, sales, 36–7,
   105, 115, 138, 199, 235, 237
Club culture, *see* Dance music
   audience
College radio, 22, 67, 109–13
Co-location, 103
Comedy, 198, 208–10
Commercial radio, *see* Radio industry
   sectors, commercial
Community:
   of interest, 113, 225–9
   online, 225–7, 229
   radio, 16, 21, 23–4, 109–13, 126–33,
     205, 211, 243
Compression, 55–6, 82, 245
   formats, *see* Streaming formats
   Computer, 4–6
   desktop, 2, 39, 43, 52–3, 65–7, 71,
     74, 124
   encoding, 81, 90–1, 95–7, 103, 111,
     124
   laptop, 65–7, 124
   palmtop, 71
   personal, 6–9, 20, 30, 40, 131, 161
   screen, 30–1, 43–9, 75, 138, 150,
     205, 234

   see also Interactivity, visual
   see also Streaming server hardware
Connection, *see* Internet connection
Contempt of court, 181, 184, 190
Convergence of communications
   technologies, 4, 28–30, 39, 48–9,
   204
Cool Edit Pro, 89, 91
Coordinated Universal Time, *see* UTC
Copyright, 155–77, 181, 223, 231,
   238–9
   current legislation, 32, 155–167
   history, 31–2, 155–160
   mechanical, 159–61, 164, 171
   music, 155–173, 199, 236
   non-musical, 173–4
   payments, 156–60, 163–6,
   piracy, 32, 156, 176
   protecting your, 175–6
CPU speed, 71, 73, 245

DAB, *see* Radio transmission routes
Dance music audience, 117, 122–5, 201
Data collection, 88, 94, 104, 121, 191,
   199, 228–9, 234–5
Data protection, 191–2
Data rate, *see* Internet connection
   speed
Defamation law, 179, 181, 183–4, 191
Democratizing medium, radio as a, 10,
   12, 23, 180–1, 189, 194–5
Diaspora, 108, 201, 225
Digital audio broadcasting, *see* Radio
   transmission routes
Digital audio production, *see* Radio
   production
'Digital Divide, The', 130–3
Digitalization, 2, 28–32, 156, 217, 241,
   246
Digital Media Association (DiMA), 165,
   167
Digital Millennium Copyright Act
   (DMCA), 161–3, 165–7, 170–2,
   246

Digital Performance Rights in Sound
     Recordings Act (DPRA), 161
Digital Radio Mondiale, *see* Radio
     transmission routes
Digital subscriber line (DSL), 52, 58,
     66–7, 71, 75, 85, 111, 120, 246
Digital transmission, *see* Radio
     transmission routes
Digitizing audio:
   degradation between formats, 96
   resolution, 96–7
   sample rate, 96–7
Direct satellite broadcasting, *see* Radio
     transmission routes
Directories of web radio stations,
     15–16, 45, 139, 142–5, 147
   Live-Radio, 16, 88, 143–4
   Radio4All, 144–5
   Radio-Locator, 99, 143
Divergence of media, 30–1
DJ, *see* Presenters
Domain name, 146–7
'Dot com' companies, 135, 153
Downloading, 54, 71, 163
   music tracks, 32–6, 63, 65, 162–3,
     199
   programmes, 38–9, 107, 127–8,
Drama, 38, 173, 198, 208–10
DRM, *see* Radio transmission routes
DSL, *see* Digital subscriber line

Edge services, 79, 103, 125, 246
Editorial responsibility, 188–9
Electrophone, 8, 246
Embedded sound files, 56, 89
Encoding:
   see Computer, encoding
   and Streaming software encoding
Encryption, 40, 192, 246
Entertainment, 1, 3, 10, 31, 42, 107,
     208–9, 223, 243
Equity (British Actors'), 173
Ethical considerations, 180, 188–92,
     231, 240

Eureka-147 standard, 40–1
Europe:
   laws and standards, 73, 157, 159,
     183, 191
   radio in, 11–12, 16–18, 40–1, 106,
     124, 129, 181, 190, 213, 224
Experimental radio, 39, 134, 198, 210,
     213–15, 231
External (radio) services, 14, 18,
     106–8, 179, 227, 235
   BBC World Service, *see* BBC
   Deutsche Welle, 179
   Radio China International, 179
   Radio France Internationale, 179
   Radio Netherlands Wereldomroep,
     see Radio Netherlands

Factual programming, 189, 203–8
Fairness Doctrine (US), 187
FCC, *see* Federal Communications
     Commission
Federal Communications Commission
     (FCC), 10, 182
Federal Radio Commission, 10–11
Fessenden, R.A., 7
File exchange, *see* MP3 file sharing
Filtering:
   Internet content, 185–6, 193–4
   sound, 95–7
Finland, 129
Firewalls, 81, 87, 192, 246
Flash, 149
FM radio, *see* Analogue radio
     transmission
Forum, *see* Bulletin boards and forums
France, 121, 190–1
Free radio, 21, 23, 144–5
Free speech, 78, 178, 180, 196, 240
Freedom of information laws, 189
Freirad.at, 129–30

Germany, 185, 190
Global to local strategies, 122, 126, 132
   see also Audience reach

Ham radio, *see* Amateur radio
Harry Fox Agency, 159
Helper application, 56–7, 84
Hill, Lewis, 23
Hilversum, *see* Radio Netherlands
History:
 of broadcasting, *see* Broadcasting,
  history of radio
 of radio, *see* Broadcasting, history of
  radio *and* Radio industry, sectors
 of the Internet, *see* Internet, history of
Home taping, 38–9, 169
Hoover, Herbert, 1, 9, 10, 23
Horizontal characteristics, 12–13
 in analogue radio, 21, 25–7, 109, 232
 in web radio, 75, 163, 178, 194, 211,
  213, 241
 of the Internet, 126, 132, 134, 136,
  156, 180
Horizontal Radio, 213
Hospital radio, 22
Host(ing), *see* Streaming host
HTML, 6, 247
HTTP, 6, 247
Hyperlinks, 56, 107, 125, 129, 138–40,
 148, 154, 219, 228

iBiquity, 41–2
IBOC (In Band On Channel), 41–2, 247
ICANN, 146–7
ICT, 3, 29–31, 51, 67, 71, 75, 126, 130,
 153, 155, 172
Idents, *see* Jingles & idents
Impartiality, 181, 187, 240
iM Radio, 69–71, 141
In Band On Channel, *see* IBOC
In car radio, 3, 14, 41, 42, 74, 220
Incitement, laws against, 179, 181, 190
Independent Radio News, *see* IRN
Information & Communications
 Technology, *see* ICT
Intellectual property rights, *see*
 Copyright

Interactivity:
 and web radio, 75, 87, 210–13, 215,
  234
 in analogue radio, 8–12, 26, 210
 on the Internet, 7, 27
 visual, 41, 44–8, 105, 108, 117, 148
 see also Audience interactions
 and Pull strategies
Internet:
 characteristics, 5, 7, 12–13, 20, 24,
  32, 136–8, 204, 233–5
  see also Horizontal characteristics
 connection, 20, 57, 156,
  access to, 23–4, 51–2, 56, 131–2,
  cost, 57–8, 114, 131, 164, 220–1,
   229
 connection speed, 52, 57–9, 65–7,
  163, 170–1, 245
  listeners choice, 142, 228
  server decisions, 83–5, 103, 108,
   111, 119–20, 129, 149, 168,
   170
  see also Bandwidth
  and Radio transmission routes,
   digital broadband
 cultures, 32, 77, 180, 195
 history, 4–5, 180
 perceptions of, *see* Public
  perceptions
 regulation, 7, 24, 72, 178–80, 183–5,
  193–6, 203, 233, 239–40
 rights, *see* Copyright
 see also World Wide Web
Internet-only stations, 35–8, 143,
 153–4, 164, 200–15, 233–4, 238,
 242
 case studies, 116–25
Internet Service Provider (ISP), 52,
 103, 120, 131
 and connection speed, 57–8, 66–7
 as streaming hosts, 78–9, 89, 129,
  195
 liability for content, 183–6, 190
Internet Service Providers Association
 (ISPA), 186

Internet Streaming Media Alliance, 65
Internet Watch Foundation, 185–6
Intranet streaming, 67, 85, 87, 193
IP (Internet Protocol) address, 5, 185,
    187, 192–3, 234, 247
IRN, 205
ISP, *see* Internet Service Provider

Japan, 20, 121, 159
Jazz FM, 20
Jingles and idents, 201
Journalism, *see* News & current affairs
'Jukebox', *see* Music channel

Kahn, Bob, 5
Kerbango, 67–9, 141
Kima, *see* Akoo
Kohnmusic.com, 158, 162
Kothmale Community Radio, 131–4, 211
KPFA, 23–4

Language, 23, 106–7, 109, 111–12,
    126, 132, 202, 206, 225
Libel, *see* Defamation law
Licence(s):
    and control of content, 21, 155,
        179–82, 187, 205, 237, 240
    fees, 17,
    to use a frequency, 11, 21, 25–6,
        41–2
Licensed broadcasters, 23, 114–5, 201,
    214,
    see also Simulcasting
Lifestyle, 36, 139, 217
Link(ing), *see* Hyperlink
Linux operating systems, 89–90, 103,
    120, 129
Liquid Audio, 65
Listening:
    at work, 67, 103, 114, 120–1, 229
    cost of, *see* Internet connection cost
    habits, 219–222, 229

patterns, 75, 83
psychology, 225–6
Live365.com, 79–81, 123, 129, 140
Live Channel, 91
Liveness, 49, 109, 117, 123, 134, 223,
    228, 238
Live-Radio.net, *see* Directories
Local to global strategies, 117, 120–1,
    205, 214
    see also Audience reach
Lycos, 211

Marconi, 31
Mass communication, *see* Broadcasting
McLuhan, Marshall, 30, 214
MeasureCast, 67, 103, 153, 199, 200,
    221
Mechanical Copyright Protection
    Society (MCPS), 159, 171
Memory, *see* Streaming server storage
Message boards, *see* Bulletin boards
    and forums
Metafiles, 56–7
Metrics, *see* Audience research
    and Data collection
Microsoft, 34, 62, 64–5, 90
    see also Windows Media Player
Miki FM, 20
MiniDisc, *see* Radio production
    technology
Mobile Internet, 52, 72, 199
Mobile phone technology, 72–5, 205
Mobility of receivers
see Portability
Modem, *see* Internet connection
Morse code, 7, 29
Motley Fool, 183–4
MP3, 63, 71, 221, 247
    file sharing, 35, 127, 161–2, 183, 239
    streaming, 58, 60–5, 85, 91–2, 124,
        128–9, 168
MP3.com, 161
Multicast, 86–7, 90–1, 93, 206–7, 214,
    234, 248

Multichannel media environment, 131, 151, 172, 181, 218
Music channels, 36–8, 117, 169, 176, 198–200, 236–7
Music copyright, *see* Copyright, music
Music industry, 31–8, 155–67, 198
   product ownership and consumption models, 172, 176
MusicMatch, 64
MusicNet, 33–4, 163
Music piracy, *see* Copyright piracy
Music publishers, 157–9, 162, 164
Music radio, 8, 15, 19–20, 118–25, 162, 168, 198–204, 219, 238–9
   formats, 19, 36, 113, 142, 151, 153, 198, 237
Music shopping, 35–6

NAB (National Association of Broadcasters), 165–6
Napster, 32, 161–2, 172, 176, 183
Narrow-casting, 20, 24–5, 114, 212, 214–15, 226, 229, 233–4
National Public Radio (NPR) network, 18
Netherlands, 101, 105–9, 114, 121, 124, 137, 195, 206, 223
NetRadio, 37, 137
New Zealand, 20
News, 107–8, 137, 142, 152, 201, 217,
   bulletins, 35, 75, 115, 206, 227, 236, 238
   & current affairs programmes, 107, 112, 132, 173, 189, 198, 203–6
Newspapers:
   online, 46, 139, 208, 228
   see also Print media
Niche:
   audience, 39, 48, 116, 145, 184, 190, 202, 210, 218–9, 239
   content, 20, 41, 55, 105, 123, 137, 205, 213, 226, 237
   see also Narrow-casting
Novelty (value), 1–4, 138
Nullsoft, 64

Obscenity laws, 181
Obsolescence of media formats, 3–4
OFCOM, 185, 248
Official secrecy, 179, 181, 189
On demand listening, 34–5, 223, 234, 236, 238
   music, 164, 169, 199, 203
   speech programmes, 108, 128, 204, 207–10, 214, 228–9
   see also Streams, archive or live
OnStar, 74
Orange 94.0, 127, 129
Outsourcing
   see Promotion strategies
   and Streaming host
Ownership, *see* Radio industry, ownership

Pacifica Foundation, 23, 24
Packet switching, 54–5, 66
Penguin Radio, 69, 141, 147
Perceptions, *see* Public perceptions
Performance rights, 157, 161, 164, 167–8, 170–1
Performing Rights Society (PRS), 157, 164, 175
Phone in, 150, 179, 184, 198, 210–13
Phonographic performance, 165–6, 168, 170, 172
Phonographic Performance Limited, 158
Pirate radio, 21, 22–3, 24
Plug in, 56, 84
Poetry, 112, 173–4
Portability:
   of radio receivers, 25, 38, 43, 52, 71
   of recorders, 25, 204
Portal site, 34, 45, 139–41, 238, 248
Power FM, 20
Presenters, 35–6, 38, 104, 117, 123, 134, 170, 175, 199–202, 212, 241
Pressplay, 33–4, 163
Print media, 28–30, 48, 180–1, 203–4, 222

Privacy, 179, 191
Production music, 171
Programmes, *see* Radio programmes
Programming, *see* Radio programming
Progressive Networks, 7,
Promotion strategies, 45, 103–5,
    136–7, 145–6, 150–4, 191, 219,
    242
Propaganda, radio as a tool for, 11, 190
ProTools, 91
PRS, *see* Performing Rights Society
Public perceptions:
    of radio, 1–2, 10–12, 200–1
    of the Internet, 1–3, 5, 10, 17, 28,175
Public radio, 18, 23, 156
Public service, radio as a, 17, 205, 243
    see also Radio industry, sectors,
        public service
Pull strategies, technologies, 136–8,
    204, 207, 219, 228
Pulse Radio, 117, 122–5, 213
Push strategies, technologies, 136–8,
    207, 219,

QuickTime, *see* Apple QuickTime

Radio, definitions of, 2, 30, 35–6, 45–6,
    49, 248
Radio4All, *see* Directories
Radio art, 213
    see also Experimental radio
Radio Authority (UK), 182, 185, 187
Radio Free Quebec, 24
RadioFreeWorld, 141
Radio industry:
    ownership, 18, 20, 25–6, 144–5,
        181–2, 194
    sectors, 13, 16–25, 100, 235, 239
        alternative or third sector, 17,
            20–5, 41, 109–13, 139, 146,
            205, 239
        commercial, 16–17, 18–21, 33,
            101–5, 151, 205

public service, 16–18, 20–1,
    106–9, 210
Radio-Locator, *see* Directories
Radio Netherlands, 101, 105–9, 114,
    137, 206, 223
Radio production technology, 39, 81, 95
    analogue, *see* Analogue radio,
        production
    digital,
        DAT, 29, 81, 96, 120
        DAWs, 29, 91, 95–6
        MiniDisc, 29, 71, 81, 96
        ripping CDs, 96
    studio, 29, 36, 44, 53, 94–7, 104,
        108, 111, 120, 129, 238
    see also Automated play-out
Radio programmes, 38–9, 48, 107, 114,
    202, 206, 208, 217–30, 232, 237
    'as live', 83, 87, 208–9, 215, 238
    built, 127–8, 209, 238
Radio programming, 38–9, 135, 197,
    208, 217–30, 233, 237
    see also Scheduling
Radio telephone, 9
Radio TNC, 213
Radio transmission routes, 1–14,
    39–43, 53, 72–5, 128, 161, 166
    analogue, 26, 195, 197–9, 215,
        232–3, 237
        cable, 58, 110
        satellite broadcast, 74, 102, 106,
          129
        terrestrial, 82, 101–2, 105–6, 110,
          126, 155, 235, 237
    digital, 39–43, 161–2, 199, 232, 235,
        237
        broadband, 52, 66–7, 71, 75, 171,
          173, 176, 211, 229
        DAB, 25–6, 40–2, 71, 102, 232,
          241, 245
        DRM, 41–2, 106, 232, 246
        IBOC, 41–2
        satellite broadcast, 42–3, 74, 102,
          126, 232, 241
RadioValve, 117–22, 221, 224

Reach, *see* Audience, reach
RealNetworks, 7, 33–4, 61–2, 65, 89, 92, 120, 153
Real software, 61–4, 89–90, 103, 120, 128–9, 168, 171
  RealAudio, 7, 61, 101, 133, 195, 213
  RealEncoder, 89
  RealGuide, 48, 141
  RealPlayer, 56, 60–4, 89, 103
  RealProducer, 63, 89, 108, 129
  RealServer, 89–91, 107–8, 111, 119
  RealSystem, 56, 61, 90
Receivers, *see* Tuners
Record companies, 31–5, 158, 164–5, 167, 170, 199, 239
Record Industries Association of America (RIAA), 162–3, 165–6, 176, 183
Regulation:
  of broadcasting, *see* Broadcasting, regulation of
  of the Internet
  see Internet, regulation of
Reith, John, 10, 11, 217
Religion, 189–90
Reputation, 150, 180, 188–9, 191, 235, 240, 242
Reuters, 204
Ripping, 171, 249
Rotation, *see* Programmes
  and Music channels
Royalties, *see* Copyright payments
RTP protocols, 63, 91, 249
Rwanda, 190

Sarnoff, David, 17, 31
Satellite:
  broadcasting, *see* Radio transmission routes
  distribution, 195, 204, 236
Scalability, 20, 39, 55, 78, 95, 97, 102, 114, 234, 238, 242
Schedule(s), *see* Scheduling

Scheduling, 217–30
  for web radio, 83, 109, 119, 124, 127, 197, 202, 238
  on analogue radio, 35, 113, 126, 197, 200, 209, 233, 241
  strip scheduling, 19
Search engines, 45, 139, 146–7, 176, 180, 219
Search functions, 169, 204–5, 207, 223
Self-regulation, 182, 187–8
SESAC, 158, 165
Shock jock, 179, 210
Short wave radio, 25
SHOUTcast, 64, 92, 141, 171
  Server, 92
  Source, 92
Side channels, 99–105, 113–4, 174, 200, 215, 236–7, 241
Simulcast(ing), 135, 165–6, 174, 198, 201, 249
  case studies, 99–115
  stations, 18, 20, 24
  strategies, 204–5, 233–7, 241–2
  see also Side channels
Sirius Satellite Radio, 42
Solaris, 89
Sorenson Broadcaster, 91
Sound art, *see* Radio art
Sound Forge, 90
Sound quality, 1, 2, 14, 41, 58, 84–5, 89, 102, 163, 168–9
South Africa, 126, 128–9
  FM, 18
  radio in, 40
Speech radio, 46, 107–14, 126–34, 142, 198, 200, 203–10, 219, 238
  see also Talk radio
  Spoken word, *see* Speech radio
Sport, 166, 198
Sri Lanka, 131–3
  Broadcasting Corporation, 132
  Ministry of Post, Telecommunications & Media, 132
State radio, 16–18, 189
Station archives, 97, 130, 223, 231, 234

Storage, *see* Streaming server storage
Streams, 34–5, 45, 49, 249
   archive or live, 35, 99, 119–20, 142,
      202–3, 214–5, 238, 241–3
     and copyright, 164, 168–71
     and defamation, 191
     and the listener, 107–9, 147, 199,
      218–9, 223–4, 227, 234
     as side channels, *see* Side
      channels
     for news and speech, 107–9,
      206–8
     serving, 34–5, 81–4, 94, 87, 91
   estimating number of, 83–4, 87–9,
     92–3, 146
   strength and reliability, 58–9, 67, 141,
     151
   see also On demand listening
   and Simulcasting
StreamAudio, 80, 172
Streaming, 7, 34–5, 52–65, 162–3, 176
   cost of, 55, 88, 93, 99, 200, 234, 236
   formats, 52, 60, 168, 222
   server:
     address, 142,
     hardware, 78, 81–2, 91–4, 97, 103,
      242
     location, 57, 94, 162, 167, 240
     managing, 88, 93–4, 104, 107–8,
      111, 140, 146, 175, 187, 192,
      239
     relay, 87, 124,
     replicating, 87
     security, 81
     storage, 93, 202, 208, 222–3, 235
   software, 59–65
     client, 52, 57, 60, 82, 149, 168,
      171–2
     encoding, 60, 82, 88–92, 124, 172
     player, *see* client
     server, 60, 82, 84, 129
     tuner, 140–1
     see also manufacturers' entries
Streaming host, 78–81, 89, 97, 122–5,
   140, 147, 172, 238

StreamWorks, 65, 92, 249
Student radio, 22, 67, 109–13
Subscription:
   for connection, 58, 66, 71,
   for stations, 40, 163–4, 167, 172–3,
     177, 193, 199
Sun Microsystems, 64, 91

Talk radio (format), 101, 142, 198,
   210–13
Taste and decency, 187, 190, 240
TCP (Transmission Control Protocol), 5
Telegraph, 29
Telephone, 4–5, 7–8, 43, 54, 57
Television, 3, 14, 28–30, 42–3, 45,
   179, 180, 203–4, 218, 223
   see also Web TV
Terrestrial transmission, *see* Radio
   transmission routes
Third sector radio see Radio industry
   sectors, alternative
Time shifting, 34–5, 39, 109, 222–4,
   229, 233, 238, 242, 250
Time zones, 83, 107–9, 119, 124,
   224–5, 228
Transmission, *see* Radio transmission
   routes
Tuners:
   analogue radio, 14, 52, 57, 68
   hardware, 39, 67–72, 141, 236
   online, 124, 141–2, 147
   see also Streaming software, tuner

UCT, *see* UTC
Underground radio, 16, 21
Unicast, 63, 85–7, 90–1, 108, 214, 228,
   234, 250
United Kingdom, 66, 69, 121, 128,
   law, 183–6, 191–4
   radio in, 11, 17, 22–3, 40, 158, 182,
     205, 209
   web radio stations, 18, 20, 44,
     101–5, 224

United Nations, 128
UNESCO, 132–3
WIPO, *see* WIPO treaties
Unix operating systems, 64, 89–92
USA:
and internet technology, 4–5, 6–7,
138, 166
radio, 1, 9, 17, 19, 22, 23, 40–2, 101,
113, 143, 158, 161–2, 165, 210
web radio stations, 15, 18, 23–4,
118–22, 142–4, 172, 174, 239
US Copyright Office, 165, 172
US Internet Industries Association
(USIAA), 186
UTC (Coordinated Universal Time), 224
Utopian visions, *see* Perceptions of
radio

Variable bit rate, 85, 120, 250
Vertical characteristics, 12–13
in broadcast technologies, 25–6, 41,
43, 75, 181, 232–3
in institutions, 18, 20, 109, 126, 194,
203, 211, 232–3
Virgin Radio, 101–5, 113–4, 148, 153,
221, 229
Visual, *see* Computer screen
and Interactivity, visual
Voice of America, 14
Voix Sans Frontières (VSF), 126–130,
213

W3C, *see* World Wide Web Consortium
Washington Post, 204
Watermarking, 176
Webcam, 44, 148
Web conferencing, 87, 211
Webmaster, 77, 140, 142
Web-only stations, *see* Internet-only
stations

Website,
as 'front door', 45, 138–40, 142, 146,
193, 222, 227, 236, 238
design, 45, 49, 100–2, 111, 147–50,
238
interactive functions, 99–109, 117,
125, 200, 226, 228–30, 234, 243
location, 94, 142
security, 180, 240
visual demands, 45–6, 49
Web TV, 47–9
Winamp, 64, 92
Windows Media Player, 56, 60–4,
90–1, 102–3, 108, 141, 168, 171
Encoder, 90
Windows operating system, 89–90, 111,
129
server software, 90, 108
WIPO treaties, 159, 161, 166–7, 172
Wireless, 251
network technology, 68–73, 75
set, 1–3, 8, 11, 14, 16–17
Wireless LAN, 72
World Intellectual Property Organisation
(WIPO), *see* WIPO treaties
World Radio Network (WRN), 107, 129
WorldSpace, 42–3
World Wide Web, 2–3, 4, 6–7, 15,
18–24, 25–6, 45
standards, 6–7
see also Internet
World Wide Web Consortium (W3C), 6
Writers Guild, 173

Xing Technologies, 65, 92
XMMS player, 64
XM Radio, 42, 74, 241

Yahoo, 34, 151

Zoning, 193, 251

You've read the book, now visit the web site!

www.web-radio-book.com

More information and resources can be found on the book's supporting web site. Benefit from:

- updates to technical information covered by the book

- latest progress of the web radio stations featured in the book's case studies

- news of changes to relevant copyright and regulation issues

- commentary on recent trends in web radio

- useful web links

- an expanded glossary of terms

- answers to your most frequently asked questions about web radio

- the opportunity to give your views on the book and website

383054